Latina Lives in Milwaukee

LATINOS IN CHICAGO AND THE MIDWEST

Series Editors
Frances R. Aparicio, Northwestern University
Pedro Cabán, State University of New York
Juan Mora-Torres, DePaul University
Maria de los Angeles Torres, University of Illinois at Chicago

A list of books in the series appears at the end of this book.

Latina Lives in Milwaukee

THERESA DELGADILLO

featuring interviews with

Ramona Arsiniega
María Monreal Cameron
Daisy Cubías
Elvira Sandoval Denk
Rosemary Sandoval Le Moine
Antonia Morales
Carmen Murguia
Gloria Sandoval Rozman
Margarita Sandoval Skare
Olga Valcourt Schwartz
Olivia Villarreal

University of Illinois Press
URBANA, CHICAGO, AND SPRINGFIELD

Support for this research received from The Ohio State
University College of Arts and Sciences Publication
Subvention Grant.

Library of Congress Control Number: 2015950154
ISBN 978-0-252-03982-9 (hardcover)
ISBN 978-0-252-08136-1 (paperback)
ISBN 978-0-252-09793-5 (e-book)

For my mother and my father,
Amalia and Sacramento Delgadillo.
Their love made all the difference.

Contents

Preface

The women who generously gave their time and thoughtfully shared stories from their life journeys in this volume demonstrate not only that achievement can come to people of many different backgrounds and experiences but that there are many forms of achievement—personal, professional, communal—large and small. The voices, personalities, political views, struggles, and triumphs in these stories reveal a diversity of Latina experience and provide a record of social changes and tensions, and ongoing debates and discussions, within Latina/o communities. These include the state of educational opportunity for Latinas/os, ethnic and racial differences among Latinas/os and between Latinas/os and other groups, limitations on economic opportunity, discrimination, language barriers and prejudices, homophobia, changing religious affinities, immigration reform, political representation, women's continued double workload, and domestic violence. In these life stories, women tackle many of these issues on multiple fronts, often working under limitations yet also contributing to efforts to ensure that all Latinas/os in the United States enjoy full civil rights, educational access, economic opportunity, and rich lives as they participate as global citizens in having a voice in the affairs of the world.

1. Latinas in Milwaukee

Why Milwaukee?

A playbill for the Palace Museum in downtown Milwaukee, open from 1883 to 1897, announces a show featuring "Mlle. Vallecita" and "performing mountain lions" as well as the "The Mexican Impalement Act" at its location on Third Street near Grand Avenue.[1] It is not known whether this was a traveling or local troupe, whether it involved actors posing as French and Mexican or actual Mexican or Mexican American performers, whether "The Mexican Impalement Act" was a tropicalized routine[2] of exotic magic and escape or a performance based on misnaming and misrecognition—as is the case with Wisconsin's Aztalan State Park—or even a collective fantasy of wish fulfillment in an era when U.S. settlers steadily and systematically dispossessed newly incorporated Mexican Americans in the Southwest of their governments, lands, and homes.[3] But the playbill, and the questions it raises, serve to prompt us to consider the possibility of many individual and unrecorded crossings, travels, and migrations that brought Latinas/os to Wisconsin; to recognize the ways that Latinas/os entered into the consciousness of societies far from Latina/o population centers and explore how that may have influenced how Latinas/os were received when they arrived in this region; and to remain attentive to the records and stories of Latinas/os themselves in the Latina/o Midwest. Indeed, it is no longer unfathomable to imagine some Mexican residents in Milwaukee in the late nineteenth century since *Latinos in Milwaukee* has identified Rafael Báez as a resident of the city in 1884, though in the main, significant migration from Mexico to the Midwest begins only in the early twentieth century.[4] As historian Zaragosa Vargas notes, "Over 58,000 Mexicans settled in the cities of the Midwest during the fifteen-year period from the end of World War I to the first years of the Great Depression."[5] Employers recruited Mexican labor in southwestern cities and towns,[6] prompting many Mexicans and Mexican Americans to migrate to the Midwest. This volume adds to our growing understanding of the experiences and histories of Latinas/os in the Midwest by making available a set of oral histories by Latinas in Milwaukee.

The participants in this project represent diverse generations, ethnicities, and occupations as well as varied political and social perspectives and life experiences. The interviewees include women who arrived in Milwaukee as migrants from another region or territory, or immigrants from another country, as well as women born and raised in Milwaukee. These oral histories provide further insight into Milwaukee's Latina/o communities in the twentieth century, with particular emphasis on the experiences of women. The women chart their family's or their own arrival in Milwaukee in ways that confirm the existing research on significant migrations from Latin America to the United States and to the Midwest in particular, as well as important research on interregional migrations of Mexican Americans and Puerto Ricans within the United States. The stories of Antonia Morales and Elvira, Gloria, Margarita, and Rosemary Sandoval confirm research on early twentieth-century migrations from Mexico to the United States with their families' arrivals in Milwaukee in the 1920s. María Monreal Cameron's oral history identifies her own family's migration from Mexico to Texas in the 1920s, and then from Texas to Wisconsin in the 1940s. These oral histories strongly suggest that the 1920s is, in fact, the inaugural moment for a Latina/o community in Milwaukee. Olivia Villareal's and Ramona Arsiniega's oral histories chart their families' emigrations from Mexico to Milwaukee in the 1940s–1950s postwar industrial boom that brought recruits and migrants to the Midwest. The migrations of Olga Valcourt Schwartz and Daisy Cubías from Puerto Rico and El Salvador, respectively, occur outside of the main, as both arrived in the 1960s for education—Valcourt in Milwaukee and Cubías in New York and eventually Milwaukee. Cubías's oral history takes up the period in the 1980s when significant numbers of Salvadorans and other Central Americans migrated to the United States, fleeing war and violence, through the impact on her family and her own antiwar activism. Carmen Murguia's oral history offers the perspective of a U.S.-born Latina/o member of a civil-rights-minded family as she tells of her life growing up in Milwaukee. Participants in this project include women in their eighties, seventies, sixties, fifties, and forties. This generational spread among women yields the set of life stories collected here that span much of the twentieth century, from the 1920s through the 1990s, and continue into the beginning of the twenty-first century. In this way, the book offers a textured view of Latina experiences in work, career, business, family, community, philanthropy, advocacy, and activism over the past ninety years.

Archival evidence of Latina/o community activities in Milwaukee in the 1920s and 1930s is scant. The two fliers pictured here from 1927 and 1933 reveal a community large enough to host activities such as dances in rented halls. The appeal to both women and men in each text, in Spanish, suggests that despite the widely held view that early migrants were mostly single men, women were obviously present in significant numbers. These fliers also suggest a growing stability to this mixed-gender population if we consider the contrast between the 1927 flier (figure 1), with limited information, and the 1933 program (figure 2), which lists multiple presenters and performers.

Research on major migration periods, major ports of arrival, and key areas of settlement for Latinas/os form an important part of piecing together the story

Figure 1. Flier announcing 1927 Gran Baile in Milwaukee, Wisconsin. Latino/Hispanic American Collection. Milwaukee County Historical Society. MSS-3035. Box 1. Folder 3. Photograph courtesy of the Milwaukee County Historical Society.

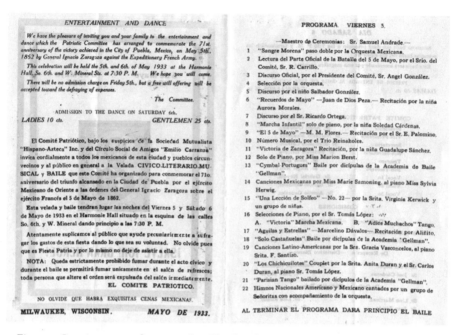

Figure 2. Interior pages of program booklet for 1933 Cinco de Mayo Commemoration in Milwaukee, Wisconsin. Latino/Hispanic American Collection. Milwaukee County Historical Society. MSS-3035. Box 1. Folder 2. Photograph courtesy of the Milwaukee County Historical Society.

of Latinas/os in the Midwest, and so, too, does the exploration of individual and smaller group migrations outside of the major periods, especially since these provide evidence of enduring transnational social and economic networks and continued cross-cultural encounters. Nor should we overlook the interregional circulation and mobility of Latina/o groups and individuals, especially in considering Latina/o populations outside of typical population centers for these groups. For example, we know more about Latinas/os in Chicago than about Latinas/os in any other midwestern city or town, yet we need to know much more about Latina/o life throughout the region. Latina/o experiences and contributions in the Midwest are only beginning to make their way into the larger bodies of knowledge about regional history, literature, and culture.[7]

In recent decades, several important histories on Latina/o life in the Midwest have emerged, including work on Milwaukee's Latina/o populations. Dennis Valdés notes in *Barrios Norteños*:

In Milwaukee, which boasted the largest concentration of Mexicanos in Wisconsin, workers were lured to Inland Steel and Illinois Steel plants during World War I, while in 1920 the largest employer of the pre-Depression era, the Pfister and Vogel tannery, initially imported a contingent of about one hundred Mexicans as strike-breakers. Others worked for local railroads, construction companies, and packing plants. By the end of the 1920s they approached four thousand residents, clustered in five neighborhoods bordering the Milwaukee or Menominee Rivers. The largest was in the factory district on the near South Side, with a second important *colonia* near the tannery on the North Side. As in many other northern cities, Milwaukee also was an important winter residence for sugar beet workers. Yet Milwaukee's Mexican population was reportedly "not well organized socially or politically" in comparison with many midwestern cities, despite its Sociedad Hispano-Azteca and the Guadalupe mission on Grove Street.[8]

Valdés's sources for this information and claim are, among others, a report by Agnes M. Fenton titled "The Mexicans of the City of Milwaukee-Wisconsin," published by the YMCA and International Institute of Milwaukee in 1930, and George T. Edson's 1926 report titled "Mexicans in Milwaukee, Wisc." in the Paul Taylor Papers of the Bancroft Library at the University of California, Berkeley. The popular photographic history *Latinos in Milwaukee* (2006) echoes these sources on the major sites of employment for early-twentieth-century Mexican and Mexican American residents of Milwaukee, but it belies the notion that these communities were not well organized: each caption's photograph provides details of family, social, religious, and economic organization among both "Los Primeros" and succeeding generations as told by those pictured in the photos themselves or their relations.[9] Discussing Milwaukee history, Zaragosa Vargas notes that "the Mexicans who went to work for Pfister & Vogel were unaware that a strike by the company's mostly Polish tannery workers had brought them to Milwaukee."[10] Valdés provides an excellent and comprehensive history of regional and interregional settlement by Mexicans and Mexican Americans in the Midwest. *Latina Lives in Milwaukee* adds to what we know about how Latinas/os in the region organized socially, culturally, and politically and how they viewed their own experiences by expanding the archive on Latina/o experience in the region. Among other things, this book allows readers to hear, from those involved, how industrial work shaped life and expectations for Latinas/os in Milwaukee—as industrial workers themselves or as the wives and daughters of industrial workers—and how the loss of those jobs, when economic restructuring affected the region, impacted Latina/o families. This book, therefore, is animated by the need and desire to hear about the history of Latinas/os in Milwaukee from those who have participated in making it.

The small but vibrant Mexican and Mexican American community founded in Milwaukee in the 1920s grew over succeeding decades to incorporate further Mexican, Mexican American, Puerto Rican, Cuban, Central American, and

Caribbean migration to this midwestern city. According to Valdés, "between 1970 and 1980" Milwaukee's Latina/o "population grew by 60 percent."[11] A flier included here (figure 3) for a 1967 program sponsored by the International Institute in Milwaukee suggests citywide interest in this growing population. Valdés notes that in St. Paul, Minnesota, the International Institute (a project of the YMCA) functions as a route toward Americanization. In Milwaukee, at least one interviewee in this book, Ramona Arsiniega, describes it differently, as a social club through which she met Latinas/os of various ethnic and national backgrounds and participated in learning about a variety of ethnicities. While the language of the 1967 flier might suggest a lack of civil rights awareness in calling the group a "Spanish Club," we might also read this wording as an attempt to find a common denominator for what is already a multiethnic Latina/o population in Milwaukee. A second 1971 flier not pictured here advertises a celebration at Trinity-Guadalupe Parish, which represented a merger of the white ethnic immigrant Holy Trinity Parish and the Mexican and Mexican American Our Lady of Guadalupe Mission—discussed by both Antonia Morales and the Sandoval sisters. It includes an explicit invitation to both Puerto Ricans

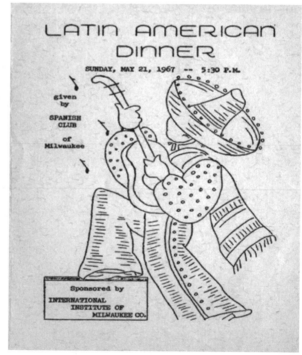

Figure 3. Page one of 1967 program sponsored by International Institute of Milwaukee. Latino/Hispanic American Collection. Milwaukee County Historical Society. MSS-3035. Box 1. Folder 2. Photograph courtesy of the Milwaukee County Historical Society.

and Mexicans as well as other Latinas/os by using the term *Panamerican*. Since the advertised "Panamerican Mass" is set to occur only a week after the national U.S. holiday of the Fourth of July, the flier might also suggest an alternative mapping of belonging and citizenship for Latina/o residents of Milwaukee and a recognition of enduring transnational ties.

Valdés notes that in the 1980s,

> Mexicans became more concentrated in the largest district, the near South Side, where they increased from 48 percent to 56 percent of Milwaukee's Latinos. Several South Side neighborhoods exceeded 75 percent Latino, particularly around Sixth and National, while Puerto Ricans, who had earlier been concentrated on the North Side, also moved into the district. The Mexican population also grew rapidly in several industrial cities in the eastern part of the state, particularly Waukesha, Racine, Green Bay, and Kenosha, where factory employment in textiles, meatpacking plants, and canneries predominated, and new work was available in many smaller enterprises, including restaurants, laundries, and nurseries.[12]

This population growth makes Milwaukee an important site of Latina/o life in the Midwest. Although Valdés highlights the region's population as being primarily of Mexican origin, countering the assertion that the Midwest is more Latina/o than Mexican, we can't ignore the significant number of "other Latinas/os" in Milwaukee in these statistics—at least 44 percent of the city's Latina/o population. Puerto Ricans, for example, began arriving in Milwaukee and the nearby smaller cities of Racine and Waukesha in the mid-twentieth century. At least twenty employers in Wisconsin were hiring Puerto Ricans at the time, and civic groups assisting Puerto Rican integration included the Spanish Club and International Institute (mentioned in figure 3), Adult Education and Recreation Department of Milwaukee Public Schools, Wisconsin State Employment Service, Catholic Welfare Bureau, and, of course, Puerto Ricans themselves, who turned out in large numbers to discuss issues affecting them. While some leaders expressed a strong anti-Communist fear as motivation for their "integration" efforts, Puerto Ricans themselves appeared to be much more civil-rights oriented.[13] As Olivia Villarreal and Ramon Arsiniega note, this era was also one of increased Mexican migration to Milwaukee, and many migrants also participated in "integration" programs.

The oral histories in this volume, from Mexican, Mexican American, Puerto Rican, and Salvadoran American women, aim to provide a fuller picture of multiethnic Latina/o life in the Midwest. Unfortunately, some ethnic/national groups from Milwaukee's Latina/o population are not included. Additional interviews were conducted with Mexican, Cuban American, Colombian American, Puerto Rican, and Mexican American women that are not included here for several reasons, including relevance, space, and withdrawal from the project by interviewees. There are also no interviews with Dominican women, a population that has grown in the city since the 1980s. In this volume, readers will find that oral history participants repeatedly refer to the significance of collaboration, coalition, and community among differing Latina/o groups in the city, strongly suggesting the necessity for collaboration across *Latinidades* in a city with a diverse Latina/o population. This study, therefore, offers a perspective on Latina/o life in the region different from that of work focused on single ethnic groups (which is the norm in the field), and in doing so suggests that the plural term *Latinidades* might better serve to account for the heterogeneity and distinctiveness of groups encompassed in the term Latina/o than *panethnic*, which tends to emphasize similarity across differences.[14]

Geography, Region, and Gender

Vicki L. Ruiz observes that "in Latina historiography, immigration, sexuality, generation, wage work, and cultural coalescence have frequently overshadowed region as a distinct category of analysis. And yet region is intricately tied to Latina identity."[15] Here I want to explore what this volume adds to existing scholarship on Latinas/os in the Midwest and in Milwaukee in particular, as well as the approach I take to geographical paradigms.

Proletarians of the North (1993) and *Barrios Norteños* (2000) bring important attention to the roles and work performed by Mexican and Mexican American women settlers to the Midwest, even though both works focus primarily on the migration, labor, and life experiences of men. Yet to be explored are the character and experience of work for Latinas in the region, what it meant for them and what unique challenges they faced, as well as how they viewed their own participation in efforts such as English and citizenship classes. The focus on male leadership, work, and activity continues in the recent popular pictorial history *Latinos in Milwaukee* (2006) as well as in Marc Rodriguez's *The Tejano Diaspora: Mexican Americanism and Ethnic Politics in Texas and Wisconsin* (2011), yet each of these volumes also provides valuable insight into the histories, experiences, and forms of organization among Milwaukee's Latina/o communities. In addition to the groundbreaking, excellent work of all these historians in exploring and making known the rich labor, settlement, political, and community-building history of Mexicans and Mexican Americans in Milwaukee and the region, documenting how migrants participated in burgeoning midwestern industries and unions and formed neighborhoods and communities, three more recent texts (all focused on Chicago) incorporate gender as a category of analysis: Gabriela F. Arredondo's *Mexican Chicago: Race, Identity and Nation, 1916–39* (2008);

Chicanas of 18th Street (2011) by Leonard G. Ramírez; and Lilia Fernandez's *Brown in the Windy City: Mexicans and Puerto Ricans in Postwar Chicago* (2012). Women's experiences and voices are also incorporated and included in recent sociological, ethnographic, and anthropological research on Latinas/os in the Midwest, such as in *Apple Pie and Enchiladas: Latino Newcomers in the Rural Midwest* (2004), edited by Ann V. Millard and Jorge Chapa, which focuses on Indiana, and Nicholas De Genova's *Latino Crossings: Mexicans, Puerto Ricans, and the Politics of Race and Citizenship* (2003), which focuses on Chicago.

As Valdés suggests in relation to the study of Chicana/o populations in *Barrios Norteños,* a variety of geographical paradigms have emerged as rubrics for analyzing Latina/o settlement in the Midwest. Two that he discusses are the "Greater Mexico" model, for bridging Chicana/o, Mexican American, and Mexican history, and the "ethnic immigrant" model. Though the former doesn't readily account for or extend to the Midwest, its transnational lens offers other advantages. The latter model suggests that the origin of many midwestern Latina/o communities in the 1920s reflects a social, cultural, and historical experience different from that of Mexican Americans in the Southwest who descend from those forcibly incorporated into the United States in 1848.[16] Marc Rodriguez's work proposes, in its very title, another paradigm for mapping at least Chicana/o settlement in the Midwest and understanding its significance in relation to regional and national civil rights movements and organizing: *The Tejano Diaspora: Mexican Americanism and Ethnic Politics in Texas and Wisconsin* (2011).

Latina Lives in Milwaukee departs from a panethnic Latina/o framework that collapses differences within this heterogenous group and instead embraces multiple Latinidades among Chicanas/os, Mexican Americans, Puerto Ricans, and Salvadoran Americans in the Midwest. Within this multi-Latina/o frame, this work understands "Latina/o" as a category that coheres not exclusively on the basis of culture or language but primarily on the basis of shared experience and status. In this respect, I follow in the sociohistorical contours offered by Marcelo M. Suárez-Orozco and Mariela M. Páez as parameters for the analytic category of Latina/o, namely: "the experience of immigration; the changing nature of U.S. relations with Latin America; and the processes of racialization as Latinos enter, and complicate, the powerful 'black-white' binary logic that has driven U.S. racial relations."[17] *Latinos Remaking America* suggests, and current events appear to confirm, that most Latinas/os are affected by these three factors regardless of their own immigration status. As the oral histories in this volume show, languages and ways of speaking languages, cultural referents, religious figures and practices, musics, foods, and social norms are as diverse among Latinas/os as ethnicity, nationality, and/or class. These differences among

Latinas/os are, in part, what make a multi- and intra-ethnic[18] focus valuable in exploring the diversity of this group. However, true to the contours of a sociohistorical analytic, in one way or another, each of these oral histories addresses the experience of racialization in the United States, the experience of immigration and/or migration—either of the interviewee herself or of her family—and the underlying power of U.S.–Latin American relations in shaping the population we today understand as Latina/o.[19]

While ethnic studies scholarship has accomplished an enormous feat in the space of roughly four decades by making known the histories, cultures, literatures, and experiences of groups who remained largely outside of mainstream systems of knowledge and knowledge-production, a limitation in ethnic studies scholarship is that while necessary attention has been focused on unique and specific ethnic/racial groups or those groups in relation to a dominant race/ethnic group, little attention has been focused on inter-ethnic or intra-ethnic experiences, histories, and cultures. The rise of mixed-race studies in the 1990s begins to address this gap, as does the emergence of greater attention to comparative racialization in the twenty-first century, and, I would argue, the growing recognition of the need for the field of Latina/o studies, which must, of necessity, take into account multiple ethnic and national subgroups.

The "Greater Mexico," "Tejano Diaspora," and "Ethnic Immigrant" frameworks discussed in histories of the region's Latinas/os work, in some cases, to name residential and migratory experiences with cultural, social, and political dimensions, while in other cases they offer a valuable interpretive lens for understanding such migrations and the ensuing kinds of settlements and continued connections to homelands. These histories offer valuable insight on the experience of specific national and ethnic groups whose histories had not been incorporated into regional, national, and transnational canons. *Latina Lives in Milwaukee* adopts a different framework, that of multiple Latinidades, to examine both the unique character of Latina/o life in Milwaukee and the gendered dimensions of this experience. I suggest here that one way the Latina/o experience in the Midwest for much of the twentieth century has been distinct from that of other regions is in the greater level of multi-, inter-, and intra-ethnic experiences. For much of the twentieth century, Mexican Americans, Puerto Ricans, groups of Mexican origin, and to a lesser extent groups of Cuban origin often coexisted in midwestern cities and towns. In the latter half of that century, this regional multiethnic mix expanded to include Central American, Caribbean, and Latin American migrants who settled in the United States as well as Latinas/os migrating to the Midwest from other regions. At the same time, other regions that were previously more homogenously Chicana/o or Mexican American (the Southwest), Cuban (Florida), and Puerto Rican (New York and the East Coast) also became ever more diverse as new Latina/o groups formed there, making Latina/o experiences in those regions more comparable with those in the Midwest.[20] The analytic of Latinidades, therefore, not only fits the history and experience of Latinas/os in the Midwest but may serve research on Latina/o populations in any part of the country.

Creating an Archive on Latinas in Milwaukee and the Midwest

In many ways, this volume was first imagined nearly twenty years ago, when, as an MFA student doing research that might serve the fictional stories I wanted to write about Mexican Americans in Milwaukee, I visited the Milwaukee County Historical Society. On the occasion of that visit, I was handed a cardboard file box of newspaper clippings, program announcements, documents, and letters related to community and social organizations; a few photos; and some souvenirs all jumbled together, none of it labeled. I can still recall the surprise and wonder of that moment, of being handed a cardboard box full of unexplained ephemera that was the only official archive on the history of Latinas/os in the City of Milwaukee, of reverently pulling out each item and reading it. Since the box wasn't full, I was soon finished. Sitting with that box in the reading room was a deeply shocking moment. I wondered then and still do: What could we know about ourselves, and what could others know about us, if so little was in the archive? What other parts of city life were absent from the historical record?

I looked for popular histories of Milwaukee and its significant industries and sites, searching for any mention at all of Latinas/os, and though a strong pride in Milwaukee's ethnic heritage looms large in much of this work, it typically doesn't include any Latina/o ethnicities and often also overlooks African Americans and Asian Americans, while relegating Native Americans to a colorful past as early inhabitants.[21] I did not return again to the Milwaukee County Historical Society until 2008, when I began interviewing the women whose oral histories are collected here. On this second visit to the more cramped temporary quarters on Clybourn Street, the Historical Society demonstrated its care in growing an archive on Latina/o Milwaukee. Not only did it now have additional materials available—including the complete archive of *La Guardia*, a Milwaukee Chicano Civil Rights Movement–era publication; copies of other community publications; and master's theses that had been written about Latina/o societies in the Midwest—but its own files were also all clearly organized and labeled. My most recent trip to the Historical Society, in December 2013, found that while there has been some change in the materials available, the collection has not grown significantly. This book contributes to the growing archive on Latina/o life in Milwaukee and the Midwest.

Today there are many more researchers engaged in generating, gathering, and analyzing information about Latinas/os in the Midwest as recognition of the longevity, significance, and continued growth of Latina/o populations in the region has increased. This new research includes studies in culture, literature, and religion; ethnography, demography, history; political and social movements; economic participation; and education. It was once common to hear, "I didn't know there were Latinas/os in Wisconsin." The current rarity of this statement, which became the title of a 1989 collection of poetry by twenty Latina/o writers in Wisconsin and edited by the poet Oscar Mireles,[22] marks how awareness of Latinas/os in the Midwest region has increased.

There is also growing community- and public-history-oriented research on Latinas/os in the Midwest, evident in the number of volumes published by the Arcadia Press Images of America Series. This specialty press, dedicated to collections on ethnic and urban enclaves throughout the United States, has brought forward several texts on the Midwest, including *Mexican Chicago* (2001), edited by Rita Aria Jirasek and Carlos Tortolero; *Latinos in Milwaukee* (2006), edited by Walter Sava and Joseph Rodriguez; *Latinos in Waukesha* (2007), edited by Walter Sava; *Chicago Latinos at Work* (2010), edited by Wilfredo Cruz; and *Detroit's Mexicantown* (2011), edited by Maria Elena Rodriguez. These photographic narratives of ethnic communities are typically supplemented by short introductory historical essays and are often collaboratively produced by community organizations and academics. They hint at a wealth of untapped knowledge about midwestern Latino/a communities.[23]

As a professor of Chicana/o and Latina/o studies for the past fourteen years, I have often encountered the dearth of materials on Latina/o groups in the Midwest readily available for classroom instruction. Several years of teaching both ethnic and gender studies courses also led me to the conclusion that a wider selection of materials must be cultivated, and research deepened, on Latina/os beyond the Southwest and East Coast. This project, therefore, began as one directed toward exploring region-specific history and experience as well as the gendered dimensions of that history and experience. Because I am not a historian, this work does not offer the kind of comprehensive overview that a history might. Instead, as an interdisciplinary cultural and literary studies scholar who regularly teaches in ethnic and gender studies, I have employed the methods of oral history, ethnography, and biography in collecting, editing, and analyzing the life studies offered here.[24]

Real Life, Oral History, Life Writing, and Literature

In 1992, the same year that Rigoberta Menchú won the Nobel Peace Prize for her work in support of Mayan indigenous rights in Guatemala—and not the Nobel Prize in Literature for her first-person *testimonio, I, Rigoberta Menchú*—the Mexican American short-fiction author Patricia Preciado Martin published *Songs My Mother Sang to Me* (1992), featuring ten first-person life stories of Mexican American women who had witnessed Arizona transform from a state dominated by rural populations and economies to one of urban centers and industrial life. Historian Vicki Ruiz notes in the foreword to that book that "Martin introduces us to ten individual personalities and experiences; yet, these women share a deep appreciation of their culture and communities. Most are superb storytellers."[25] Ruiz also notes that the "rhythms, expectations, and cultural practices" described by the women "no longer exist," and therefore their testimony constitutes a valuable archive of Mexican American life in Arizona.[26] Recent events in Arizona highlight for all of us how this archive, these voices, and this occluded history remain highly problematic for many in Arizona. In the preface to *Chicanas of 18th Street: Narratives of a Movement from Latino Chicago* (2011), Leonard Ramírez notes that his oral history project emerged from a group of women who had been activists in 1970s progressive political movements in Chicago who wanted to "highlight their individual accounts" so that their "personal reflections might reach a broader audience, particularly new generations of social justice activists."[27] Preciado, Ruiz, and Ramírez recognize the women in these oral history projects as narrators and storytellers who speak themselves into history in order to voice their claims and clear paths for future generations.

Rather than employ oral histories as historians do, as evidence or data informing a more comprehensive and general historical analysis or narrative,[28] *Latina Lives in Milwaukee* situates its narratives in an interdisciplinary framework, as texts that participate in genres of oral history (history) and life stories (auto/biographical literature). This recognizes the complexity of both the information that oral histories provide and the narrative performance of each interviewee who offers her story at a particular moment in her life, colored by a set of considerations unique to that time, and to specific listeners Their accounts of important events and daily Latina lives in Milwaukee provide a textured view of Latina/o life in the city throughout the twentieth century.

At every stage of this research—planning, study, collection, interviewing, editing, and analyzing—an interdisciplinary approach has been key. Here I want to discuss some of the interdisciplinary considerations that have been foremost in this work, exploring how a multifaceted analytic frame might also make a difference in how readers understand these oral histories.

The "autobiographical desire" of the women in *Songs My Mother Sang to Me* and *Chicanas of 18th Street* as well as the women whose stories are collected in *Latina Lives in Milwaukee* parallels that of earlier Mexican American autobiographies in which, as literary scholar Genaro Padilla notes, minority status appears to drive the autobiographical subject's need to establish a historical presence.[29] Often read strictly as ethnographic material, according to Padilla, those earlier autobiographies or oral history/as-told-to narratives had the power to shape perceptions of the collectives to which individual narrators belonged, but because scores of Mexican American personal narratives were, intentionally, never published—because they "were meant to function only as supplemental material for American historians," theirs was a latent power. Padilla calls scholars to rescue "our autobiographical literature from such archival incarceration" and reminds us of the value of autobiographical narrative to reveal an "individual contending with social, cultural and ideological forces," asking us not to dismiss collaboratively produced narratives but instead to remain attentive to the conditions of their production, including the individual and personal voice as an aspect of the collaborative authority of these texts.[30] He argues:

> As more and more autobiography scholars, especially feminist and third world practitioners, are arguing, traditional genre constraints have been exclusionary and must be renegotiated, wedged open to alternate forms of self-representation— historiography, cultural ethnography, folkloristic narratives—which do not focus exclusively upon the development of individual personality so much as upon the formation, and transformation, of the individual within a community transformation.[31]

Padilla's call not to ignore collaboratively produced narratives in autobiography studies runs up against Rosaura Sánchez's observation in *Telling Identities: The Californio Testimonios* (1995) that "collaborative efforts of the type generated" by Hubert Howe Bancroft's nineteenth-century historiographic project produced life narratives "mediated and filtered through a second, more powerful agency, that of the interviewer/editor," which, she argues, do not fit into the standard definition of auto-biography as a self-generated text.[32] Sánchez points out that the names of Californios who participated in Bancroft's oral history project were subsequently erased from history as authors of their own life stories in Bancroft's publishing projects, and later their narratives were frequently cited in historical works as anonymous sources.[33] Sánchez's critique echoes that of Padilla in calling attention to the elimination of self-authorizing Latina/o voices and texts from research, as it joins in Padilla's implicit argument that this loss is not only one of perspective and nuance but also constitutive of inequalities and domination. While the two scholars may disagree on what term to apply to collaboratively produced narratives, they agree entirely on the need for researchers to function with an awareness of the power dynamics at play as well as an ethical acknowledgment of the contributions of individuals and groups to making history.

In particular, Padilla's work on Mexican American autobiography matters here, because he has devoted considerable attention to how the life narratives and stories of Mexican and Mexican American subjects appear in ethnographic, sociological, and psychological research. In tracing out the genealogy of the modes in which Mexican and Mexican American life narratives are gathered by social scientists and made available to researchers from the 1920s through the 1970s, and comparing these with the modes of fiction, biography, and autobiography, Padilla delineates the ways that Latina/o subjects have been erased and silenced in that research:

> I am interested in identifying the specific discursive practices by which a voice is projected into a body in order to tell a story that serves sociology as a representation for a set of generalizations about immigration and immigrants. As a scholar of autobiography, I also wish to discover how this process is resisted—how and when the immigrant Mexican ceases being the object about whom the social scientist can "formulate scientific problems," the embodiment of the discipline's typical concerns, and becomes, rather, the autonomous subject of his or her own narrative fascination, an autobiographical agent rather than a de-named object of speculation.[34]

Padilla describes the method that Manuel Gamio articulates and later researchers of Mexican immigrant life adopt in the course of their "objective observations" as a kind of "anthropological hypnotism." In that method, researchers initiated conversation with potential "informants" about interests, then introduced comments and questions about other persons and lives to suggest indifference about the informant being interviewed, then waited for responses. Once the interviewee was engaged, direct questions were posed, often of a type that "implicitly derided" the informant or questioned their loyalty.[35] As Padilla suggests, this "scientific method" relied on the "objective researcher" to bring forth "data" from an unsuspecting informant, thereby eliminating that subject's autobiographical agency.[36] As Padilla argues:

> However, the immigrant subjects of Gamio's study—as well as those subjects of succeeding studies—in responding to the social scientist's systematic perturbation of memory have had their painful experiences of liminality and cultural difference structured in a particular way. The construction of the immigrant subject was not

intended to open sustained, self-authorizing, autobiographically free terrain for immigrants to think about the fullness of experience in any sustained manner: memory, rather, was orchestrated to produce data in a form that could be contained, an account of cultural otherness, a narrative of the immigrant subject as marginal, suspended in a stasis between two cultures, not an active participant in the life of the United States.[37]

The fake names ascribed to interviewees by researchers such as John Poggie, Robert Redfield, and Oscar Lewis (to protect the confidentiality of participants in these studies) emerges, in Padilla's analysis, as something that has "developed into a self-authorizing instrument for deciding what is in the best interest of the human subject, for dominating the human subject, for controlling discourse about the human subject" rather than strictly protecting the interviewee from political persecution or deportation.[38] In this scenario, the anonymity of the subjects and questionable tactics for "extracting" information from them are interwoven, and of this Padilla is quite critical.

In contrast, historians of Latinas/os in the Midwest have taken the opposite approach. Rather than engage in suspect practices, they carefully document Latina/o voices where these appear in the record, name individuals who speak about important experiences and events, and make both Latina/o individuals and groups known to us. Yet, Padilla places greater value on the autobiographical voice than perhaps many social scientists and historians and asks us to seek out this "self-fashioned and self-empowering formation" in mediated life narratives: "This story contains its own logic, its own necessity. The original subject's need to tell this story, this basic narrative desire, as I call it, invests narrative performance with a claim to presence in the world that it is our responsibility to help validate in the act of reading."[39] In one reading, Padilla locates this self-fashioning and the power of voice in one subject's expression of negotiating loss and familial trauma rather than in his discussion of intercultural experiences, because it is in "the disclosure of formative personal experience, the crises and achievements that shape personality and the emotional life" that we recognize a person and not a category.[40]

According to literary scholars Sidonie Smith and Julia Watson: "In autobiographical acts, narrators become readers of their experiential histories, bringing discursive schema that are culturally available to them to bear on what has happened."[41] But they also observe: "The life narrative and the novel share features we ascribe to fictional writing: plot, dialogue, setting, characterization, and so on."[42] Padilla and Smith and Watson recognize oral histories and collaborative life writing as complex and creative narrative constructions driven by a socially conscious autobiographical desire.

Robert Folkenflik argues in *The Culture of Autobiography: Constructions of Self-Representation* that "autobiography is a battlefield on which competing ideas about literature (and for that matter history) are fought out. It is a highly problematic form (some would say genre) that encourages the asking of questions about fact and fiction, about the relations of reality and the text, about origins. Is autobiography to be found in referentiality, textuality, or social construction?"[43] The concerns of ethnography, oral history, and life writing have merged in recent decades, informing each other in unique ways including the paradigm shift from objective to participant observer, the expansion of biography/autobiography genre to life writing, the shift from viewing individuals who share their histories and life stories with others from informants or research subjects to participants and speaking subjects.

In exploring the lack of research in oral history, Ronald J. Grele examines disciplinary biases that still remain, although they were more prevalent in the 1980s than today. Writing in the late 1980s, Grele discusses the disdain with which oral history is viewed in traditional history departments. As Grele outlines them, traditional historians have a number of theoretical and methodological questions about the "subjective" nature of the oral history as well as concerns about the historian him or herself making choices of what to preserve rather than coming upon what is "already there."[44] Yet Grele's critique, considering my earlier discussion regarding the lack of archival resources available about Latinas/os in Milwaukee, also suggests that we cannot ignore the "subjective" nature of what is preserved at present, by whom, and for whom, and the ways that power structures the creation of archives and of knowledge. This volume represents only one piece of the work underway today to collect, archive, and circulate the oral histories of Latinas/os in the Midwest, but that work is presented here in a decidedly unique form as a set of edited life stories, modeled after Preciado Martin's 1992 *Songs My Mother Sang to Me*, so as to be widely available and easily studied.

As the above discussion illustrates, oral histories and collaborative life writing projects partake of two discourses: history and literature. They are forms that disrupt the unities of both fields and prompt "a whole cluster of questions" about the self-evidence of each discourse.[45] In both the interviews I conducted and in the subsequent editing collaborations with the women whose life stories appear in this volume, attention to elements of storytelling were as central to how the women described and knew themselves, and key in my own interpretations of them as I edited, as were considerations of dates, events, and memory. From the beginning, questions of mediation, archival significance, editing, and performance were in play. When I entered the transcribing and editing phases of the project, the more literary concerns of representation, narrative, and storytelling gained prominence in the work. Life writing has gained a new prominence in literary study recently, and its literary theory has attuned us to the significance of the creation and possible reception of these life stories among readers. Life writing in its many forms—autohisteoría, autobiography, memoir, biography, testimonio, and now oral history—has entered the interdisciplinary Latina/o studies classroom. My hope is that these life stories will be studied in many contexts, including history, literature, gender, and ethnic studies.

Feminism, Gender, and *Latinidades* in Research Method and Findings

An awareness of race, ethnicity, gender, class, nation, and sexuality as socially constructed boundaries of difference or categories of belonging and identity, as well as politically salient discursive constructions with real material consequences, undergirds this project's focus, framework, and findings. This awareness also emerges repeatedly in the oral histories collected here as participants offer self-definitions, remark upon exclusions, recognize desires and ambitions, and map their lives. Since this project collects the oral histories of Latinas, it necessarily focuses on women who, following Kimberlé Williams Crenshaw's theory of intersectionality, experience their lives in multiple registers at once. More importantly, taking an intersectional approach in this study militates against, for example, separating the gender issues in Ramona Arsiniega's life story offered here from those of her Mexican ethnicity and nationality, and immigrant status. Such a separation would only reinscribe what Crenshaw states as "the descriptive content of those categories and the narratives on which they are based [that] have privileged some experiences and excluded others."[46] Instead, these oral histories are offered in line with Crenshaw's project of developing "a political discourse that more fully empowers women of color."[47] For example, several women speak about life-long efforts to redefine an ethnic category to one that can be inclusive of all genders and sexualities. This project also takes seriously the distance that Crenshaw takes from identity politics, which tends toward a homogenous view of a group. As she states, "ignoring differences within groups contributes to tension among groups."[48] Several of the narratives collected here reference histories of intra-Latina/o and interethnic tensions, but they also reflect changing attitudes and understandings. Crenshaw's analysis of intersectionality on structural and political planes is not simply an application of a theory of identity but an analytical focus on "how the social world is constructed" through "multiple grounds of identity."[49] The participants in *Latina Lives in Milwaukee* reveal the operation of powerful social constructions in real lives as well as the ways that they work to limit, contest, or alter those social constructions in their daily lives, demonstrating the fluidity of cultural change.

The Interdisciplinary Research Process: Method and Theory

In the first stages of the project, between 2008 and 2011, I interviewed select participants to create a pool that would represent the ethnic, generational, and occupational diversity of the Latina population of Milwaukee. Initially I was most interested in researching Latina leadership, but I soon found other important themes emerging. While I studied interview and oral history methods in advance, I also learned a great deal in the process of the work itself, and I thank every participant in the project for her patience and cooperation. I listened for syntactical or linguistic clues and threads of stories separated by tangents. I recognized, as the editors of *Women's Words* note, that the interview was itself "a linguistic, as well as a social and psychological event."[50] For the women who participated in this project, this first stage of the research meant setting aside time for interviews, considering possible questions before the interview, and gathering professional and/or biographical information to share with me. The participants also likely researched *me* to ensure that I would be a worthy collaborator in what they would share. Preparation and planning was involved for those on both sides of the microphone. I informed all participants that I sought insight on Latina leadership and that I imagined younger Latinas as the audience for this book. Participants were also informed that their oral histories would be edited for publication, and I invited their collaboration during that process. Finally, everyone agreed that their audio interviews and transcripts would eventually be deposited in an archive for future research.

The Mission Statement for this project that I distributed in 2008 to all possible participants in the project stated:

> The purpose of the Latina Oral Histories of Milwaukee Project is to document the unique history and experiences of Latinas in Milwaukee and the contributions of Latinas to both Latino/a and Milwaukee city communities through the accounts of the women involved in or directly affected by these experiences and events.
>
> Designed to encompass Milwaukee's Latino/a community and specifically Latinas in Milwaukee as a study area, the project's period of significance is 1940 to the present, and the project's focus is on the lives, daily activities, challenges, ideals, leadership, and civic contributions of Latinas in Milwaukee. Because women's work and women's concerns are often overlooked in histories and because women often contribute to family and community survival and success in ways not visible to the public yet important for succeeding generations to know, this project will be an

important addition to existing histories of Milwaukee, its ethnic communities, and its Latino/a communities. Through this project information about Latina lives in Milwaukee, including homemakers, community activists, professional and career women, not available or documented elsewhere will be gathered and published in an edited volume primarily aimed at an academic audience of scholars, teachers, and students. This collection will likely also have some broader appeal among Latino/as. All work will be performed according to the guidelines of the Oral History Association.[51]

The most common locations for interviews were the homes or offices of the participants who agreed to join in the project. In two cases, interviews were conducted at a library or community center. Some participants brought photos with them, but in most cases photos were gathered after the interviews. Since the project was framed as one that focused on women's leadership of families, communities, organizations, and/or professions, many of the questions posed to participants centered on their journeys to leadership and their experiences in leading.

Next, I began the lengthy process of transcribing, translating, editing, and revising. This included further collaboration with the many women who participated in this project via mail, telephone, and email, gathering their feedback on the edited versions of their life stories, ensuring accuracy, and researching references in the stories. This process provided multiple opportunities for interviewees to collaborate in shaping the narrative while respecting the difference between interview and edited text. Alessandro Portelli notes that "the transcript turns aural objects into visual ones, which inevitably implies changes and interpretation." Creating a transcript, according to Portelli, requires the insertion of punctuation and the "flattening" of emotional content to create a standardized written document.[52] Transcribing and editing the interviews required constantly questioning what was being said, something that isn't always self-evident.[53] As scholars in this field have noted and this brief description confirms, oral history involves analysis and choice in several stages of the process. This book of first person life stories represents my, and in some cases our, translation of the aural transcript into a more standardized narrative form.

The methodological, theoretical, and ethical questions that feminist scholars and researchers have struggled with in recent decades resonate in distinct ways in this project, focused as it is on telling the life stories of Latinas in Milwaukee, Wisconsin. Oral history and testimonio have emerged at key moments in the past century as vehicles for documenting the experiences of those whose lives were often overlooked in history, whether they were rural workers during the Depression; lesbians in the closeted mid-twentieth century; African American, Chicana/o, or Puerto Rican civil rights activists; or women building the feminist movement. As both articulations of a historical imagination and methods for the construction of history, oral history and testimonio have made significant inroads in the academy since the 1970s, particularly among scholars in interdisciplinary studies who have recognized these as vehicles for self-representation among disenfranchised groups. Scholars Doris Sommer and John Beverley remind us that testimonio represents collective experience in an individual story in a way that appeals to readers as equals.[54] Sonia Saldivar-Hull argues that testimonio is particularly valuable in making women's social movement visible.[55] Elizabeth Kennedy notes that oral history is often dismissed as subjective, yet therein lies its power: oral history reveals an individual experience of broad social questions, an aspect of this methodology that she values more highly than the new facts it contributes.[56]

Concerns of ethnography and oral history in recent decades have merged with the narrative concerns of life writing and memoir as these latter forms have flourished in the late twentieth and early twenty-first centuries. We now conduct research in a disciplinary and narrative environment that has shifted from objective to participant observers, from biographers to autobiographers and memoirists, from informants to testimonio—with a newfound focus on the voice of the speaking subject. Our speaking subjects are engaged in a complex process, as Katherine Borland reminds us: the narration of a life story is a complex event in itself and, when recorded, occurs simultaneously with another event of some complexity, the preservation of that life story through documentation by interview.[57] Marianne Hirsch and Valerie Smith note that "acts of memory are . . . acts of performance, representation, and interpretation," a view that I apply here in recognition of the power of the participants in this project to shape their life stories in ways that convey their agency, insight, and analysis.[58] Research on the complexity of life writing and its narrative and representational strategies has grown, and this has given varied forms of life writing—including oral history and collaborative life writing—new purchase in the Latina/o literature classroom where it joins growing numbers of memoirs, autobiographies, and testimonios. Doris Sommer's trenchant argument about how we might read testimonial life stories is as applicable to this oral history volume as it is to the testimonio of Rigoberta Menchú or the fiction of Toni Morrison: the silences and moments of refusal that a text presents may not be "simply a barrier to enhance desire for the chase. It is also a barricade against the rush of short-lived sentimental identification that oversteps restricted positions and lasts hardly longer than the reading. . . . It is a self-authorizing strategy that incites desire in order to chasten it."[59] While I am not suggesting that these oral histories are testimonios, a point I discuss further in the next section, they do have testimonio-like moments, and they often enjoin us to listen carefully through their moments of refusal to elaborate in a way that would make them spectacles for easy consumption while also insisting on making known their lived experiences. Asking participants to discuss their paths to leadership and their experiences of leadership prompted them to analyze their lives as they narrated them, theorizing about their own journeys. These narratives, therefore, might be usefully read as "autohistorias," as Gloria E. Anzaldúa defines this: "The concept that Chicanas and women of color write not only about abstract ideas but also bring in their personal history as well as the history of their community. I call it 'auto' for self-writing, and 'historia' for history—as in collective, personal, cultural, and racial history."[60] The method of autohistoria blends many of the critical considerations addressed here.

As I hope this discussion of methodology and process makes evident, readers of this book are encountering a series of life stories cocreated by the participants and myself in a way that owes much to feminist and ethnic studies scholarship on how to gather historical, ethnographic, and autobiographical research from women of color in a way that respects the agency of participants in research, and following Rina Benmayor's model, in a way that allows participants "to make meaningful contributions to their own well-being" as well as that of the families, communities, and future generations with whom they share commitments.[61]

Findings: *Latina Lives in Milwaukee*

This project departs from more "traditional academic approaches" wherein analyses "move toward comparison, tend to simplify, aggregate, and reduce experience to variables," as the authors and editors of *Telling to Live: Latina Feminist Testimonios* explain.[62] Instead, this project offers multiple oral histories, full life stories that in their rich and textured detail illuminate some important Latina experiences in Milwaukee and present significant new insight on Latina/o life in the Midwest. This project follows the impetus to illuminate women's lives more fully evident in the work of Vicki L. Ruiz and Virginia Sánchez-Korral, and extends this to include Latinas in the Midwest region.[63] Like the work of Ruiz and Sánchez-Korral on Latina biographies, *Latina Lives in Milwaukee* includes women from different classes and occupations.[64] However, in addition to the organization of subsections in each oral history, and by way of providing readers with a guide to the chapters that follow, this section offers readers an overview of what these oral histories offer and how they offer it.

As a scholar of fictional testimonio,[65] I recognize testimonio as a unique narrative form whose contours scholar John Beverley and others have carefully delineated. The features of the form include the presence of a mediating scribe recording another's story and the telling of a journey to consciousness about social or political oppression in a way that invites readers to join in solidarity with the cause of the testimonial subject. The women interviewed for this project, however, are not engaged in a specific shared social movement but instead in more general cultural shifts, and their narratives do not always adhere to the overarching frame in testimonio of developoing a movement consciousness, nor do they necessarily see themselves as a cause with which others can align. Rather, these women share their life stories with many details of family origins, relations, and conflicts; jobs, careers, and interests; and opportunities and lost opportunities, in a way that makes their community building and history-making evident to larger audiences. As noted above, these oral histories do have testimonial moments, that is, times in the story when a woman is aware of narrating an experience shared by many, and, therefore, a representative one, or instances when a woman relates a particular social or political epiphany she felt at a certain moment in her life; however, these narratives are primarily about individual experiences of general social, cultural, and economic life at particular periods.

In 2008 when I began interviewing Latinas in Milwaukee from three different generations, I suspected that they might be able to shed light on events important to communal histories, but I hoped that they could also share their lived experiences of gender, sexuality, and race, especially in relation to their leadership of families, organizations, businesses, and communities. In the first person life stories of this book, women discuss their participation in educational, professional, commercial, social, and political organizations; multiethnic political and civic movements; family life and religious community; movements for lesbian rights and against domestic violence; and transnational migration and immigration. Listening to these women throughout the past several years—in person, on tape, and on the page—has been both a privilege and a learning experience and has contributed to my own appreciation for the many fronts on which women, generation after generation, seek equality.

In both their individual stories and taken together as a volume, a strong sense of everyday Latina/o life in Milwaukee emerges from the mid-twentieth century forward, including the key industries in which Latina/os found employment, and in the latter half of the twentieth century, the professional careers that opened up to include Latinas/os; the social clubs, religious groups, and community organizations around which Latinas/os coalesced and where Latinas, in particular, found support and friendship; the changes in educational opportunity afforded to Latinas over the course of the twentieth century; the political and social movements in which Latinas participated and how these impacted both individuals and the broader populace; immigrant and migrant experiences for women; the significance of transnational ties in family and communal lives;

and the way that Latinas in Milwaukee participate in national and regional economic, literary, and political movements.

In some ways, these stories are my stories, too. I grew up in Milwaukee and participated in the social, cultural, and political life of the city and Latina/o communities until moving away in my early twenties. My familiarity with many of the places, events, and periods discussed in these oral histories, yet unfamiliarity with others and the many changes in Milwaukee since I last lived there, gave me both entry and inspired caution.

Readers will learn much from the life stories included here, narratives that often disrupt more commonplace understandings of Latinas/os and present new perspectives on Latina/o experiences and history. One way that this book stands out is that in addition to the generational and occupational diversity of the women speakers, it collects the voices of Latinas from across the political spectrum in a way that might illuminate why the intersection of gender/race/ethnicity continues to matter so much in the United States.

Migration

Historical studies show that Latina/o migration to Milwaukee and settlement there was spurred by the recruitment of Latina/o workers to the United States and the region as well as political and economic turmoil in Latin American countries. Several of the Latina oral histories collected here, however, disrupt popular conceptions of migration and settlement as driven exclusively by male breadwinners by telling the stories of their mothers' and foremothers' roles in migration. Antonia Morales tells us that her father arrived in Milwaukee first, and she and the rest of the family arrived a year or two later, including her mother and two brothers. Yet, when her father died just nine years later, the family did not return to Mexico but stayed in Milwaukee where she participated in a growing Latina/o community. María Monreal Cameron describes her mother as the catalyst for the family's move to Milwaukee, where her father and older siblings secured industrial work, as well as her mother's role in later building a family business. Ramona Arsiniega recalls that though her husband's work was in Milwaukee, she preferred to stay in Mexico, and it wasn't until she was sure of a network of support from women peers that she decided to join her husband. Arsiniega's oral history also includes discussion of her U.S.-citizen husband's move to Mexico with his parents in their 1954 repatriation, illuminating the back and forth of U.S.-immigration policies in constituting a Latina/o population, as well as enduring transnational relationship. Olivia Villarreal's oral history tells a more traditional tale, like that of Antonia Morales, of her father migrating to Waukesha for work ahead of the rest of his family and then later bringing them all to live in Waukesha together; yet in describing what made it possible for her family to thrive in Milwaukee she notes the importance of both her mother's role in raising and supporting the family, as well as supplementing the household income with summer agricultural work, and her father's multiple jobs.

In these oral histories, both Antonia Morales and Ramona Arsiniega describe living in rented flats in the 1940s, 1950s, and 1960s that in some instances did not provide hot water and in others lacked sufficient heat. This required that all water for bathing, cooking, and washing had to be boiled on the stove. In addition, some flats did not have bathtubs, requiring women to bathe their children in tin tubs purchased for this purpose. These elements of their stories highlight that life in the United States was not automatically superior in all aspects to their previous lives in their home countries, though that was frequently what potential immigrants heard and anticipated.

In these pages, the importance of support networks among migrant mothers and working women emerge as significant factors in individual and communal success, and as essential components of decisions to migrate. These narratives depart from the focus on male breadwinners alone to recognize more complex patterns of migration and the multiple sources of economic and social support that made life in Milwaukee for Latina/o communities possible. As discussed earlier, some of these oral histories reveal migrations that occurred outside of the major periods and in response to other factors than the lure of steady and well-paying industrial or agricultural work. In the oral histories of Daisy Cubías and Olga Valcourt, education is the primary reason for migration, and their narratives speak to the diversity of class and ethnic/national background among Milwaukee Latinas/os. The participants in this project acknowledge the hard work of both their fathers and mothers in sustaining family and community, and often specifically praise their mothers and grandmothers as models.

Multiethnic Latina/o Life

As I noted earlier in this chapter, Latinidad in Milwaukee has long incorporated a diversity of racial, ethnic, and national backgrounds. The earliest Mexican and Mexican American residents were soon joined by Puerto Ricans, Cuban Americans, Central Americans, South Americans, and Dominicans. The selection of interviewees for this book reflects, in part, this reality, but so too do the stories they share. In relating their experiences in the Milwaukee Public School system both Elvira Sandoval Denk, who is Mexican American, and Olga Valcourt, who is Puerto Rican, make plain that collaborations among Puerto Rican and Mexican professionals, parents, and students were vital to the success of the bilingual education program and its students. Valcourt also stresses this intra-Latina/o cooperation as essential to the success of a key Milwaukee Latina/o community organization, the United Community Center (UCC), as well as the success of its programs serving diverse Latina/o communities. A longtime participant in the UCC as well as other initiatives, Valcourt describes inclusion and respect for Latina/o diversity as central to her life's work. Daisy Cubías echoes this commitment in a later era when discussing her outreach work to involve Latina/o parents in K–12 educational settings. Cubías, who is Salvadoran American and whose professional career was varied, also discusses her employment advising Mexican agricultural workers and her role as an assistant to the mayor on Latina/o affairs. In the business sector, Olivia Villarreal, who is Mexican American, attributes the success of her family grocery store business to Milwaukee's Latina/o communities, while María Monreal Cameron, Mexican American and former director of the Hispanic Chamber of Commerce, describes efforts to support all Latina/o businesspersons as well as Latina/o professionals.

However, if we are tempted to think that intra-ethnic collaborations are more common among professional classes, we would be mistaken. In describing her experience of assembly, service, and industrial work outside of the home, Ramona Arsiniega remembers meeting women from other ethnic/national backgrounds in each of these workplaces, including Puerto Rican and Cuban American women. The workplace was not the only site of intra-ethnic encounters among Latinas. Arsiniega also recounts her participation in events sponsored by the International Institute that brought together Latina/os from diverse national/ethnic backgrounds. In general, the participants show awareness of processes of racialization or of strict black/white binaries, though not always. Unfortunately, I did not directly ask any questions about Latina/o and African American interactions, and there is little here about these relations except the recognition of segregation or mention of civil rights struggles. Nonetheless, from these oral histories, it appears that Latinas who exercised a variety of leadership roles in the city did so as a result of their ability to remain attentive to all of the city's Latina/o constituencies.

Intersectionality

When Carmen Murguia states that "it was okay to be Mexican, but I wanted more," she voices a recognition of her own multi-dimensionality but also captures the way that an intersectional analytic—one that considers gender, race, ethnicity, class, sexuality, and nationality in relation to each other rather than in isolation from each other—informs the oral histories collected here. These intersecting experiences shape both the access to opportunity and the character of that opportunity for the participants in this project, and because of this the interviewees often describe their lives with an intersectional lens. Murguia's oral history includes the story of her and her family's successful journey toward mutual acceptance and their embrace of all of her identities, including her identity as a Mexican American lesbian.

As the earlier discussion on the topic of migration in these oral histories suggests, an intersectional approach to migration stories and histories reveals the significance of women's roles in making migration possible and success-ful—through work inside and outside the home, with willingness and inspi-ration, and via networks of support these women established. Every woman interviewed for this project worked outside of the home. That is, working out-side of the home was not confined only to those in the professional sector, nor was it exclusively generational since the Sandoval sisters, Olivia Villarreal, and María Monreal Cameron each recall their own mothers working outside of the home at different points in their lives. The jobs available to migrant women of an earlier generation including agriculture, janitorial services, and restaurant service were most often not unionized, and therefore workers in these industries did not enjoy as much of a public presence as those in unionized industries. Women's work both inside and outside of the home was not readily visible or acknowledged, which is one reason why these oral histories repeatedly do so. When Ramona Arsiniega describes her factory work outside of the home as an opportunity for her to have her own money and not an economic necessity, she seems to adhere to the script of minimizing the importance of women's labor, but she also describes in her life story how her salary concretely mattered in the household and in the well-being of herself and her children, a sentiment that Antonia Morales also echoes in describing her work outside of the home. Although this book does not include the interviewees' many expressions of pride in the education and economic independence of both their male and female children, every participant expressed this in the interviews and viewed themselves as having made an important contribution to that next generation, including often of having imparted a different attitude about gender, a project they continue here in sharing their oral histories.

The Latina participants in this project did not dwell much on personal encounters with discrimination or domestic violence, and many resist seeing themselves as victims of discrimination, yet both issues came up in several inter-views as enduring, unsolved problems Latinas face. Nearly all the oral histories collected here suggest an instance of discrimination due to language/ethnicity/ race that in its openness seems to have also been highly gendered, or an incident of gender discrimination compounded by ethnicity, race, or class. Daisy Cubías describes several such moments with both righteousness and humor, and in her stories prejudiced people are silenced by her wit or outmaneuvered by her honesty and forthrightness.

Education

It was striking to me that Olga Valcourt's experience as a college student of being explicitly steered away from math echoed Antonia Morales's experience of not being awarded the top marks she had earned in mathematics. As today's efforts at recruiting more women and underrepresented groups into math and science fields show, we all lose when we actively discourage young women of color from pursuing these educational paths. A path that was open to women—and much more so than government or leadership of social service agencies—was the field of education, and several participants in this oral history enjoyed long and illustrious careers in education in Milwaukee. In fact, Elvira Sandoval Denk and Margaret Sandoval Skare were among the first Latinas hired by Milwaukee Public Schools (MPS), as counselor and librarian respectively, while Olga Valcourt was the first woman to lead the bilingual education program for MPS. Each of these women also describes their extensive efforts to ensure educational opportunities for younger Latinas/os including creating and administering programs, writing grant proposals, leading workshops, advising and mentoring students and faculty, raising scholarship funds, and promoting the successes of their students. Their stories show us that if we want to identify and study Latina leadership, looking at the areas where Latinas *were* allowed to lead is crucial.

"The Firsts"—Latinas in Professions

In addition to the "firsts" in education discussed here, María Monreal Cameron, although now retired, was the first Latina to lead the Hispanic Chamber of Commerce (HCC). Monreal Cameron describes her efforts to center support for women and Latina professionals in her work at HCC through her extensive work building an educational scholarship fund for Latina/o college students in Milwaukee. The routes toward becoming the first Latina counselor, first Latina librarian, first Latina executive of the HCC provided in this volume, while unique to each individual, also resonate beyond the individual experience for many other Milwaukee and midwestern Latinas who have been "firsts" in new fields and areas. These are not the elements of history or experience of Latinas/os in the Midwest that currently prevail in our own stories, narratives, or consciousness about our lives in this region, and that makes them important stories to share.

Americanization or Leadership?

While adult education programs may have been aimed at inculcating anti-Communism and enforcing assimilation according to one prominent Milwaukeean describing them in the early 1950s, what they meant to the women who participated in them was another matter.[66] Antonia Morales relates with great pride how her mother enjoyed decades of adult day school education, learning everything that her children learned in K–12. Her description allows us to envision her mother not merely as a passive Mexican recipient of Americanization but as a parent actively maintaining a family and household by studying in day school, preparing herself to understand and assist her children in their own U.S. educations. While the emphasis in Americanization and adult day school classes appears to have been on imparting education and language rather than incorporating the immigrant's knowledge and language, Antonia Morales's story suggests that we know more about how mainstream organizers and educators viewed these programs than we do about the difference they made in the daily lives of new immigrants. As a young mother, Morales also participates in parent-centered activities, which are important to assisting her own children but that also provide an opportunity for her as a stay-at-home mom to expand her social network and develop friendships. Ramona Arsiniega also describes her participation in English classes as an avenue for expanding her social networks among other newcomers to the city, networks that we know are critical in seeking employment, housing, and opportunity. In the experience of these two women, community adult education classes allowed them to make connections with other Latinas/os and immigrants, learn about housing and jobs, and take pleasure and enjoy a social life with other adults in situations where they might otherwise have been socially isolated in the home. Since Arsiniega also describes her enduring attachment to her home country of Mexico and her family's frequent trips there, which were critical to sustaining family relationships across borders, the paradigm of a transnational life has greater salience in her experience than that of an exclusively U.S. life. As research in Latina/o Studies has shown, transnationalism is not uncommon among Latinas/os in the United States. We might view Daisy Cubías's antiwar activism against U.S. support for the Salvadoran regime in the 1980s as an element of her transnational life, since her family in El Salvador was directly harmed by the war. Cubías and Valcourt migrated to the United States for education, but in ways unique to their specific national contexts. They arrived as already educated subjects seeking a U.S. education, and they worked to understand the United States as well as its relationship to their home countries. In these oral histories, the women suggest that both higher education and adult education programs were ways to know both what their children were learning in U.S. schools and how to assist their children; a way to establish greater mobility for themselves and, by extension, their families via language acquisition and an avenue to meet other Latinas and build social networks.

Conclusion

Given the limited number of life stories presented here, this book is a partial contribution toward understanding the Latina experience in Milwaukee and the Midwest. *Latina Lives in Milwaukee* begins with the life stories of women whose families arrived in Milwaukee in the 1920s and concludes with the life story of a Mexican American woman born and raised in Milwaukee, thereby providing a chronologically ordered view of everyday life throughout the twentieth century for Latinas in Milwaukee through the lens of complex, individual oral histories.

2. It Wasn't Bad to Live without a Car

ANTONIA MORALES
Interviewed on August 21, 2008
Homemaker, Retail, and Office Worker

Learning English

My father, Luciano Haro, was living here before my mother, Norberta, and my two brothers and myself came to live in Milwaukee. We came in April of 1926. My father had been here a year or two before that, or maybe longer. He was working at the Pfister and Vogel Tannery. We came from Tepitclan, Zacatecas, in Mexico.

We had a portrait picture taken within a year of arriving, and in it I must have been about a year and a half or two, and my brother was three, and the other, I think, he was four and a half. My mom stayed at home all the time. I think she started working when she was about fifty years old.

I started kindergarten when I was about three and a half years old. I don't really remember the first school I went to because I was in kindergarten, but I remember that two of the girls in the neighborhood would always be arguing about who was going to take me to school—that's when we lived on First and Orchard in what must have been 1928. Then we moved over to where the grocery store was, over on South Fifth Street, and I went to kindergarten there at Vieau School.[1] I wasn't quite four. I went to Vieau School until seventh grade, and then in eighth grade I went to Holy Trinity School for my last year. Well, the pastor of our Church at Our Lady of Guadalupe wanted the Mexican children to get a Catholic education, and I guess he talked to the pastor at Holy Trinity so that we could go there without paying tuition. At Holy Trinity, there were a few other Mexican students—maybe three or four others. I can remember two others in my class. I graduated from Holy Trinity and then I went to Mercy High School.

Well, when I went to kindergarten I didn't know any English at all. I learned English from kindergarten on, I think, because I don't remember not knowing

English and only knowing Spanish. My mother always wanted to be a citizen of the United States so she would always tell us, "Don't speak to me in Spanish. Speak to me in English." That's why my Spanish isn't that good.

My mother went to school for about twenty years, attending adult education classes at Vieau School so she could get her citizenship papers, and she got them when she was fifty years old. It was important to her. I remember she was always going to school, and in the daytime. I don't think she went to night school. I don't think they had night school. They had day school. After she passed away we had a lot of her things, and there were so many of her notebooks on history and geography and things that I had learned years before when I was in high school, but that I had already forgotten because I was older. She had it all written down.

When I changed schools, I left so many of my friends at Vieau School. I really didn't like it, but when I went to Trinity some of the popular girls became real good friends with me so then I didn't mind being transferred.

The Changing Ethnic and Racial Composition of Catholic Parish

My family belonged to Our Lady of Guadalupe Parish—actually, at that time it was called a Mission: Our Lady of Guadalupe Mission. I think they called it *Sanctuario de la Señora de Guadalupe*. That was the name. It was on Fifth Street. It was just a storefront building. They had converted the first floor into a church, and the upstairs was where the three priests lived. There was a basement, too, and that's where we had our catechism classes.

In 1946, the *Sanctuario* moved over to Third and Washington, and in 1966 we moved over to Holy Trinity Parish. The last move was with a procession; it was on a Sunday afternoon, I remember, and it was a big procession, because we were so glad to be able to go to Holy Trinity, because our church was too small for us; it was just getting too crowded. Meanwhile, a lot of the parishioners from Holy Trinity were leaving, because they were moving away from the area. But what happened was that the pastor at that church didn't tell his parishioners that we were coming, so when we arrived there, I think, after one of the masses, all the parishioners were surprised. I don't think they liked us. Or maybe it was just that they weren't told that we were joining them, so it was unexpected. If they would have been told they might have felt differently about it, but not being told and just all of sudden on the front door steps there we are, the whole congregation—well, that was a surprise. The procession had been about a block long; there's a picture of it in *Latino Milwaukee*.

I think that the parishioners never really accepted us. They never said anything to us, but there was that feeling that they wished we weren't there. How

Figure 4. Antonia Morales in foreground with siblings and
parents. Photo used with permission of Antonia Morales.

can I describe it? It just seemed like we weren't welcome. I don't know how long
that feeling stayed, but by the time our children started going to grade school
then there wasn't that animosity there any longer.

Excelling in Math at Mercy High School

For high school, I didn't really know what school to go to, but the pastor who
had directed us to Trinity, Father Gonzales Serapio, also saw to it that I learned
about and got into Mercy High School.[2] My brothers were already in high school.
One went to what was then Boy's Technical High School and the other went to
Bay View High School. When I went to Mercy, I participated in a lot of school
activities. I belonged to a lot of the clubs at Mercy. I was real active there. I also
worked an hour after school to help pay for my tuition. There was another girl

and I who were assigned to clean the chapel after school for 45 minutes to an hour. I remember that out of all the subjects I liked math the best. I saved all my report cards, too, from school. I remember that in my algebra class what the teacher used for our final mark [grade] would be our test scores, and mine were perfect so she said to me one time, "Well, I can't really give you a hundred on your report card because that wouldn't look good." So she only gave me a 98! I just loved algebra. I got good marks in geometry, too, but geometry is so different. Yes, I really liked math, especially algebra.

My sister-in-law's sister was also there at Mercy. Then later on there were more Mexican girls going there, but the year that I started high school I think there were only three of us. But, you know, I never in all my life felt—how can I describe it? where you don't feel you belong because you're a Mexican? I never felt like that. I never felt like a minority. I never felt discriminated against.

Helping Mother as a Girl and Young Woman in the 1930s and 1940s

When I was a kid, Vieau school, across the street, had a big playground and field house. Once when I was in school they flooded the whole park and had ice skating. I never liked winter. I didn't like sports. I liked to read, instead. I was glad to stay home and read; I was that kind of person. My brothers and sisters all went and they skated; that was their playground over there, but I wasn't into that. I didn't do much with the kids because I liked to read and I would read anything. I stayed home but my brothers and sisters enjoyed that playground.

My dad died when I was ten, and I had two older brothers and I had three younger sisters. We went to school and then came home to Mother. She was a housewife and she did all the work, and when I came home from school at five o'clock she already had supper for us. I never really helped with the housework. She never made us do chores. We had to clean the house and all that, but we never had to wash the clothes or cook because she had the time.

After high school I started working. I would have wanted to go on, but we wouldn't have been able to afford it because there were six of us in the family, and my mother got what they called Mothers' Aid for Dependent Children. When my brothers and sisters and I started working, we would contribute half of our paychecks to my mother. We received aid from the State, but when we started working we would have to contribute half, and then the State would take away that amount from what she was getting. I worked at a couple of offices, just office work, for about four years until I got married. My husband's cousin was my best girlfriend. That's how I met him. She lived in the same building that I lived in so he came once or twice when he was a teenager to visit them. That's how I got to know him.

There was a group then called the *Estrellitas* [Little Stars]. It was a Spanish-language group for teenagers. I would like to have joined, but my mother didn't let me; she just didn't want me to join. She was just strict with me, but later with my three younger sisters she wasn't as strict; I kind of broke the ice for them. I tell you, I couldn't go anyplace unless I took my sister; even when I was about twenty years old I had to take her to the movies with me. My mother was real strict with me, even when I was working.

Activities as a Young Woman in the 1940s

After I got married, I still got together with my cousins for a few years, and the girls that we used to hang out with when we were teenagers at the church. During the war years, when the fellows came back they started getting married and then they started moving away, and some of the girls even moved out of the state. You didn't see many of them anymore, because they moved maybe three or four miles away from you and they had different friends so you sort of lost touch with the girls who were your friends when you were teenagers. We all married later and we knew all the different girls and guys in our circle. I got married in 1947.

During the war, however, everything was rationed. If you wanted silk stockings you could hardly even get them. There was a store right across the street from Gimbel's[3] on Second Avenue downtown, and if you went to get stockings the line would be around the block to get a pair of stockings, and then after that you couldn't get any silk stockings. There was always something; sugar was rationed, everything was rationed; gasoline was rationed—you got a certain amount of everything. Most of my brothers went to the war and most of their friends went, too. They all came back at different times; nobody came back at the same time. We just were glad when they did come back.

After I married, I belonged to a group called The Society of Our Lady. Well, we used to meet once a month and maybe more often. We'd have sales at Church, different things to sell at the parish. We had a bake sale every so often to raise money for our society. I joined it because everybody else joined! That was my only social life, really, the church groups were the only social life then for me.

When My Children Entered Schools

When I got married I had eight children, and I tell you, if I had to describe how my life was I would say I was a single mother. No help from my husband. I did everything. When my oldest son went to second grade at Holy Trinity then I got active in their school. At that time, the parents would meet once a month or so, during the day. I remember I'd go and have to take one of my kids with me all the time! I liked it because I got to know different mothers of the kids in school. Some of them became my best friends, for the rest of my life. I don't remember much about the meetings except that I liked going to them, because then I got out of the house! I don't think other women brought children, but I always had to take at least one.

I was less active in their high schools because I was working outside the home by then. I never went to PTA meetings at the high school; I'm not sure they had them. Five of my kids were involved in wrestling, and their matches were in the nighttime, always at a different school. I went to their matches. My oldest son was the first one to get involved when he was just a freshman. He was a wrestler that year. He got to be—at that time they never had such a low-weight class: he was 98 pounds and he won City that year. The second year he didn't go into wrestling, because he wanted to work and get a job. He quit wrestling, but all the other boys continued. He did it just the first year. When I went to see him, I went alone. At that time I was working in the evening, so I went to see him wrestle after work. When I didn't have to work I'd go directly from home to the high schools where they would be wrestling.

The Early Years of Marriage and Children with No Water Heater

From 1948 to 1953, I had five children. That was my work then! I cooked, and washed clothes; it was hard, because when I first got married and for about six years after, I lived in an upper flat that had no tub or no hot water. I had to warm up all the water on the stove. I used to buy one of those big tubs for washing the kids. By that time I had a washing machine in the apartment, so I didn't need the tub for that. Before that, I used to go wash my clothes by my mother's because she only lived five blocks from my house. I'd take my laundry in my little stroller—there was a basket behind it. I'd wash clothes over there twice a week until I got my own washing machine.

I saw my mother just about every day. She'd come over, too, just about every day. When I had my children she'd come over for a month after each child was born to help me with all the housework, because she always said that after giving birth you shouldn't be doing housework, so she'd come over for a whole month and help me.

I lived on East Washington, a half block east of First Street, and I'd shop up on Ninth and Mitchell. I'd pull my wagon with my boys in it and shop that way. They hated it—"What if we see some of the kids from school?" they'd say, and I'd say, "I don't care. I'm not going by myself!" They helped me pull the wagon and all the way they'd be complaining, "It's not my turn," and I would be scolding them that "I'm not going by myself!" [*laughs*] What a time! But we didn't have a car. We never had a car.

It wasn't bad to live without a car, because it was just thirteen or fourteen blocks to Mitchell Street: Gimbels was up there, Schusters was up there, Goldmans was up there—all the big stores.[4] We had five or six bridal shops up on Mitchell Street and we had some fancy places—a First Store was up there, until about two or three years ago. Later, when the kids were more grown up, I would just take my shopping cart there on one of the buses and carry things back in it. It was too heavy to pull up onto the bus when it was full, so I took the bus with the shopping cart empty and then just rolled my shopping home in the cart on foot.

Managing Tuberculosis in the 1950s

I got TB in 1953. Then, I had the three boys. I had had four boys, but one had already passed away in infancy, and I was pregnant with my fifth boy. I was about five months pregnant when I found out I had TB. My boys were two, three, and four years old. When I found out about the TB each of my three sisters said, "We'll take one of the boys." I said, "No, I don't want to separate them." There were only two sites where I could place them through Catholic Welfare Services and they would be together. One was where the UMOS[5] building is now and that used to be St. Vincent's Orphanage. They had children from one to six years old there, but they were separated according to age, so they'd be in the same place but separated by age and I didn't want that for them either. The other option they told me about was the Carmelite Home out in Wauwatosa [a western suburb of Milwaukee], where maybe they would take them, because they accepted children there from after they were potty-trained to about the age of twelve or fifteen. First they asked me—because my youngest was just about two and half, "Is he potty-trained?" I said, "Yes." So that's where the boys stayed, at the Carmelite Home in Wauwatosa. It's still out there now, or was for a long time, though later the Carmelite Home focused on taking care of children who were in trouble.

I was out at the Muirdale Tuberculosis Sanatorium[6] during my illness. Before I went, the boys all had to have health examinations to see that they hadn't contracted the disease. They were all fine, though. Then I went into the hospital at Muirdale in November, the day of my birthday, and the boys went to the Carmelite Home. About two months later they called me down to the office and they said, "Well, we have some news for you," and I thought, "Well, what could it be?" Well, they brought in the three boys because they had sore throats and in children TB starts in the throat, in the bronchial tubes. The boys stayed there and they took tests and the oldest boy didn't have any germ in the body at all, but the other two did; so they kept the two. One boy stayed six months and the other boy stayed nine months, and I was there for the whole year.

I couldn't do anything because at that time, and in the years before that, the only cure for TB was rest; so if you had the TB, then you'd be out there at Muirdale for three or four years. What they would do, I think, was put some things through your lungs and then keep you there for three or four years. But the year that I went out there, they had started experimenting with drugs. They offered treatment with INH (isoniazid), streptomycin, and something else. They gave the different patients different medications to see which would work out best, and it turned out that the INH pill was the one that worked out best, though the one I got was streptomycin. Nowadays, if you get TB that's what they give you: INH. Also nowadays you're not confined. Before if you had TB you had to go out to Muirdale, but now if you have TB they give you INH, and I don't think you're quarantined. I'm not sure about that, though, because nowadays there's not too many cases. Anyhow, that's what I had. They also offered you surgery back then, depending on how your TB was. My TB was in a small section of one of my lungs. If you had the surgery to take the TB out, you could leave two months after. If not, you had to stay there a lot longer. Some of the girls were afraid of surgery so they would stay longer, but I wanted to get out sooner so I had the surgery.

When I entered Muirdale I was five months pregnant and I had my son while I was out there. I had to go out to Misericordia Hospital at that time, to give birth, and then when Gary was born they kept him at the hospital a week longer and then they put him into a foster home, where he stayed until after I got out of Muirdale. The lady and the family kept him a year longer so that I could have even more rest instead of jumping back in to taking care of this little two-year-old.

I was confined from November to November: one year. After I gave birth to my son in March, then I had the operation, because I figured if I didn't have it that the TB might come back. You see, what the medication does is it builds a wall around your TB, but I thought, well, what if that wall breaks? Then I'm going to have TB again. I decided to have the operation, because I didn't care about the scar or anything. I would get out of there sooner, too. They had surgery three days of the week; a doctor from Columbia Hospital would come and do the surgery. Then the week before my surgery, one of the girls died. Well, you can imagine how I felt, but I wanted to get out of there so I decided on my own to go ahead with the surgery. It was scary.

At Muirdale I lived on the third floor and the nurses would take the children for a walk every day, and they'd send me a note saying, "We're going to pass your building today at about two o'clock." Then I would stand by the window and wave to them. Well, they couldn't see me, but I could see them. At that time they had a children's cottage out there at Muirdale, so they were near me, but I could only see them from afar. There'd been too much trouble for it to be any other way—because what if they were getting healthy and you visited them and gave them the germ again? They just never let you see them in person. I never saw them in person when they were out there living in the cottages. No.

In my section, I happened to be in a solarium with about eight other ladies, from all over the city. It was a fun group! [*laughs*] There were some crazy girls in there, young girls, and they'd do some silly things that they'd get away with. Like you weren't supposed to have any electric appliances, so this one girl—she's such a daredevil, she's about eighteen or nineteen—she thought she'd bring in a toaster. She got away with it for one day. The second day they said, "Jeannie, what are you doing with that toaster? We can smell it down the hall!" [*laughs*] Jeannie said, "Well, if we can't use these appliances how come those girls in the other ward can use their hair appliances?" She was talking about black girls in the other ward using curlers to straighten their hair, which we could smell, and she insisted, "If we can't use our things, how can they use theirs?" They said, "Well, that's different." It just so happened that all the black girls were in one ward. I don't think they would have felt comfortable if they were in one of the other wards. There were different ages in the wards, too.

We had our activities, too, and we could do needlecraft, play cards, or anything like that. If you did do sewing, like me—I made some clowns for my boys—then you had to do all your stitching by hand. You couldn't use a sewing machine, because that was too much energy. I had fun! I really did have fun. These two girls on my ward they were so funny. There was a pizza place near, across the street from Muirdale, and they'd call up and say, "Send us over a pizza," and they'd wait downstairs for it to be delivered! These two girls, their mothers would come a couple of nights a week and bring them a big bag full of sweets, and the girls would tell the nurse to go down and meet them and bring the things up to them. The sanitarium didn't mind, because they wanted us to gain weight. It was a fun ward. I think if I'd been in a place with just two people I would've hated it, but there were eight of us and that made it more entertaining. Unless somebody had surgery and then they went home . . . the eight of us stayed.

I'm glad I got TB the year that I did, because that's when they started with the medication. I don't think I would've liked to have been there before; all they did was lay in bed and do nothing. But when I went, I was glad to be out there. I mean I didn't like the fact that I was out there, but if I had to be out there it was a good rest for me. I like my children and everything, yet because I was sick I needed to be away from them, and it became a rest for me. I missed them a lot, though. When I found out that they had to be there at Muirdale for a while, that made me really sad that they had gotten the TB.

Working Outside of the Home

I started working in 1969, when my youngest was five years old. I couldn't start working earlier than that, because I didn't have anyone to take care of the children. My husband said he would, but I think he took care of them for just one week and then I had to quit my job. I had to wait until the older ones could take care of the younger ones, and that's when I started working: when my youngest was in kindergarten—she was five or six.

I worked for about ten years for Doctor Dundon. Well, I worked there from about 1970 to about 1980. Well, he just had the one girl—that was me, taking care of the office and the building. He made house calls. He made a lot of house calls to people that just couldn't go to the office or just didn't have transportation.

I found out about the job from Sister Patricia who was head of Head Start over here, because she knew Sister Dundon. Sister Dundon was Dr. Dundon's daughter, and she knew her Dad was looking for somebody to work. She was friends with the principal of the Head Start, Sister Patricia, so Sister Patricia recommended me for the job.

A lot of times he'd go up to a house call and there'd be three or four other ones there and all they wanted was diet pills and sleeping pills. They abused him. They really did. I used to tell him, "You're going to be sorry if you go there." But he was that kind of doctor that he didn't care about money, or about who paid and didn't pay. I stopped working for him when some of the male patients started getting too abusive, because I wouldn't let them see the doctor when they didn't have an appointment. I knew what they were for, but they'd come back to see the doctor after I had left for the day. Then the next morning doctor would say, "Why did you do that to me?" I'd say "What?" He'd say, "You let all those people in." I said, "No, I didn't. You only had patients until five." But they would come after five.

One day I just quit. I was afraid. I said, what if someday I go home and somebody is down there waiting for me because I didn't let them in? I couldn't put them in there. Dr. Dundon refused to give me unemployment. His daughter and his son came to help and after they had been there for a week or two they said to me, "Toni we know why you quit and we don't blame you." Then he gave me my unemployment. I liked working for him.

About three months later, Dr. Dundon had a stroke. After he had the stroke, he passed away, but up until the time that he had the stroke he made house calls. He was making house calls when he was 80, 81, and 82. I think he died when he was about 83.

Well, then I started working part-time at Arlan's, the discount store. I worked there for about ten years. Then when they closed down, I went to work at Red Owl, a food store, cashiering, for about eight years. I liked cashiering. Both jobs were part-time. My youngest son said to me a few years ago, he said, "I know what you were doing, Mother." I said, "What?" He said, "All of sudden you would disappear, but I knew you went to work. I knew you went to work." When I came home I used to have my big TV there, and all the kids would be huddled in front of it, looking like they were waiting for me to come home! But my little one, I didn't want to upset him, so I just would disappear; I didn't think he would know when I left the house. But a few years ago he told me, "I know what you were doing. You thought you were fooling me, but I knew you were working."

They didn't like for me to be away but they liked when I was working, because then we had money to do things like we didn't have before, to buy what I wanted, and my kids could get shoes when they needed them and not wait until forever to get them. It made a whole lot of difference—different life altogether when I was working. Before that, I was always begging my husband for food money because I wasn't getting enough, but I had to be satisfied with what he gave me.

A New House

My marriage was not an easy one, but another thing that made a big difference was when we moved to this house. I met the woman who had lived here. Her dad used to be the principal of what was then Boy's Technical High School back in 1926, and then he had passed away maybe about fifteen years later and she lived here with her mother. Her mother had died about two years before I met her. She was 94 years old, the mother; she had broken her hip and I think she never recovered. The daughter lived alone by herself here for two years. She invited me into the house saying, "Oh, come in and see the house." In the other house we only had one closet. It was a long skinny closet where you couldn't even hang your things properly because there was no rod. Instead, you had to place the hangers side-by-side, flat and forward facing. Only one closet in that place! Well, when I saw this house I thought, "Oh, all those closets!" Then she showed us the whole house, a closet in each bedroom. The best part, I'll tell you, was that there were front stairs and back stairs within the house.

3. *Hilitos de Oro*

ELVIRA SANDOVAL DENK

GLORIA SANDOVAL ROZMAN

MARGARITA SANDOVAL SKARE

ROSEMARY SANDOVAL LE MOINE

Interviewed on Friday, July 2, 2010

Singer, Beauty Queen, Artist, Homemaker,
Counselor, Teacher, Small Business Owner, Librarian,
Real Estate Broker, Landlord, Volunteer

Immigration to Milwaukee in the 1920s and 1940s

Margarita Sandoval Skare:

Our papá, Pedro Sandoval, came to Milwaukee with his brother, Vidal Sandoval, in 1924. Papá came to Milwaukee as a teenager since he was born on September 9, 1906, but the Border Crossing Manifest lists him as twenty-one years of age. The Milwaukee City Directory lists him as "Pedro Sandobal" at "723 Kinnickinnic Ave" and lists his occupation as laborer, so he came directly to Milwaukee from Mexico in 1924. That's why he is referred to as one of "*Los Primeros*" or the first Mexicans to come to Milwaukee in the early 1920s. Yet we know that Papá was born in Alamo Gordo, New Mexico, where his father Isidro Sandoval was working as a laborer and that his father, Isidro Sandoval, was born in Nochistlan, Zacatecas, Mexico. The family returned to Zacatecas when my father was a child.

In 1924, as my cousin Carlos later told me, Papá was working for the Greenbaum Tannery while his brother Vidal worked at the Plate Glass Company.[1] The tannery work was very difficult; you were always inhaling noxious fumes and working with chemicals. Papá was injured at the tannery after a few months, and then he did look for another type of work and acquired a job at Allis-Chalmers, where he worked as an electrical assembler. He was also a union shop foreman at Allis-Chalmers, which at the time employed ten thousand people—one of the largest employers in the State of Wisconsin.

When he was about thirty-five years old, he decided to go to Mexico. It was 1941 and he had been ill, with pneumonia, and the doctor told him that he needed to go to a warm climate and rest. He drove to Aguascalientes, Aguascalientes, Mexico, in his Ford automobile. The story is—and my mother would tell us these beautiful stories as we were growing up—that he was driving past her family's home when he saw this lovely lady through the window, drying her hair. That was our mamá, Margarita Díaz de Soto. Papá had relatives there as well as relatives in Zacatecas, and he asked to be introduced to Margarita, whose father was Miguel Díaz. Her mother, also named Margarita, was much younger than Miguel Díaz. Through the family introduction, Papá met our mamá, who was then eighteen years old, and they courted—of course, always with a chaperone along.

Before they went to the altar to say the "I do," they had to go through all of the permissions of the Church to marry. In addition, our *abuelita*, Margarita Soto de Díaz, who was very concerned that they did not know this man coming from the United States, hired a private detective to confirm that Papá was, indeed, a single man, and that the Ford was his vehicle. They also wanted to know his family background. Pedro Sandoval and Margarita Díaz were then married on April 14, 1941, in the Cathedral of Aguascalientes, and we have lovely photographs of their beautiful wedding day. Mamá had a gorgeous long-sleeved gown with an eight-foot-long train, a tiara with droplets of dripped wax and a bouquet of calla lilies. Papá wore a black suit with a boutonniere also made of beads of dripped wax. Papá was a very handsome man. Until the day he died, he had his full head of hair.

Rosemary Sandoval Le Moine:

For their honeymoon, they toured Mexico by train. Mamá entered the U.S. for the first time at Laredo, Texas, as Mrs. Pedro Sandoval on June 1, 1941. At home in Mexico, Mamá had been taught crochet, swimming, sharp shooting, and horseback riding. She had been trained to manage a household of servants. She was not trained in cooking, cleaning, ironing, and laundry. When she was brought here to Milwaukee it was very sad for her, because here there were no maids to do anything. My father was a factory worker. They were expected to do everything themselves. She always said that the first year here was extremely sad until she became pregnant with Elvira—that finally gave her joy. My oldest sister Elvira was born in 1942, and the next oldest, Gloria, was born in 1943. Margarita was born in 1948, and I was born in 1951.

It took her a long time to become friends with the few people who were around her that were Hispanic, and there were very few Hispanic families. They were living in what was the Hispanic neighborhood then, which ran from about Sixth Street to First Street between National and Scott Streets—where Vieau School is located, but there were very few Hispanic families.

There was no expressway then through the neighborhood. Much of the community was removed then when the expressways were developed in the 1960s. One of the landmarks at that time was the local family grocery store, the Cardenas Grocery Store at 911 South Sixth Street, which stood where the expressway ramps are now. That was a wonderful place to gather, and my mother became great friends with José and Mercedes Cardenas, because she shopped at their store. The Cardenas family loved Elvira and Gloria as little children. Another landmark was the Bruce Publishing Company, owned by a gentleman named Mr. William Bruce in that neighborhood.

A Family Hobby: Musical and Cultural Performance

Elvira Sandoval Denk:

Our papá, Pedro, and our mamá, Margarita, both loved music, and we were raised on the music from Mexico. We frequently performed together, and one of our songs was a Mexican song about a train going to Atotonilco, where there were beautiful girls. The four of us would stand in formation, behind each other, and do the train motion with our arms while we sang.

Rosemary Sandoval Le Moine:

We started singing at a very young age. We performed on the radio, on the stage, at the South Side Armory, and everywhere they requested us: picnics, gatherings, weddings, funerals, birthday parties, the *posadas* [reenactment of biblical story of Joseph and Mary's attempt to find lodging in Bethlehem] at La Misión de la Virgen de Guadalupe. Usually, at events, people ask us to do a couple of songs.

Elvira Sandoval Denk:

Rosemary was two years old when she started performing, and we had many requests to perform over the years. Our Tío Salvador Arellano, who passed away just two weeks ago, asked us to sing to him on his deathbed.

Gloria Sandoval Rozman:

The church had many celebrations, and we would dress up in our Mexican outfits for them. I remember carrying *las charolas*, which are our Mexican trays that are beautifully decorated and painted, with fruit piled high upon them, into the Church to offer to Our Lady of Guadalupe. All of us participated in that ceremony. Mom made our Mexican dresses by hand, with little sequins, applying all these little sequins. Just beautiful. We still have some of those original costumes.

Elvira Sandoval Denk:

Just beautiful. Of course, along with it came the singing. My father just loved to play the guitar and my mother loved to sing the Spanish songs. We learned from them and we enjoyed singing with them. We sang them on the radio in 1955, on the Dante Navarro[2] radio program on WRAC, Spanish Radio of Racine, and at all the fiestas. We could go on the stage and each one of us would do our little part. Rosemary had the *claves—el clavel.* Margarita played maracas. All of us would sing the songs and we enjoyed that very much.

As we grew a little bit more, we continued by serving the food at the church, and then, of course, cooking at home. We celebrated Christmas beautifully with *las posadas* at home and at church. We knew how to make tamales, mixing the *masa* and spreading it on the husks, and we've enjoyed these very much since we were little. We went to *la Misa de Gallo* [midnight mass], then we would come home and celebrate the great feast of Christmas by having *tamales* and *buñuelos* and *tostadas,* and other relatives would come over. It was always a very joyful experience.

Rosemary Sandoval Le Moine:

We were fortunate that in the house it was all Spanish, and the customs were still there. We do as much as we can to keep up the food, the music, the culture. In 1977, we started the Christmas tradition of the posadas when our children were tiny.

Margarita Sandoval Skare:

All of us sewed costumes. Oh! I did the actual booklets for the posadas—our posadas are bilingual because our husbands speak English, so our whole book is bilingual.

Rosemary Sandoval Le Moine:

In Elvira's basement we have over fifty costumes, for every age: Baby Jesus, the Three Kings costumes, King David, the shepherds, and we have angels. We have all the costumes for the posadas.

Our family gathering spot is Elvira's house. Elvira built her home thirty-four years ago to hold fifty people dancing for that reason! She said, "We will gather at my home." Yes. Okay. That has been the house of gathering for all of us.

Margarita Sandoval Skare:

Because this is the middle of winter and it's cold, we do the posadas indoors and all in one day. We are there all day, eating tamales that were made at a separate gathering weeks before.

For the posadas we reenact Mary and Joseph's search for lodging by using different rooms in Elvira's house. In between each knocking, we're singing the songs from our booklet.

Rosemary Sandoval Le Moine:

I don't remember doing the posadas when we lived on Thirty-First Street and Lapham, but they did them in the neighborhood around Third and Washington at the Mission of Our Lady of Guadalupe.

The Creation of a Mexican American Parish

Elvira Sandoval Denk:

When Papá came to Milwaukee, he soon realized that all the Catholic parishes were either English-speaking or they were German-speaking, and there was really no church that Mexicans could call their own. He got together with several of the Hispanic men from other Mexican families in the area and they went to the archbishop and appealed to him, and eventually the Diocese brought a missionary from Spain. The first Church for Mexicans was in a little storefront at 313 Grove Street, which is now Fifth and Pierce Streets, between Washington and Scott. The Church bought it. That served as our church. It was dedicated on December 12, 1926, to Our Lady of Guadalupe on her Feast Day. I think our first priest was Padre Ernesto Ossorio Aguirre. There began the first masses in Spanish, and the families were very happy, because the religious life was very critical for them. They wanted to have a place that they called home. Well, as the years developed, the parish grew a little bit more. Then they appealed again to the archbishop to, please, locate a place that would be a little bit larger. In 1945 they were able to get a building that had been closed; it was the former telephone exchange building at 239 West Washington Street.

The archbishop then bought the building on Third and Washington. We had our grand opening, of the new Mission of Our Lady of Guadalupe, and I was the first little girl who cut the ribbon for the great celebration. I was about three years old, you know, a tiny little thing. We have some pictures of that in which I'm wearing a kind of a little flower girl dress, and my little bonnet, the ridge, was shaped into a heart. It's very, very sweet, and it was matching. I was the ribbon cutter for that ceremony. We had a beautiful church and another priest

Figure 5. Margarita Sandoval (mother) with daughters Gloria and Elvira (standing), and Margaret and Rosemary (seated). Mitchell Park Colonnade 1957. Photo used with permission of Margaret Sandoval Skare.

who came as a missionary from Mexico. Those were the early beginnings of our mission.

Cultural Practices in Kitchen and Cooking

Rosemary Sandoval Le Moine:

In the early 1970s Mamá would take us down to the manufacturing plant where the *masa* was being made for the tamales. Now we go the convenient route and go to El Rey Supermarket at 7:00 A.M. on the first Saturday of December, and we get all the ingredients we need: seasoned lard from *chicharones*, *chile ancho*, *hojas* and *masa*. By then Elvira's made twenty pounds of pork, and I've already made two gallons of *chile salsa*, and we gather at one of our homes, and we put together those fat little tamales and take them home to be steamed, but before we break up we have a wonderful homemade soup that Margarita has made for lunch and our husbands join us. It's a day that I absolutely love! We usually make about four kettles that yield about two hundred tamales.

Margarita Sandoval Skare:

Here in Milwaukee Mamá became a fabulous cook. We are very fortunate in that we have our *Mamá's* recipes because of Rosemary's effort.

Rosemary Sandoval Le Moine:

As Mamá cooked, I would ask her how much of each ingredient she was using and I would write it down. I would just ask and make estimates, because she was doing a pinch of that, a handful of this. We probably put together about twenty recipes in that way. That was in the mid-seventies, about 1978, and I was stopping over at home to help out Mom and Dad more regularly then—to take them to the store or the doctor—and my two children at the time were just toddlers. When we were little we often ate in the kitchen, while she was cooking, but we had never paid close attention to the whole composition of a meal. I wanted to write down those recipes to make and to hand down to our *hijos*. We have her recipes for *tamales, frijoles, sopas de fideos, albondigas, papas, caldo de res, chile salsa* made in the *molcajete* and many others.

Gloria Sandoval Rozman:

My, you know what I remember about Mamá? She would be baking, she would be cooking, she would be making the tortillas while we were eating, because she wanted us to have fresh tortillas right off the *comal*, or the gas stove.

Rosemary Sandoval Le Moine:

She never sat down to eat with us. She stood next to the stove. She would always be standing next to the stove making sure she waited on us. She served us. We were raised like that and we sort of do the same thing. We do. Absolutely, with joy. Cooking for us is a joy.

Later, I included some of Mamá's recipes in the St. Rita Cookbook,[3] which was a fundraising project for the kids' school. My sisters all have copies of her recipes from the year 2000 when we put together a binder of poems, songs, and recipes from our parents.

Living on Sixth Street: A Microcosm of the Changing Ethnic Landscape of Milwaukee

Gloria Sandoval Rozman:

Well, I'll tell you something. We had the front home, didn't we Elvira? We lived in the home at the front of a lot and then the owner of the property lived in a cottage at the back of the lot. She was an older lady, with grey hair already. She probably was a little disoriented, or perhaps she was a little mentally sick. I don't know. But one day Elvira and I were outside cleaning the house. We had little buckets and we had little brushes, and we were washing our house down with water. She came out and saw us and she became very angry. She thought we were painting the house. Here we were painting with water! She scolded Elvira and then she grabbed Elvira by the neck and shook her and tried choking her. That was it. I don't think we lasted more than two weeks there after that. At that time Mom and Dad had made some friends, and after the landlady on Sixth Street mistreated my sister, Elvira, "Well, that was it," Dad said, "We're buying a house."

So this is how we came to our first house on Third and Washington at 306 West Washington. It was a duplex, and we always had some very nice tenants who lived upstairs. One thing I remember about the home is that it had a big front porch, and that when Mom and Dad would have company the men would always be on the porch playing their guitars, with Mom, or us, singing along. Elvira and I grew up in that neighborhood.

We sort of hated to leave that neighborhood because right next door was Cardenas' grocery store. The owners of the grocery store were dear friends of our parents: Mercedes and José Cardenas. We loved going there because Mercedes, who we called *madrina*, was godmother to Elvira. Even though she wasn't my godmother, I called her *madrina* also.

We'd go in there and we could pick out our penny candy for nothing. [*laughs*] Their sons would spoil us, lift us up, swing us, and babysit for us. They nick-named us, too. Elvira was called "*el gallo*," because she was the leader and I was the follower, so I was the "*pato*." And they would say, "*Aquí vienen el gallo y el pato*" when we went to the store.

Elvira Sandoval Denk:

We also went to the corner park, and the five-cent movies at the Royal, too, where we saw scary movies and wartime movies.

Gloria Sandoval Rozman:

Something very traumatic happened when we were living on Sixth Street. We were crossing the street and, Elvira, you slipped out of Dad's hand, the way all kids do, and a milk truck came and hit you. I know that I was able to talk and I ran back home and told Mom—your name is Elvira but I called you *Vida*— "Mamá, Mamá, Vida boom, Vida boom!" Then, of course, Mom came out and Elvira had to go to the Emergency Room and she had a broken jaw, a broken leg, and she was already also suffering from a weakness in the right eye.

Elvira Sandoval Denk:

Yes, I was. I was at Children's Hospital. It took me many years to recuperate from that. I remember even in fifth and sixth grade that my jaw was braced, and I was drinking through straws.

Gloria Sandoval Rozman:

Mom and Dad took very good care of you.

Entering School, Learning English

Elvira Sandoval Denk:

Okay, so we were living at Third and Washington and, of course, Mr. Bruce went to his company, Bruce Publishing, every day, wearing his black round top hat, *el bolero*, a wool coat and carrying *el bastón*. He walked very rhythmically and he always walked past our house and we would always go out there and say . . .

Elvira Sandoval Denk and Gloria Sandoval Rozman (together):

Good morning, Mr. Bruce!

Elvira Sandoval Denk:

Yes, we would say it together. Mr. Bruce would respond, "Oh, good morning to all the girls. What wonderful young ladies you're growing up to be." He would pass, and we just loved to do that, loved to exchange greetings with him. We were enrolled at Vieau School, and we were taking English as a second language, because we didn't know how to speak English. We had grown up in a Spanish-speaking home, with my mother speaking Spanish to us, always, and my mom and dad speaking Spanish to each other 'til the day they died.

Elvira Sandoval Denk and Gloria Sandoval Rozman:

We always spoke Spanish to them, too, out of respect.

Elvira Sandoval Denk:

Among ourselves, we only spoke Spanish at home. It was so sweet. Then, of course, when we got to Vieau School, we had to learn English. We were taking our English as a second language with our wonderful English teacher, Miss Mondry. She helped us learn. We must have been so young that I don't even remember that we were learning another language, we just did. We loved Vieau School. We had wonderful singing and dancing and coloring and painting.

Well, one evening Mr. Bruce came to our house looking very serious and knocked at the door. He said he wanted to speak to Mr. Sandoval. Mr. Bruce said to our dad, "Well, I think it's time that you consider putting your children in the Catholic School." Then my father wondered where, because Our Lady of Guadalupe didn't have a school. He asked Mr. Bruce which school did he recommend? "Well," Mr. Bruce said, "I recommend that you put them at St. Patrick's." If we did that we would have to walk from Third Street to Seventh Street, out of our neighborhood.

We were accustomed to staying within two blocks of the house; we never walked beyond that—it was forbidden to us, and we always walked together in pairs. To walk to Seventh Street was out of the neighborhood and something that we were prohibited from doing. But upon Mr. Bruce's urging, my father decided to send us there. In the third grade, I transferred over to St. Patrick's. I must say, it was a very difficult transfer. We did study our religion, but that was the end to singing and dancing and being tulips and butterflies on the stage. From there on, it was taking notes and learning our English and writing things on a little piece of paper with the word and a definition, because we did not know English that well. It was a lot of writing. We would also keep this little sheet of paper, a little slip measuring two inches by four inches, in our pocket, and we would practice our English on the way to school, the words and the meanings, especially for our spelling tests that we began having every Friday. Yes. There began our academics, with the nuns from the Order of Our Lady of Mercy. They were hard on us, strict.

Gloria Sandoval Rozman:

I always went where Elvira went so I transferred, too. She was the *gallo*, I was the *pato*. So I transferred! There was no separating us. Like Elvira said, the transition was really not that easy. We learned how to speak English using phonics. We had some friends, but basically we were our own best friends. There were a few other Hispanic kids at St. Patrick's, but just a few. We had some turmoil with some girls there. I think that was the first time we had ever encountered that, well, besides the crazy lady who lived on Sixth Street.

Elvira Sandoval Denk:

Yes! Yes! There was a problem, because we had gone out of our neighborhood. They wanted to beat us up a couple of times.

Gloria Sandoval Rozman:

I remember that. Not everything comes up roses, does it? No. I don't know that it was discrimination. I think it was more . . . jealousy, or new neighborhood.

A Big Family in a Small House

Gloria Sandoval Rozman:

Years later, in 1998, we girls went back to see that two-bedroom home at 306 West Washington as part of the Tour of Milwaukee. We were so surprised to see how small it was. There was a living room, dining room, two bedrooms, and a kitchen. In the back we had an area where there was a porch and small yard, Mamá had her flowers. She had a plant called *Las Ramas de San José*. They called them hollyhocks, but Mamá always said that was the plant that bloomed when St. Joseph found that Mary was with child.

Rosemary Sandoval Le Moine:

Yes, the house was so small. It was 800 square feet in the City Assessor's Records.

Gloria Sandoval Rozman:

Back then, we didn't think it was all that small. We all lived in it and my mom helped people. If somebody was sick, she brought them in to stay with us and helped them, especially Kika, as we used to call her. Kika would often stay on our roll-away couch. She raised canaries so Mom always had a canary in the house.

There was a little closet in the bedroom, and Mamá had a *castaña*, which would have been a flat chest in there. Mom didn't have a lot of clothes for us, but she made sure we had our everyday clothes and that we had our Sunday best. We dressed quite nice on Sunday. We had our hats and our coats and our gloves and our muffs—in the warmer months, little sandals. Around the house, we were just in little panties, maybe little aprons or something like that. When we went out of the house, we probably had little shorts and tops or little one-piece outfits. Elvira, you and I were dressed like twins. What you had, I had. We did everything together.

We were naughty sometimes, but Mom disciplined us in a nice way. She would give us "the look," and if we continued to misbehave she'd take off her slipper and we'd get it on our little heinies. Every once in a while she'd pinch me. Dad would just have to say, gruffly, *"Muchachas!"* We used to jump on the bed until we'd break the bed boards! Mom never allowed us to fight. If we fought, she would put an end to it. Because of that, to this day, we have always cherished one another, all of us including my brothers.

There were bums in the neighborhood and Mom would feed them, but then during the polio season she got strict with us and she didn't let us run around or do too much. There was one man who she used to call the "boogeyman," and if we were naughty she would tell us that the boogeyman was going to come and get us, but every once in a while we would see him and we would say, "Ha, ha, boogeyman, you can't catch us!" and we'd run on our porch and run in the house.

We had lots of time to play with our cousins, too. Tío Vidal was my father's older brother by about four or five years. He had a little home on First and National. Sundays were family days, so Mom would cook or we'd go to a park or we would go visit Tío Vidal. It was wonderful. The cousins always got together. Tío Vidal was married three times. He had two children with his first wife: a boy and a girl. Then she died. That's probably when Elvira and I came into the story. We were born probably when he was married to the second wife. Her name was Mariquita, little Mary. He brought her into a family of two children, and they had four more children together. She was a wonderful lady, who took care of all six children. As years went on, she had some heart problems. She passed away of a heart problem. Tío Vidal now had six kids to raise. No woman in the house.

Elvira Sandoval Denk:

Well, then, Tío Vidal told my father, "I'd like to get a wife, but I'd like to go and get a wife from Mexico, so that she knows the language and the customs and the food." My dad said, "Bring your children over to the house and you take as long as you want to meet a future wife in Mexico." That was 1950. Our cousins moved in with us on Third and Washington while Tío Vidal went to Mexico. As children, we did not travel to Mexico much at all, and when we did, we did not all go together. No, it was very expensive.

After the eleventh grade, I went to Mexico for a summer with my Tía Rutilia, Tío Vidal's third wife, to Zacatecas, where my father's family is from. Rutilia was going back to visit her parents, and Dad and Mom said I could go along. It was a very rural *pueblito*. I was about seventeen or eighteen then, and for me, it was a wonderful experience.

When our cousins moved in and we had beds everywhere, every room had a bed. We stored all the furniture in the basement and every room became a bedroom. Of course, we kept the kitchen table because we needed to eat. They were there many months and we loved it! We were all in school. We would go to the grocery store every day to keep stocked up, but it was a beautiful experience. At night, we would go to The Fruit Boat, next to the Milwaukee River, for free popsicles and to buy fruit and vegetables, and we'd see the seagulls on the river. Oh, that was fun. We got to know our cousins very well and be with them. Later, our relatives Jesus and Estela Sandoval stayed with us after they emigrated from Mexico, and then later the Villaseñors. We used to go on picnics to Bradford Beach and Greenfield Park—wonderful places.

Keeping Family Together in Changing Economic Times

Elvira Sandoval Denk:

We're all still together here in the Milwaukee area, and we have really made an effort to be here together, because our husbands have all had employment opportunities elsewhere. In my case, Caterpillar Tractor closed here in Milwaukee, and then we were offered a position in Detroit so we would have had to move. We didn't. My husband, who is a mechanical engineer, went through the difficulty of finding another company and another job, and then went to work for ABB Robotics in 1986, just to stay in this area.

Gloria Sandoval Rozman:

We cannot live without our sisters! My children will tell you that: "Mom can't move away, because she cannot live without her sisters."

Rosemary Sandoval Le Moine:

My husband was working for American Motors when they closed in 1988, and he needed to go to Detroit. We looked there, and I said, just in tears, "I can't go." He said he would find another job in Milwaukee, and he did.

Margarita Sandoval Skare:

My husband also was laid off, in 1980, from the Ladish Company, a large employer in Milwaukee. They were all told to take a month of vacation, and then during that month they were all called on the phone and told not to come back, because the plant had been purchased by a Texas company. My husband also had to find another job, and he stayed in the Milwaukee area working in sales, then in 1987 he started working as a letter carrier with the United States Postal Service.

During World War II Papá worked seven days a week at Allis Chalmers. There was no break. He earned a living wage. There was a union then. In 1956 the union went out on strike and we had no income. We drank powdered milk, and received flour, cornmeal, and cheese from the union. Their wages were what we now call a "living wage," that is, they could raise a family of seven children on one salary, on what my father made. On his salary. This was true throughout Milwaukee regardless of whether you were Polish, German, Italian, whatever. Those jobs were very important: Allis Chalmers, Briggs and Stratton, and others were big manufacturers here.

Rosemary Sandoval Le Moine:

Yes, and now those jobs are all gone. A lot of loss.

Margarita Sandoval Skare:

All of us lived at home until the day we married. After marriage, we moved into our own homes with our husbands but we stayed in the Milwaukee area.

Rosemary Sandoval Le Moine:

I don't know if all of our family will remain in Milwaukee. My daughter is still here because she works for the State. Nowadays, mobility, and going where the job is matters. Two of my children live out of state. They have to go where the jobs are.

Margarita Sandoval Skare:

Back then the Hispanic people could work in the factories and educate their children. But now, we don't see that employment anymore. The large factories are gone. They're gone.

Cultivating Economic Mobility

Gloria Sandoval Rozman:

I am a widow. I've been a widow for close to eight years, but my husband Vern was in the real estate business, and we've continued his business. We moved to Waukesha, because we bought a lumberyard there, and sell lumber, hardware, and cabinets. To this day, my son Philip Rozman runs it.

I'm still in real estate and I'm glad that I am! When I first met my husband, he was going into real estate school to become a real estate broker. He asked me, "Would you be interested in doing that?" I thought, yes, I would! So the two of us attended classes at Spencerian and got our broker licenses. We decided a little bit later to buy some income property, and I still have about thirty-one tenants in the West Allis historic neighborhood on 65th and National. It's something I recommend for all women to have: property. Yes. Absolutely. Real estate. You can always clean and paint and fix it up a little bit, but it's good for ladies to have income coming in.

Margarita Sandoval Skare:

Well, we all have income. We all received an education.

Gloria Sandoval Rozman:

Mom was absolutely adamant about us all going to college. We were told that from the time we were little, that we were all going to college, and we all had the ability to be the presidents of a company. She had no doubts. No doubts. All the children: we never thought, even once, that we were not going to college. We never considered ourselves underprivileged. That's a word that I learned when I was married and older with children. I thought, "Underprivileged? Who would ever consider us underprivileged?" Not the way that we were raised, with the gift of being bilingual.

Moving into an All-White Neighborhood

Rosemary Sandoval Le Moine:

I was five years old when we moved to Thirty-First Street and Lapham, and Margarita, you were seven. When Daddy bought that home in 1955 for $8,200 he thought it was the palace, of course. It was a huge, huge property. It had three full floors. It was a wood-frame duplex built in the early 1900s. On the first floor we always had a tenant—the Murphys, and the Pouros, and Ruth Hines. We had the second floor where we had a spacious dining room and living room and two bedrooms and nine of us in one bathroom! Poor Daddy, he's the one who had to deal with that. Then we had two more bedrooms up on the attic level. The best part was the second floor balcony, where you could survey the whole neighborhood, and Mamá loved to sit on that porch and talk to everyone in the neighborhood as she got older.

Elvira Sandoval Denk:

We moved into that big duplex on 3113 West Lapham Street in 1955 . . .

Rosemary Sandoval Le Moine:

. . . out of the Mexican community. We were the only Hispanic family in the new neighborhood and school.

Gloria Sandoval Rozman:

When we moved we were in a new parish and a new school: St. Lawrence Church and Elementary School on Twenty-Seventh and Greenfield. Then Mom and Dad had three more children. We all went to elementary school at St. Lawrence, then the four of us older children, the girls, we all attended Our Lady of Mercy High School, an all-girl Catholic high school. Our three younger siblings eventually attended Pius High School. Elvira and I were at Mercy at the same time, and Margarita and Rosemary were there at the same time, so we overlapped.

Elvira Sandoval Denk:

We were the only Hispanics in the new neighborhood and school. It was interesting. I was really looking forward to going to Mercy with its beautiful campus, the flowers, and the beautiful statue of Our Lady of Fatima. It was a beautiful, park-like setting. I was looking forward to that. When we moved it was a good experience. I felt good about it.

Rosemary Sandoval Le Moine:

When we moved to Thirty-First Street and Lapham, my mother won over all of the neighbors with her food and her happiness. *Platillos* of food. Platters of food. They did not know who we were, and my parents were not speaking English then, but my mom would send us over to the neighbors with platillos of food. She would say, "Now go to this neighbor's and take this food," or "Now, go to this one's house and take this food." Before long they were waving and friendly.

Margarita Sandoval Skare:

The whole neighborhood went to St. Lawrence Elementary School and we had our friends in the neighborhood. We played together in the alley in winter, spring, summer, and fall.

Rosemary Sandoval Le Moine:

That helped. Most of the families in the neighborhood were large, too, and we had seven kids, and other families had six, seven, eight kids, so there were lots of friendships among the children.

Margarita Sandoval Skare:

Yes, we all went to St. Lawrence Elementary on Twenty-Seventh Street and Greenfield. I remember registering for school there with Elvira and Gloria on that first day and being so nervous that I peed in my pants. Gloria and Elvira had to mop it up! What can you do?! [*laughs*] I think we managed the school a lot on our own, because you and I were the main translators for Mom and Dad.

Rosemary Sandoval Le Moine:

It's possible they weren't with us that day because Mamá was very shy when it came to the English language. At that time she wasn't practicing it much.

Margarita Sandoval Skare:

Do you remember when the farmer would deliver dozens and dozens of eggs per month? It was like a pallet of eggs because we were so many. Vegetables would be delivered, and orange juice, and milk in those glass containers. Do you remember that chicken we had under the front porch? [*laughs*]

Rosemary Sandoval Le Moine:

That was the egg man that brought that one summer. We got to raise her under the porch and feed her. Oh, she was beautiful! She loved Michael and followed him around. The two were inseparable all summer.

Margarita Sandoval Skare:

She never ran away because Mamá fed her the scraps! We had all sorts of pets under that porch!

Rosemary Sandoval Le Moine:

We had so many activities in the neighborhood with the other kids—kick the can, ice skating, swimming. Then later as we got older the fun of the CYO [Catholic Youth Organization] dances!

Margarita Sandoval Skare:

Oh yes, at all the Catholic church halls. How about Daddy? Now we had to pay to get into the CYO dance and we didn't earn our own money yet, either—we didn't work—and there was no such thing as an allowance. So we'd go up to Papá and ask him if he would drive us to the dance and also if he would give us money to pay for the dance, and he'd very slowly reach for his wallet and open it up and very slowly he would lick his thumb and then very slowly pull out a dollar for each of us. I think a dollar included a soda, too! We danced every dance and sweated up a big storm at those dances.

Developing Artistic Inclinations

Elvira Sandoval Denk:

During the time we went to Mercy High School, I enjoyed it. First of all, because I became a photographer. For example, I took every picture in the yearbook one year, with the old-fashioned camera, and the battery pack, and so I was really loaded up. I did all the darkroom developing, too.

Rosemary Sandoval Le Moine:

Mamá would have us take supper to you at school, because you never came home! We would take the Mexican basket, the *canasta*, up to Elvira, who was working late at Mercy, with her rice, beans—*arroz y frijoles*—and the *carne de puerco*. "Rápido," Mamá said, "rápido" so it wouldn't get cold for her.

Elvira Sandoval Denk:

Yes, she had to run to deliver it, so it wouldn't get cold. I was busy, busy, busy. During the four years I worked as staff photographer, staff artist—and did all the little drawings for the yearbook. As a senior, I was the editor. I was so proud at graduation. Then I went on to Alverno College.

There were a couple of things that led me to photography. Remember that my mother had those calla lilies for her wedding bouquet? Historically, Diego Rivera made them famous, okay, but they were the Aztec wedding flower. All these kinds of connections for me were very important like religion is important, because they developed a Mexican woman. I actually thought in terms of my mother; I still to this day have the box; it's a box from *Francia*, of her oil paintings. It's her oil painting box. She painted all my father's handkerchiefs with a little design—a cactus or a little sombrero or some flowers. She would hand-paint that. She took the time to do that. I saw that painting and I liked that. In addition to the singing, I saw this painting. For my wedding I had calla lilies too, and I wanted that connection for myself, too, to the Aztec. My artwork is clay and painting. All of it has a Spanish connection. I really enjoyed that.

In the third grade, I was recommended for an art scholarship to the Layton School of Art. Here I am with ten cents to put in for carfare to go downtown on the trolley, and I'd go to the Layton School of Art, which was located downtown

Figure 6. Elvira Sandoval graduation picture in Mercy High School Mercia Yearbook 1960. Photo used with permission of Elvira Sandoval Denk.

near Wisconsin Avenue. Mother taught me how to make the trip two times, then after that I would do that on my own. I painted for one hour at the Layton School of Art. After that I would walk all the way to the museum on Ninth and Wisconsin, because they had more activities there that I loved. There's where photography came into play. They had a science show with photography and art. I would go into these dioramas that they were making then with the Indians in them. I loved that. I said to myself, I want to do something with museums, with teaching. I really enjoyed that.

Mercy was an academic school, and I took Latin, logic, English, geometry, et cetera, and it was a very classical education. But I also signed up for art. I liked it very much. One art class.

Dances, Marching Bands, and Beauty Pageants

Gloria Sandoval Rozman:

I am sixty-seven years old. Even though Elvira and I were very close as we were growing up, I did not follow in Elvira's footsteps. I had a different outlook on life. I think it was more of a lighter side of society that I was interested in. Of course, we went to the same schools from elementary through high school. Sometime in the fourth grade, we took a folk-dancing class. We enjoyed it very much. I loved it! My father would take us, and then every once in a while some of the boys would bring us back, but we were not allowed to date until we were sixteen years old. We learned folk dancing and we learned some of our traditional Mexican dances, and we danced for the Folk Fair.

I did take up the guitar—not that I'm good at it—sometime in the third grade. I have still retained some of the knowledge but not the love like my father had. Papá was a musician. He played the guitar and had two of them, which we still own: a 1942 Gibson and a 1935 Martin. He played well. Papá also played the banjo and the trumpet. He was very active as a musician with several different groups in Milwaukee, in particular, The Bill Carlson Band, which was the Allis-Chalmers band—back then factories would have their own orchestras, and the José Martinez Orchestra.

I first took guitar lessons at the Accordion School in our neighborhood. I still have my first music book. I learned my notes and I wrote my notes F-A-C-E and I repeated and repeated. I played with two other guitarists. The polka music would be going along and we would be strumming along on the guitar. Well then my father thought that it would be better for me to get a little better education, so he did send me to the Wisconsin Conservatory of Music at 1584 North Prospect Avenue. He would always take me and wait for me. It was a really wonderful time to spend alone with my father. That's what I liked.

I probably started in third grade and took lessons steadily for two years and then kept it up off and on after that when I played with father in the José Martinez Band. Then the *hermanitas* Sandoval would be invited to sing with them up on stage and I loved that! My mother did not sing with us on stage but she was always there, with us.

From there we went to Mercy High School. If I recall, our *madrina* Mercedes Cardenas had a daughter, Elita, who went to Mercy; she was probably one of the first Hispanic girls who went to Mercy High School. I'm sure that's one of the reasons why Mamá and Daddy decided to buy that house on Thirty-First Street and Lapham, because they knew that was a good school and they knew that soon we would be going to high school. Of course, Elvira was very busy in high school—in the photography and arts and designing dance costumes. Elvira made our costumes! She would put us on the floor and make a pattern and make the dresses. I mean this girl can sew. This girl could do that. I loved it. We would go to all the folk dances, and, of course, she made all of our dresses and Mom would help and manually stitch on all the sequins. Sixteen was the age at which we could start dating. We did not have *quinceañeras*. You have to remember that my father was the only working person in the family and he had to support us all. Allis Chalmers, where he worked, went through some tough times, too, when they had the *huelgas*, when they had the strikes.

Elvira Sandoval Denk:

They went through three of them, each of them many months long.

Gloria Sandoval Rozman:

But my mother always held her head up high and told us to do the same, that the Lord would protect us and allow us to finish our educations. My mother always had food on the table, as I mentioned before, she was always warming the tortillas for us. Well, I went to Mercy High School and before I knew it, a girlfriend of mine from school said, "Why don't we look into the Drum and Bugle Corp?" I joined and for four years those nuns had us practicing every day! In the morning it was bugle, in the evening it was marching. It was Our Lady of Mercy Drum and Bugle Corp and we were the best in the country! We won all the competitions. I still remember the competitions in South Milwaukee—whoa! where we met more boys! The boys from Don Bosco and St. John's Military Academy would invite us out. But Mom always said not until we were sixteen. Then when we started dating, we always had beautiful dresses. It was one size fits all.

Elvira Sandoval Denk:

Oh, she could kick those white boots!

Gloria Sandoval Rozman:

It was an army. Regimented. People today say, "Gloria, how do you get ready so fast?" I say, "I was in a Drum and Bugle Corp and when they said 'Jump,' we jumped!" The inspection had to be perfect. Margarita and Rosemary were always helping me out, and I owe them a lot. If it wasn't the Drum and Bugle Corp, it was school activities, and we were on prom committee, and Elvira was in Latin Club and making toga costumes for us. There were beauty pageants on top of that! In the city, there were beauty pageants for the Hispanic girls.

Elvira Sandoval Denk, Margarita Sandoval Skare,
and Rosemary Sandoval Le Moine [together]:

Yes, yes, the beauty pageants. There were many, many!

Gloria Sandoval Rozman:

My father and mother helped the Villaseñors to settle in the United States, and they came to live with us for a while in that little house that we told you about. Elvira and I and Betty Villaseñor were usually involved in various beauty pageants. I'm sure my mother really had to figure out how the money was spent, but we were never without the party dance dresses. We had our gloves and our hats.

Rosemary Sandoval Le Moine:

We had the undergarments to push and squeeze, too—and none of our girl-friends had those.

Gloria Sandoval Rozman:

Now you have to remember there was one bathroom. By this time there were nine of us in the house, with one bathroom. Mom had a white dresser there with five drawers. The top drawer was the padded bras. The second drawer was the garter belts and girdles. The third drawer was the nylons and the slips. One of her customs was that when we became teenagers, at about twelve or thirteen, Mom would put a band on us that was maybe an inch or an inch-and-a-half wide and it had little clips on the end, and we would put that around our waist so that it never grew. We were all very small waisted. Yes. Many Mexican women do have small waists. I don't anymore because once you take that off, it's gone forever—except for Margarita. She still has a small waist! Margarita has always stayed slim and trim.

The Miss Horse Show Contest was held in 1962 at the West Allis State Fair. I placed first in that, and one of my gifts was that I had a riding horse all summer long. It was a wonderful time in my life, because I would go to the YMCA and the Joy Bus would come, and we would go to the Joy Farm and we'd do the horseback riding. Well then Jim Muellenbach[4] made my dress for this competition—which was considered a "tulip dress," and they're popular again—then he made me another beautiful dress and we did more beauty pageants. The gals in these contests were leaders of the Hispanic community, such as Betty, Elvira, and María Monreal. There was a beauty contest organized by LULAC and other civic organizations. We traveled to Chicago for them. Hispanic girls were getting married at a young age then, but most of the Mercy girls did not marry until after high school, and some went on to college though not all. As a young woman I had three priorities: beauty pageants, acquiring good grades, and Drum and Bugle Corp. It was a fun life for me. I liked the beauty pageants!

Elvira Sandoval Denk:

I photographed them.

Gloria Sandoval Rozman:

Yes, Elvira took the photographs, and did the developing and enlarging and everything that had to be done. We were also in the Miss Mexico contest. On one occasion, we wore dresses that were designed by Jim Muellenbach for Gypsy Rose Lee when she came to town. We all appear in a picture together wearing those Muellenbach designs. If one of us did something, we all did it together.

Changes in Work, Leisure, and Family Life over the Decades

Gloria Sandoval Rozman:

Now, we girls always also had jobs. I liked cleaning. I don't know why, but I liked cleaning. My mother would hire me out in the neighborhood, and I would clean and I would iron clothes at 50 cents per hour, and I liked it. We did some babysitting, too. Then when I was close to sixteen years old, one of the gentlemen in the Cardenas family hired me to work for him at a National Food Store right on Twenty-Seventh Street and Wells. Right after practice from the Drum and Bugle Corp I would take the bus, or my boyfriend or my father would drive me over to the National Food Store. Those were the days when food stores were not open on Sundays. I thoroughly enjoyed it because I enjoy people. The nice thing about it was that when they closed the store on Saturday night, the meat was taken out from the meat counters and employees could go and pick out the meat that we wanted. I love pork chops and steak! Mom would take that steak and take the knife and thinly slice it and she'd make fajitas for us. We just loved it. It was a way of contributing to the family and I enjoyed it. I worked there until I was about seventeen. Then I graduated. Well, Elvira had graduated from Mercy in 1960 and I graduated in 1961. I had pretty much a steady boyfriend, and he gave me an engagement ring and he went away to the Air Force and, of course, I got involved with other things and decided not to marry. During high school and afterward, Mamá always encouraged us to go dancing. She would say, "Pete, take the girls to the dances," and my dad would take us and pick us up from the dances. Elvira and I would go dancing to the Eagles Club! Back in those days, there were also church dances.

Rosemary Sandoval Le Moine:

My mother and father treated us very well, didn't they? Our parents catered to us, they took care of us, as we now take care of our families. They taught us that. That's why our husbands have been with us for life, even the old boyfriends would come around years later.

We always enjoyed dancing through high school and college; in fact, I think that's how I met my husband.

Margarita Sandoval Skare:

I met my husband Kenny dancing! His full name is Gordon Kenneth Skare and he was born in Milwaukee, too. Before I had met him he had finished serving in the Vietnam War from 1967 to 1969. We met at Counselors on Forest Home Avenue. He was attending MATC [Milwaukee Area Technical College] at the time, taking Traffic and Transportation classes, and I was attending UW-Milwaukee. We danced a lot throughout our whole courtship, going out every Friday or Saturday. During the week we studied because, of course, we had to get good grades. After graduation I worked at Pulaski High School and he worked at the Ladish Company. Then we were married in December of 1973. I had already graduated from UW-Milwaukee, and after we were married I finalized the Master's Degree in Library Science in 1974. We have one beautiful daughter.

Rosemary Sandoval Le Moine:

I met my husband Tom, who also studied Transportation, at MATC. I was studying marketing back then, in 1969, at MATC. When he heard about how much fun we were having going to the different places dancing he asked me for a map and he said, "Well, maybe I can meet you sometime." He lived in Cedarburg then and that was a long way to drive in. He met us, and we went dancing, and courted, and fell in love, and by gosh, by 1972 we were planning our wedding. We've been married for thirty-nine years and have three children.

One thing that Ken and Tom have in common is that they love to laugh, and they have been friends since we first started courting. My mom would always invite everyone over for Sunday dinners and the boyfriends always came. In fact, they stuck together when Margarita and I went off to our European vacation.

Margarita Sandoval Skare:

Oh, yes, our big trip as *solteras*!

Rosemary Sandoval Le Moine:

Yes, yes, before we got married. Well, Ken and Tom decided they would still go to Sunday meal at Grandma's house for those three weeks. Then they would go down to the corner tap on Thirty-Fifth Street and Lapham, Zeke's Tavern, and visit for a couple of *cervezas*. Oh, they were worried and they were anxious for us to return. All those things are such happy memories.

Then as time progresses and age takes over we had Mom's and Dad's health starting to deteriorate.

Margarita Sandoval Skare:

Well, Papá worked at Allis Chalmers from 1934 to 1968. He put in thirty-four years of service as an electrical assembler. He had numerous health issues over the years with his back and his heart. When he retired at the age of sixty-two, Mamá decided to go to work outside of the home, because the three youngest were still in high school and they needed income to support them. So she started working second shift cleaning classrooms at Marquette University. After that, Mamá went to work for St. Mary Hill Hospital and soon became head of housekeeping where she worked for thirteen years. She did work hard. After that, in her sixties, was when she realized that she needed to get her driver's license and she needed to get her citizenship. She realized that Dad was not a very healthy person, and she couldn't count on him to be available. And she knew that the transportation element was very important for them to be able to get around to doctor's appointments, and church and other things. So she got the driver's license.

In 1974 she passed her citizenship test and she told us that when she was being tested, the Judge asked her, "Now Mrs. Sandoval who was the first president of the United States?" She was so nervous she couldn't remember. The Judge said, "His first name was George." Then she remembered and answered Washington. The Judge said, "You passed. You're now a citizen."

In 1977 she took her driver's license test and learned to drive. She had never driven in all those years. I helped Mamá with her driving. I took her out for driving lessons. Then I got pregnant and she said, "No, Maguito, you can't take me out for driving lessons anymore," because she was worried about me getting into an accident while pregnant. Then all of us pooled our money and we bought her driving lessons.

Rosemary Sandoval Le Moine:

Mamá asked us to plan a big wedding anniversary celebration for their forty-second anniversary, and we did. She didn't want to wait for the Fiftieth Anniversary, because she didn't think that Papá's health would be there. We had a big celebration for them in 1983, and out came the Sisters Sandoval and we sang and danced and performed poems for them and everybody loved it. We sang "*Atotonilco*," "*Allá en el rancho grande*," and others. We had a great time. Mamá must have known, because by 1985 we were all there regularly helping them as their health failed. In 1987 she had the second pituitary tumor that caused blindness, and we hired people to help us but Dad didn't like it when others were in the house. Then in the spring of 1988 we helped them relocate to Clement Manor in Greenfield. Mamá loved it and she had the red bus to take her to arts and crafts classes, which *Papá* didn't like. One of us went every day and we kept a log there of our visits. Papá loved our visits, and called us his "*hilitos de oro*." Papá died in 1992 and Mamá died in 1993. They are buried at Forest Home Cemetery.

Teaching in the 1960s and the Creation of Bilingual Education Programs

Elvira Sandoval Denk:

I went to Alverno College and I majored in art education and Spanish, and I graduated as an art and Spanish teacher in 1964. Two years before I graduated from Alverno, the State wanted to open up the first Head Start program for the State of Wisconsin. They called me. The nuns at Alverno had recommended me, because I spoke Spanish and they wanted someone in education to work with the migrant-worker children. They started the funding for Head Start in 1962, and then I worked with that program. It was the first in Wisconsin, in Wautoma, Wisconsin. Every year after that, that's how I earned my tuition; I actually saved every penny from that job to pay for the following year of school at Alverno.

Head Start began in Wautoma, Wisconsin, on the initiative of the Wisconsin Department of Health and Family Services. They needed Spanish-speaking teachers and I was hired, with some education coursework under my belt, to become a Head Start teacher. That was the first time it was tried in Wisconsin. We picked up the children at 5 A.M. when their parents went to the fields. We had a whole program for them until 6 P.M., and then at 6 P.M. we started returning them to the camps and their parents.

I started working for MPS as an art teacher at Kosciuszko Junior High in 1964; I believe that I was one of the first Hispanics who was hired by MPS as a teacher. At Kosciuszko the administration always needed help with the new kids who were arriving in greater numbers who didn't speak English. I was called out from the classroom and asked to please translate, please do this, please help register. Then the Principal recommended that I pursue a degree in counseling so I enrolled at UW-Milwaukee and received an MS in educational psychology. My first Guidance job was in Bilingual Counseling at Washington High School in 1974. The first Bilingual Counseling Program in MPS started at Washington High School in 1968. The high school had been one of the city's finest high schools, and at that time integration was starting and it was changing in composition from an all-white school with a big Jewish population to one that was predominantly a minority and black-student population. That was when we began having the riots that we had in Milwaukee. It was that turbulent time. I was at Washington High School for about seven years. From there, I moved with the Bilingual Counseling Program to West Division, then from there I moved with the Bilingual Counseling Program to Riverside High School. In 1984 I was hired as the South Division Bilingual Guidance Counselor, and I became the Guidance Director there in 1988. I was there for about fifteen years before retiring, then I worked as a consultant with Pulaski High School in developing their bilingual program and in training bilingual teachers. In total, I worked thirty-five years with MPS and three years as a consultant. I'm now retired. It was a wonderful career! I loved it!

Bilingual education didn't just happen, and I was at both ends of the creation of the bilingual program. First of all, when it started, blacks didn't like Hispanics. We weren't really a part of the movement for integration. It wasn't an easy thing. You had to work with white students and teachers, and black students and teachers. I participated yes—and it was difficult on both ends because one of the techniques for calling attention to the need for bilingual education was to have the kids walk out of school. Then you're torn by the fact that they're not in geometry class and they're not going to pass their geometry tests and then the Hispanic community wants them out on the streets. On the streets you don't learn anything. So, yes, I had mixed feelings. I tried to participate in the positive aspects of it, for instance, I felt our students needed to enroll and ask for scholarships but in order to do that they needed to write English, express themselves, have a good academic background, have algebra, geometry, and advanced mathematics. With the bilingual students in front of me I tried to do two things: I tried to have them academically move forward and at the same time have them be aware of what's happening on the outside. The outside was very active. We had everything in those days: we had fires, we had gunshots, we had people that died. A friend of mine, Aurora Weir, was murdered.[5] It was very difficult. Very difficult.

And yet to proceed to try and get the things that you wanted the kids to have was certainly important: to work with kids to be well-prepared for the future, and for them to see a future, to avoid the kids being assimilated into gangs. There were challenges. The time was not an easy one. I willingly chose those schools. I could have very easily gone and transferred to a school that was not having this kind of fiery experience in that period. I could have asked for a different school, but I stayed in it and I spoke Spanish 90 percent of the time. That meant that everything I learned in school had to be translated and presented in Spanish.

I must say that I have gotten a great deal of satisfaction from this work. I was very happy to have lived through this very difficult period. The bilingual program was the end result of all that, and so it came into being in 1968, ten years after the turmoil began. It's a slow process. The whole thing, the development has been slow. The people we had speaking out on the street were stretching themselves, and we have to be grateful for anybody who was available at the time to speak out, and did.

In my role, I developed students—their talents and abilities. I felt that the way for us to move away from poverty, as Hispanics, was to move into the educational system and from there funnel our activities into other areas. That was my vocation in life.

Gloria Sandoval Rozman:

It was. We needed good dedicated leaders who had the initiative to stay there, to stay where you were, to stay in that place, and not to give up.

Elvira Sandoval Denk:

Yes. To not give up. As a result it's kind of interesting. You get "Good Morning" from some people and you don't get any "Good Morning" greetings from other people. If I had ever shown any tears or hesitation, my husband would have said in a minute, "Quit." He always wanted everything 100 % safe—so he always made sure that I had a good, safe car, that things were taken care of; he has always been very helpful. He was worried. Well, we got pretty close to it. When you're standing next to a casket with your friend in it, that means something. Aurora Weir, a friend of mine who was killed, ran the Community Enrichment Center on the North Side, on Richards Street. She ran the center there. She was murdered for her voice, for her leadership, and she was one who was out on the street, fighting for bilingual education and other things.

It's interesting because we were divided. During that time Aurora used to say that if you're on the South Side you're Mexican and if you're on the North Side you're Puerto Rican. Then they said, well, your mother, we will say, is Puerto Rican, and your father, we will say, is Mexican, so then you can be on both sides. It was interesting because it was a strategy that was made in that period.

I, myself, in order to be more "authentic," and even though my parents were both Mexican, I was Puerto Rican when I was on the North Side and Mexican when I was on the South Side. I could be "one of us" in both places. But then Riverside High School was on the North Side, and it had a mixed population, so when I was there it was said that the "word" was that my mother was Puerto Rican and my father was Mexican, and that circulated. But it was planned and I knew about it, and that opened doors. Through constant interaction over time, then finally one day there was greater unity between Puerto Ricans and Mexicans, then finally one day someone says "Good Morning" to you.

I wanted to provide all of our students the same courtesy, the same ability, the same opportunity. If they wanted it. I would break, even, with the Bilingual Program, or be with it, on these questions, depending on what the student needed. I was creative with it. But that wouldn't always sit right with the public, because someone else would hear about it, and it might be this organization or that organization. Some Hispanics, even relatives, would be angry and would not talk to me, or my mother, because they heard this or that.

Rosemary Sandoval Le Moine:

A very political time. Families were divided.

Elvira Sandoval Denk:

In all of this time, I kept my name and address and phone number in the telephone directory, because I had students who needed me and who would call me at home. I finished thirty-five years. It was my vocation. I kept the name and address, my husband's name and address, in the telephone book, and I said, "Well, the Lord will have to bless." It never came to be that I was harmed or that our family was ever harmed, which is the Lord's blessing.

Entering the Work World in Business: From the 1960s to the Present

Gloria Sandoval Rozman:

The nuns at Mercy also took care of us. They wanted us to go out for interviews, but you couldn't go out to the interview unless the nuns approved of the outfit that you were wearing! Did she like the hat? Was it too wild? Was it prim and proper? Was the suit matching? Were the gloves and shoes okay? Then they sent you out. I went out, and everybody called me back. I was accepted at every single one! I'm telling you, I had a good life.

I don't know what it was, but I loved working with people. I accepted the job at First Wisconsin, and I told them that I was in the Miss Mexico competition and that if I won I would have to have two weeks off for that, and they said okay, they said, that would be fine. Mr. Brumder was the President at the time, of the bank. He thought it would be good to have a receptionist. They built a half-moon-shaped desk for me, which they've now taken out of the bank, and I was the receptionist. I loved it! Met people, men galore! Men would come in from the service. People sang to me there. The First Wisconsin was the bank of its day. Well, then I met Mr. Harnischfeger there and he said, "You know, I've lost my receptionist. I would like you to come and work for me." I said, "Well, you're going to have to ask Mr. Brumder and Mr. Simpson if they would let me go." They said, yes, they would let me go because it was closer to my home and they would get another receptionist. Then I became the receptionist at Harnischfeger Corporation. Once again, men galore! It was just a wonderful job for me. My girlfriends still remember, "Oh, my gosh, you have the life of Riley. You're in a reception room where you don't have to compete with anybody." At that time I did some modeling after work. I dated a lot. At Harnischfeger I met a lot of wonderful men, and dated a lot. The people from Harnischfeger generally also remain good friends in my life.

Then my mother met my future husband! She came to one of his open houses and she told me, "You know, I didn't know he was having an open house, but I saw this tall, slim guy pounding the "For Sale" sign into the ground and I said, 'Pete, *vamonos*, let's go take a look at that house. It's a bigger house than what we have. It's time that we get a larger home'"—by then we had seven children in the family. She met him. She said to him, "I need a home for my daughters." She didn't use our names; instead she said, "I have my artist, my beauty queen," and so on. Mamá called Margarita her "Cinderella."

Margarita Sandoval Skare:

No, I'm five years younger, so she wasn't offering me. She was offering you two!

Gloria Sandoval Rozman:

He, Vern, called the house and I'm yak, yak, yak, and he asks, "Could I speak with your father?" I said, "Oh, no, I will interpret for them." He said, "I showed them a house. I was wondering if they're interested." Well, I think we were on the phone for hours. Then Vern said, "Gloria, you work at Harnischfeger and I've been there a couple of times but you sent me out to a different department, and I really wanted to ask you out but I figured you'll never go out with me. Well, now I've met your mother! I want to offer you this: I'm going to come to your house. I'm going to ring your doorbell. I'll probably have my little dog with me, and you don't have to feel embarrassed. We've talked for so many hours already, but if you don't think you like me you just close the door and you go back upstairs." Well, I never closed the door and we married. Vern and I married in 1964, and he loved Mexican traditions.

He was in real estate. Of course, then we went to real estate school together. He had an office with his uncle, and later he started a blueprint business with him. I would help them with open houses. Then five years later, I had three children, who are now all grown with their own families. Then Vern's brother told him about an old lumberyard in Waukesha for sale. His brother said, "Why don't you bid on it?" Prior to this, we were moving every year. I lived in thirteen different houses in twelve years. Some were beat-up. Some were nice. I was good at cleaning. He was good at painting. We worked together. We fixed them up and sold them. That's how he made his money, enough to get the down payment on this lumberyard, and that's how we started with our business there. My children loved the lumberyard! The business experienced a terrible fire in 1994.

Vern was diagnosed with Parkinson's disease in 1993, which I had never heard of before then. I thought whatever it was, that we were going to save him. Well, he actually lived with Parkinson's until August of 2002, and that's when he passed away. I was involved with the Parkinson's Association and went to many meetings and talked to many people about the disease. I'm proud to say that between my family, my sisters included, that we were able to take care of him at home until his dying day.

After my husband died I did take some grieving classes at St. Williams. I was alone, you know. Then my brother, who is the ballroom dancer, came over to the house and said, "How about taking some dance lessons?" I said, yes, and I signed up at Casa di Danza in Waukesha, and I'm very proud to say that I love ballroom dancing! It took me two years to get into the dancing, but it's where I met my fiancé Norv. At first, I didn't know how I was going to fit in because I didn't have a partner. My brother said, "You don't have to worry. They'll have a mixer." The line of men on this side is this long, and the line of women on the other side is that much longer. My brother said, "You just tell the men that your name is Gloria and you're a beginner."

My fiancé Norv introduced me to fishing and hunting, so we have fishing and hunting and dancing and we really enjoy our grandchildren. I took the DNR courses on hunting but the deer meat stays on his side of the family. I still have our business in Waukesha and all of my children have worked there and are all still involved in it. Every once in a while there is business turmoil, but I've kept the real estate business, the property in West Allis, and the lumberyard.

Working as a Librarian for Milwaukee Public Schools from the 1970s to 2004

Margarita Sandoval Skare:

I was born in 1948. I am not sure what school I started at as a child, but I do know that I was quiet, shy, and didn't talk much. I cried a lot because I didn't want to be in school. I repeated the first grade at St. Lawrence Elementary, where I sang in the choir. We had the School Sisters of St. Frances nuns in every grade, and the classrooms must have had thirty to thirty-five students each! I enjoyed school and went on to high school at Mercy in 1968.

At Mercy High School, I took the college and business classes in my junior and senior year, so I even learned shorthand and learned how to type, which came in very handy later in life with the introduction of computers into every aspect of life. Each of us paid our own way through college. I also paid my own way through Mercy High School by working there. I swept the cafeteria floor, a job I didn't like because it prevented me from doing other things after school, but the nuns wanted the floor swept right after school and it took an hour and a half to sweep. My mother did not charge us room and board while we went to school so that was a great help. I graduated from Mercy High School in 1968. I went to UW-Milwaukee, and the first two years I took classes in general education. I became very interested in teaching because of Elvira—she was already teaching. I decided on a Spanish teaching major and a minor in library science, because I liked doing research in the library.

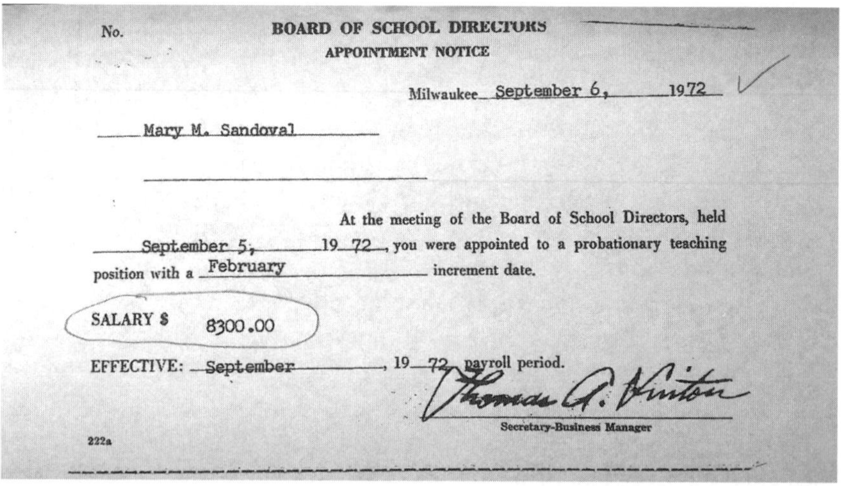

No. BOARD OF SCHOOL DIRECTORS

APPOINTMENT NOTICE

Milwaukee September 6, 1972

Mary M. Sandoval

At the meeting of the Board of School Directors, held September 5, 1972, you were appointed to a probationary teaching position with a February increment date.

SALARY $ 8300.00

EFFECTIVE: September, 1972 payroll period.

Thomas A. Vinton

Secretary-Business Manager

222a

Figure 7. Appointment Notice for Mary M. Sandoval. Photo used with permission of Margaret Sandoval Skare.

I was at the university at a time when protests and picketing were taking place. Some Hispanic university students who were picketing were trying to bring in more Hispanic-themed courses into the university, but I did not picket.[6] My father didn't want us to be in harm's way. Because I lived at home it was already hard for me to get to school every day; I took two buses and it was an hour ride each way.

I did a lot of studying in the library and graduated from UW-Milwaukee in 1972 with a degree in Teaching Spanish K–12. I did my student teaching as a senior at Pulaski High School in Spanish and in the library, which was my second area of specialization—library sciences. When I graduated from UW-Milwaukee I was hired by Milwaukee Public Schools for Pulaski High School and I started on September 5, 1972, at a salary of $8,300 per year working in the library. At that time, there were very few Hispanic students at Pulaski, but over the years, and once integration started, then more and more went there. I spent my entire career of thirty-three years at Pulaski. "Margarita, go train the new principal," the head secretary would say.

Along with my colleague Sandy Petricek, we developed the library into one of the best-run libraries in the district. By 1974, I had completed my MA in library science, the master's degree required for the position of high school librarian. That was the same year that Elvira finished her master's degree in educational psychology; we both graduated together and had a great party.

In the late 1980s and early 1990s, we worked on introducing new technology into the public schools. For example, we converted the card catalog in our school library into an online catalog system and bought the first computer we bought for the library at a cost of $2,500. We approached our school principal and then the school board requesting money to create the library of the twenty-first century. We then became great grant writers! We had a teaching library with classes in every hour, and we developed lesson plans in coordination with classroom teachers. We brought in funds from federal and local school grants, and we also received grants from private sources such as the Ameritech grants and the Herb Kohl grant. Over the years we raised enough funds for twenty computers and the purchase of online research databases for the students.

In the 1990s, Sandy and I received a number of awards for this work, including the Council of Great City Schools Award and the National Urban Education Technology Award, which were based on technology and lesson-plan integration. I also won a Crystal Apple Award from Ameritech for $4,000 for the integration of technology into the teaching curriculum, and the President's Award from the Wisconsin Education Media Association. I was active in several educational and computer information organizations.

A priority for me was teaching our staff at Pulaski High School, and in MPS, on using technology and integrating it into the classroom. We took many classes at Alverno, UW-Milwaukee, MATC, and MPS that we paid for out of our own pockets so that we could learn the software and we became technology leaders. Then we taught the other teachers in our building. Eventually we set up numerous computer labs for instruction for the students.

We also taught technology to students, including the software programs. The English department eventually made it a requirement that students turn in essays in Microsoft Word. Since most of our students did not have computers at home, we kept the library open until 5 P.M. even though the school day ended at 3:30 P.M. Students would work on their homework after school. We also taught technology to students and parents in Spanish. I always encouraged parents to keep up the Spanish at home, and encouraged students to remain bilingual.

Another special area for me was the responsibility for coordinating ethnic cultural events and programs at Pulaski High School. Programs included European, Hmong, and Hispanic traditions; food; music; and performances. We held some of these in the library, too, since it was a large space, and on parent-teacher conference nights we held events in the hallways. Mexican programs were wonderful, because I always involved my family in these. For example, we had a "Tortilla Program" for three classes at a time where we taught students how to make *tortillas de harina* from scratch. Rosemary, Mamá, and I led the class. We used Mexican cheese to make quesadillas from the finished tortillas and we all ate. As part of it we sang a little song and talked about our Mexican culture. We taught five periods in a row—the whole day!—for students in Spanish, Home Economics, and Special Education classes. We had thirty rolling pins going in those classes with fresh dough. Mamá was in her sixties then and she loved it! She was so excited to be invited to do it that she would be dancing. That lesson developed a following, and the students all knew when Mamá Sandoval was coming to school.

I retired in 2004. They brought a ten-piece mariachi band to the school for me at my retirement and honored me in the auditorium with the whole student body present! I thoroughly loved my job! After my last day on the job, my husband took me to a Fish Fry and when he got the check I started to cry. He said, "What's the problem, Margarita?" I said, "I can't believe I handed in my retirement paperwork. I've been teaching for 33 years. I've been going to school year-round for all these years since I was a child; I don't know what's going to happen to me!" He said, "Stop crying, Margarita; people are going to think we're getting a divorce." I said, "But nobody knows us in this restaurant!" He said, "You're giving me a headache." I cried all the way home in the car. When we got home, he said, "Margarita, you've now given me a headache. I'm going to take a nap." After fifteen minutes he came downstairs and he said, "You're crying too loudly and I can't fall asleep." I said, "Okay, I'll go cry in the kitchen." I relocated and went to the kitchen. He went back up and took a very long nap and when he came back down two hours later, I was done crying. I haven't cried since, because I love what I'm doing in retirement!

Raising Family and Selling Real Estate from the 1970s to the Present

Rosemary Sandoval Le Moine:

My baptism certificate name is Rosa María Sandoval. Everyone called me Rosita or Rosy when I was growing up. I'm number four in the family so I was always in the middle and very fortunate; there are three sisters older than me, and two brothers and one sister younger than me.

At Mercy High School, I was always involved in all the musicals, Glee club, singing in every form. I loved the stage. After school I would scurry over to Alverno College where I served supper to the nuns and cleaned up after the meal. My Papá would take me there. I don't know how he did all that, but he would take me and then pick me up two or three hours later to take me home to do homework. He was always driving! Mamá didn't drive until her sixties, and we only had one vehicle.

I attended Milwaukee Area Technical College (MATC) and received an Associate Degree in Marketing. My first job was as an Assistant Buyer at Gimbel's in Ready to Wear and Sleepwear. It was fun. It was a good job. Then Gimbel's and Schuster's closed. At MATC I met my husband-to-be, Tom, who had returned from Vietnam in 1969 and enrolled at MATC to study Traffic and Transportation. We dated and danced and fell in love and were married in 1972. I was the only one in my family who had a big mariachi band at the wedding! It was Nacho Zaragoza's Band, and he guaranteed it was a thirteen-piece band for $190 for four hours of music! Tom and I have been married thirty-nine years and our children are all grown now and have their own lives.

I returned to MATC for a second degree in real estate. Then I went to work for the same company that I still work for now, Bauman Realty, Inc. I've been there since 1979. Being bilingual has been helpful all the way through this occupation. I am more successful because I speak Spanish. I work with bilingual customers. I also do volunteer presentations in Spanish for first-time homebuyers at the United Community Center, Walker's Point, Select Milwaukee, and Housing Resources—all organizations that offer first-time homebuyer classes in several languages. That's ongoing volunteer work; it never stops. I have also given back to St. Rita's and have been a volunteer teacher for ninth- and tenth-grade catechism classes for thirteen years, on the weekends. At some point long ago, there was a request from the pulpit that they needed teachers and my heart jumped: it's something I can do! I can do that.

Generational Changes in Raising a Family

Rosemary Sandoval Le Moine:

When I was starting out in my career, I found that my hours in real estate were very flexible. I would take my daughter to work with me. I could structure my day so that I could deliver my children to school, pick them up from school, prepare a hot meal, and make sure my appointments started again after 6 o'clock in the evening.

Margarita Sandoval Skare:

My school day was structured: I started at 7:00 A.M. and I worked until 5 P.M. When my daughter was born, I had a neighbor lady come in and take care of her, in my home, for three years, and then from there she went to kindergarten, and I did enroll her in a Spanish immersion program with Milwaukee Public Schools, and that's why she's bilingual.

Rosemary Sandoval Le Moine:

Somehow the family has helped out when necessary. My two boys cook so very well. They cook and keep up the family recipes. Now as our daughters are getting into their thirties it's clicking with them, too, that this is really important to pass on. I think that happens naturally when you get to your thirties and forties, that realization that what you have is absolutely very special, and yes, you want to carry it on. As Gloria was saying earlier: now her daughter is starting to be very interested in her Mexican culture—that's how it happened.

Rosemary Sandoval Le Moine:

Having a family was very important to us, and there was much juggling that was necessary with our work and family needs. I mean I got up at five o'clock in the morning to do what I needed to do. The kids never went to school without everything done. There was food being prepared in a crockpot in the morning for an evening supper. Margarita never even bought baby food!

Margarita Sandoval Skare:

No, I make everything from scratch. Yes. We like our recipes for everything!

Rosemary Sandoval Le Moine:

Our husbands are the most wonderful, spoiled men on earth, and they love it. All of our husbands. That's how we were raised.

Margarita Sandoval Skare:

But that's because we're organized. We saw the organization at home, and we're all organized to do this juggling. We wait hand and foot on our husbands. It's how we were raised.

My mamá would, of course, have Sunday dinner. When we were courting, the boyfriends would come over and they would all be well fed. Before dinner, my papá would take the *novios* into the pantry and my dad would say, "Now we're going to have our little shot of brandy." They would have Five-Star brandy that had been bought at National Liquor. As children, we all went along for the drive to get the case of beer and the bottle of Five-Star brandy at National Liquor.

Rosemary Sandoval Le Moine:

Oh, how they liked their little ceremony!

Margarita Sandoval Skare:

They would come out of the pantry all happy, ready to eat! [*laughs*]
　　Now, with our children—that's a different story!

Rosemary Sandoval Le Moine:

Yes, we raised our children to be totally independent. We raised our children to function independently—to cook, to clean, to sew. For both boys and girls! Absolutely.

Margarita Sandoval Skare:

Among our children, there is no one spouse that caters to the other spouse. It's equal.

Rosemary Sandoval Le Moine:

Absolutely! Because I knew that this was not going to continue. My sons will never find a wife that will work as hard as I did. My boys are so appreciative, and their wives are so appreciative! They laugh at me now that I used to tell them we're going to do Ironing Shirts 101, and they were in seventh grade. Then we did Laundry 101 and one son did whites every night, and one son did colors every night. We did Cooking 101. My sons would ask, "What are we going to cook?" I'd say, "Let's open the recipe book and you pick." When they were young I brought out drying cloth for dishes and some big buttons and they learned to sew by attaching big, colorful buttons to every corner of the towel.

Margarita Sandoval Skare:

Independent and self-sufficient, they all went away to college—Madison, Stevens Point, Portland, Denver, Platteville, Ann Arbor, Winona, and Tampa.

Preserving the Story of Mexican Milwaukee

Margarita Sandoval Skare:

In retirement I took free genealogy classes at the Milwaukee Public Library once a month. I wanted to learn how to do everything correctly. At the end of that ten-class series, the president of the Milwaukee County Genealogical Society said, "Margarita you're the new secretary for our society." I said, "But, Arlene, I don't know anything; I just finished taking the classes." She said, "That's okay; you will learn and we will all help you." That's how I became the secretary and I am still the secretary; this is my fifth year.

With that initial training, I was inspired to start the first ever Genealogy Booth at Mexican Fiesta in 2007. As was true with my school activities, the family gets involved in my projects so they've all become active in volunteering for the Genealogy Booth at Mexican Fiesta. The booth is located in the Potawotami Building, which during Fiesta is called the Culture Building. Our eighty volunteers include my family, Genealogy Society members, and members of the Church of Latter Day Saints. Their volunteers are very knowledgeable, because this is part of their beliefs, that they find their ancestors through genealogy and bring them into the faith. Our greeters explain what the booth offers, then we have eight computers in the booth with Internet connections where we can search for vital records of border crossing manifests between the U.S. and Mexico. We can also access copies of documents using Ancestry.com and Familysearch.org and we print everything for free. We can help visitors locate the meaning and origin of their last name. We provide handouts on genealogy for beginners—all materials are bilingual; I've prepared those myself. On one side of the booth, we have examples of documents and maps, and on the other side of the booth we feature family photos of "*Los Primeros.*" Sunday is family day: that's when the Sandoval sisters, our husbands and children, all volunteer for Mexican Fiesta. We spent a lot of time building an attractive booth. The other thing we do together as sisters is to teach cooking classes at the Milwaukee Public Market down on Water Street. In 2005 Mexican Fiesta asked us to do a tortilla demonstration at the Milwaukee Public Market to help promote Mexican Fiesta and we said yes. We did that presentation for a small group of people. Since then the Milwaukee Public Market has developed a list of cooking classes that they offer to companies interested in having a group cooking lesson at the market. They have a web site on it, and they do all the advertising. We might do that once a month. We come in full costume for these events.

These lessons are for private company parties or business meetings. We've done this for Kraft, Rexnord, Rockwell International, attorney's offices, and other businesses. Usually they start their business meeting at 9 A.M. and at 11 A.M. the Sandoval sisters come in. We might have a group of fifty-five people and divide them into smaller groups, working with each of us on one dish for the meal so that I might be making the *arroz mexicano* or *arroz verde* with them, Rosemary is usually the tortilla dough maker with another group; sister Elvira might be working with a group on making the *chile salsa*, and sister Gloria will be helping them with the guacamole or the little galletas, the *polvorones*—powder cookies. We might have cilantro salad with *jicama* and other ingredients on the menu, or *chorizo* or tostadas, depending on what the company requests. If they ask for flan that will be made in advance. We bring the *molcahetes*, the roasting peppers, all the ingredients, and utensils they will need. They cook for 1 ½ to 2 hours, and then we set everything out buffet style and everyone eats. If they have funds they might hire a mariachi trio to serenade them during lunch, led by Alberto Cardenas, one of the instructors of the Mariachi Juvenil at the United Community Center. We always make genealogy a part of these cooking programs as well. We talk about our family, bring in photographs and artifacts, and we talk about Mamá *y* Papá.

In retirement, I have taken guitar lessons through the Milwaukee Public Schools Recreation program, then with Alberto Cardenas—who helped me find just the right guitar, and also at UW-Milwaukee. Alberto encourages me in so many ways and is very supportive of my late entry into the guitar and music world and it's been great fun! I also write for the Milwaukee County Genealogical Society Newsletter. I'm the first Hispanic to be a member of this organization and the first Hispanic to be on the Board.

4. On the Shoulders of Women

MARÍA MONREAL CAMERON

Interviewed on Monday, December 29, 2008,
and Monday, January 12, 2009

Waitress, Homemaker, Volunteer, Executive Director

Taking the Helm of the Hispanic Chamber of Commerce

I took over the Hispanic Chamber of Commerce of Wisconsin on September 8, 1989. I can't believe it's been so long! The organization began in 1972 with the name the Latin American Chamber of Commerce, but the name had changed to Hispanic Chamber of Commerce well before I came onboard. At that time, my daughter Becky was going to start high school, and I got a call at home from the chairman of the board of directors. He said that they'd like me to come down and talk to them about heading the Hispanic Chamber of Commerce of Wisconsin. As much as I was involved with the community, I didn't know much about the Chamber even though my older brother Joseph Monreal had been one of the founders of the organization.

I met with them and I thought it sounded interesting, but I wanted to think it over. After that meeting I could see two things: that it had been functioning as a "good old boys" social organization and they were not adhering to their mission of business, and that there was some division—that people weren't really together in this thing. I wondered what that was all about. I talked it over with my husband, Edward Cameron, and I told him that I thought I wanted to take the job. He said, "They don't have any money. They're not established. Nobody knows about them." I said, "If I could guide and nurture and direct and keep us on a budget to raise six children and to get them all educated, then I think I can do that job"—because at that time we had two kids in medical college, one undergraduate, and one about to enter college. I thought I would try it. I decided to sign a short-term contract with them. By the end of the first month I knew I had found my calling and a cause to which I wanted to commit. At that time we didn't have two nickels to rub together, and I mean that: I had to sit on my checks because there was no money in the bank account. Why cash them to have them bounce? I knew that we weren't even a little speck on most people's radar screens, and I knew that I had a huge task in front of me, but I also knew that the Hispanic Chamber of Commerce could be an important business organization.

When I came onboard, I started getting the house in order. There weren't a lot of documents and there wasn't a lot of backup, because nobody had stayed in that position for longer than eighteen months, so I decided that I was going to do this slowly, very slowly. First was to get us on the radar. I got out of the office and began advertising our presence, letting people know that there is a Hispanic Chamber of Commerce here where "business is our business." We started growing and recruiting new members. We had about eighty members at that time, and about thirty businesses that belonged to the chamber, including some corporate members. I thought, "Okay, this can't just be a 'good old boys' organization." I knew things were going to be tough because the board of directors didn't have a single woman on it. It was an all-male board. I started restructuring little by little. One of the first things I did was to apply for a business development grant from the Community Development Block Grant (CDBG) program, to see if they could help us so that we could start our mission of providing businesses with assistance. CDBG allocates funds for social services or development or things like that. The very first grant was for $25,000 and to me it was $25 million! It was a good grant. We were in the old business incubator space on Eleventh and National, where we paid a minimal amount of rent.

I next worked to forge relationships with all the elected officials, sending out letters to them introducing myself and letting them know that I would appreciate a one-on-one conversation with them. I knew what the organization could do, and I worked to make believers among other people. It didn't happen overnight, and there's some supporters of this organization who I had to bring in kicking and screaming, yet they are still supporters to this day. It was not an easy task because the chamber didn't have an established reputation and record of credibility. Nobody knew it. So I started forging my relationships and, of course, I was already connected to elected officials because of my husband Ed's political involvement. Ed was very active politically, and he had very good connections with the governor, with the mayor, with the county executive, with all the men who were supervisors. Whenever there were political functions, I was there as Ed Cameron's wife, and I knew many of the elected officials. My older brother Frank was also very politically connected. I took advantage of those connections and slowly started establishing the credibility of the organization, slowly started recruiting new members to the organization.

If somebody would have told me nineteen years ago that we would be where we are today, I would have said, "Dream on. You know that's never going to happen." But it did. Today our organization has seven hundred members, is on everybody's radar screen, and we are housed in our own 2.1-million-dollar facility. We are highly regarded and respected throughout this community. It took a long, long time, but we have remained steady. We have established that credibility, and a reputation second to none. We are considered by all sectors of the community as a respected voice of this community. The media calls us. When there's an issue in the community, our perspective is sought and the Hispanic Chamber of Commerce is right there waving the banner. Although business is our priority, we also care about the community, and we've been active in all issues. I always remind people: "This is not a one-woman show. I've been assisted, encouraged, and blessed with outstanding support. Our slogan, *Adelante Juntos* [We go forward together], reflects that support. I am grateful for the past, proud of the present, and optimistic for the future."[1]

An Ethnically and Racially Mixed Marriage

I met my husband, Edward R. Cameron, at our family restaurant, Monreal's El Matador Restaurant, where I worked. That's where I met him. We courted for a little more than three years. At the time it was not as common as it is now for a Mexican American to marry an Anglo-Saxon. It was not a very common thing. He was divorced and had three children of his own; we courted and the rest is history. My husband has just celebrated fifty years of law practice.

At the time, my older brother Joseph was a close friend and client of Ed's, who was his attorney. When we opened Monreal's El Matador Restaurant in 1962, Ed Cameron was a frequent customer there. He came not only to go over the legal matters with my brother—whatever needed to be addressed—but he also went there to socialize, and that's where I met him. When we got married, he took me out of the community—I moved from our family home above the restaurant in the Hispanic community to the nearby suburb of Greendale, Wisconsin, with him—but he recognized and was very sensitive to the fact that although he took me physically out of Milwaukee's Hispanic community that my heart remained there, that I wanted to remain active in the community, and that one day I wanted to return to it. Nonetheless, we relocated to Greendale, Wisconsin, and that's where the two of us raised six children, three of his own from his former marriage, and then three of our own. That's how it was. I had the luxury and the privilege, truly, of remaining at home for nearly seventeen years to be a stay-at-home mom, to ride and guide and nurture our six children.

Throughout those years, though, I remained very active in the community. For instance, in 1986 I worked with the INS on the year of the amnesty. As a volunteer, I worked from the Rectory of Our Lady of Guadalupe Parish, and I headed that effort in the community to convince people that the amnesty was real, that there was not anything to fear in the process, that if you proved that you had entered illegally and had been here for so long, then the INS was ready to grant you amnesty. I also sat for a year or two on the United Migrant Opportunity Services (UMOS) Board of Directors as a volunteer board member.

From Fiesta Mexicana to Mexican Fiesta

Another community activity during those years of being a stay-at-home mom was my involvement in Fiesta Mexicana, which was encountering some financial and leadership difficulties. Summerfest had alerted the then-leadership of Fiesta Mexicana that they, in fact, were going to take away Fiesta Mexicana for nonpayment of rent and for other difficulties that they were having. Ed and I, my husband and I, were contacted by María Flores, who was married to Professor Salomon Flores then, and asked if we would be part of a new group to save Fiesta Mexicana at that time.

We agreed to do that, and we went to court and we saved Fiesta Mexicana. One of the conditions was that we couldn't use the name Fiesta Mexicana anymore, so all we did was translate it into English, and that's why it's known now as Mexican Fiesta. The name changed and the past debt was forgiven, and Ed and I became extremely involved in putting this ethnic festival back on track. We insisted that an audit had to be done each and every year, and that our efforts to secure sponsorship for the ethnic festival would be made more credible if we were backed by an official audit. We did it.

We were probably there for ten years before we tendered our resignations from Mexican Fiesta. We wished them the best and all, but they have kept everything pretty much the same. To me, it's important to get any organization, no matter what area, but especially community-based organizations, to recruit new blood, new energy, new thought, new ideas.

Years later, after I was here at the chamber, the former executive of Summerfest, Bo Black, came to me and asked if the chamber would be willing to take it over and provide a new vision for the festival. She encouraged me to submit a proposal, so our board of directors discussed, it and we submitted a proposal to create "Fiesta Caliente," which would shift away from the exclusively Mexican focus to include every single Spanish-speaking country represented in the City of Milwaukee. In fact, Milwaukee has large Peruvian, Dominican, and Cuban populations, and we imagined a festival that would appeal to those segments, too. We had some really creative ideas for it and submitted the proposal, but then that blew up, because Mexican Fiesta then said that we in the chamber were trying to take the festival away from them. We brought all the parties together and we said, "Wait a minute, we never went after it, we never looked for it; we were approached, we were asked to submit a proposal and we did, but our intent was never to take anything away from anybody. We'll back out." We as the chamber backed out of the situation.

Learning Organizational Skills in the PTA

When I was a stay-at-home mom, I was active in my children's activities and lives. When my youngest one, who is now an attorney, started school, I volunteered at her preschool, then when she started elementary and through junior high, I was a teacher mom. I went in and I volunteered in reading and math, and then later in Spanish. I brought in examples of Mexican culture and taught about some of our traditions. I was the PTA chairman for years and years. There was another woman who was also a stay-at-home mom, and the two of us volunteered a lot for our children's activities, all the way from kindergarten through high school. When the older ones were in high school, I also volunteered to help the Spanish teacher there. I did things to keep the culture and traditional language alive, to create an awareness and a positive feeling about our people. I took Spanish language periodicals and publications into the classes to help create a better understanding of other ethnicities. I was extremely active in their education.

My years in the PTA taught me patience and organizational skills that were very important. I learned to create a comfort level with youngsters who weren't my own and create positive interactions. I think the experience honed skills that I already had, and it was a nice feeling to walk into a school and to hear numerous students say, "How are you, Mrs. Cameron?" That kind of rapport is very important. I was so actively involved in my children's lives that the Monreal Cameron household in Greendale was always a meeting place, which was important to me, because I knew who my children were hanging around with and got to know their closest friends. Working with kids you have many different personalities, different characteristics, all kinds of family environments and family backgrounds to learn about; plus you have the naughty ones and the well-behaved ones, and you learn to manage a lot.

Challenging Sexism among Hispanic Professionals

When I came to work here at the Hispanic Chamber of Commerce nineteen years ago there was an organization called CHAD, Coalition of Hispanic Agency

Directors, and I had just started here and heard of this meeting and I thought, "Hmmm. They must not know that I've already started my tenure here, so let me just head over there." I went to the meeting, and, of course, I knew all of the people at the meeting already, because my family was here since the early 1940s so we knew everybody. Our family was huge, and had a lot of networks, and I already knew my colleagues who were heads of organizations, either because they were friends or they had some kind of relationship with one of my older siblings. When I arrived at the meeting I was greeted with a question: "María what are you doing here?" I asked them, "Isn't this a meeting of the Hispanic Coalition, of CHAD?" "Well yes," they answered. "Well I'm the head of the Hispanic Chamber of Commerce, which is a community-based organization, although it's a chamber organization," I replied. They said, "Oh no, your organization is different. These are all social service organizations." And they were all men at the meeting! "Yours is a business organization," they added. I clarified for them, "Mine is a Hispanic-based organization, community based, here in the heart of the Hispanic community." They said, "Oh, no, but it's very, very different." I said to them "Okay." I picked up my purse, and as I was walking out I let them know that if they didn't come up with a good, legitimate reason for my exclusion that I would challenge them legally. They all knew that Ed was an attorney. I picked up my purse and I walked back to my office. When I got back to my office the phone rang and it was the Chairman of CHAD, who said, "María, you know, we just talked it over, and we decided that yes, you should be included in this organization."

I bit my tongue and I said, "Okay, very well, I'll walk back up there." When I returned to the meeting, they said, "*Ay María, que bueno que regresaste* [Oh, María, how nice that you returned]." I said, "Wait a minute. I know that my gender was the reason for my exclusion; that's why I told you to come up with a legitimate reason for my exclusion, because I knew what it was."

I was at a disadvantage because I was, and still am, the only Latina that's the head of an organization in Milwaukee. Yes. I said to them, "I know the reason," I continued, "And shame on each one of you. I plan to come to the meetings as they are called and I promise you I will be a constant reminder about diversity, about acceptance, about the value that a Latina can bring. As the first girl after seven boys in a typical Mexican family there isn't a pair of pants that intimidates me, so get that. If you think you're going to make life miserable for me, if you think that you're going to challenge me: take your best shot because I don't back down. I don't back down."

Growing Hispanic Women's Leadership in the Professions

After I joined the Hispanic Chamber of Commerce, another Latina, Denise Wise, became the head of an organization, and led the Walkers Point Redevelopment

Corporation for about six years before it folded. She was a Latina from California. After they folded, I was again the only Latina heading up a community-based organization. Then Rosa Dominguez took over as head of the Council for the Spanish Speaking, and was there for just a year, so during that time there were two of us. She was then replaced by a good friend and good colleague, Tony Baez.

Today, the Hispanic Professionals of Greater Milwaukee (HPGM), which was founded and established by the Hispanic Chamber of Commerce, is now led by a Latina. We established that organization as a networking venue for young professionals who don't necessarily have businesses. Members might be employed by large corporations, for example. Because our focus here is business, the board of directors of this organization saw it fitting to establish such an organization. When HPGM started out, the chamber was the fiscal agent because they weren't established yet. For seven years we acted as a fiscal agent for them, until they started spreading their wings and they thought it'd be a good idea to establish their own organization. Now we have the Hispanic Professionals of Greater Milwaukee with its own president and board of directors, its own bylaws and tax exemption. It started out as an offshoot of the Hispanic Chamber of Commerce of Wisconsin.

At the time, the board of directors of the Hispanic Chamber of Commerce (HCC) was noticing that a lot of our young professionals don't golf or know how to do business after hours and the benefits of that. We felt we needed to establish an organization geared toward the young professional who is not necessarily a business owner. Our membership, the HCC membership at that time, became the first HPGM memberships; if you were a member of the chamber you were a member of the HPGM. Well then, of course, they realized that they had a lot of drop-off, because our business organization had been established for a long time and our members weren't just starting out, so they didn't remain in HPGM. That was in the first few years, when they had membership drops, but then the leadership of the Hispanic Professionals of Greater Milwaukee started recruiting on their own, and they started going to major corporations and companies like Morgan Stanley and Chase to recruit them. Now the majority of HPGM members are not chamber members but their own recruits, which is great for the city.

To me it's very, very important that we have this young professional group. They have two or three very nice social events each year, they get involved in community events, but their focus is on networking and establishing business contacts. To retain young talent we need to focus on that. The Hispanic Chamber of Commerce saw the merit in creating such an organization; we knew that we needed to do that and that's why we helped it get established and supported it for as long as we did. We think it's important to help any organization focused on the best interests of the Hispanic community, to help each other to ensure continued Hispanic progress. We think that's important.

In terms of the HCC, 51 percent of our board must be from Hispanic-owned businesses, and because we are the Hispanic Chamber of Commerce, that makes sense. Currently we have seventeen board members, so that means that nine of our business owners must be Hispanic. Just recently, Latinas have started to grow businesses, but male Hispanic business owners far outnumber the Latinas, although that is changing, that is changing. The majority of my Hispanic business owners are male. Of nine Hispanics on the HCCW Board, two are women. I've always tried to champion board involvement, but I also recognize that a Latina runs a business very differently than a man. She truly does not tend to socialize and to commit. Her priority is still her family and her business, and sometimes there is not enough time to do outside professional work. This year we have elections to fill six board positions whose terms have expired. Members elect the board. This year we have a Latina candidate, and hopefully she is going to be elected to that position. Every year I ask for candidates. I call people to ask them to consider running and explain what's involved. Sometimes they accept the nomination and sometimes they don't. Nine members of the board have to be Hispanic owned businesses, but eight can be corporate professionals, so we have those eight other positions that are open and these are the slots where women are more likely to serve. This year Ruta Vastos, a Latina and Senior Vice President for Associated Bank, is running for the board, as is David Ruiz, the Vice President for the Wisconsin District of UPS. There is also a candidate from American Family Insurance and others. I champion and encourage Latinas to get active in the board because gender diversity is also very important. The fact that I have been the only Latina head of an organization for many years is an indication of how much the effort on gender diversity is a work in progress.

Advocating for Business Opportunities for Hispanics

My approach has never been that I want you to change criteria, that I want you to lower standards. Absolutely not. I don't want anybody to lower any standards or to change criteria to let us in the back door because we're Hispanics. I don't want that. What I want is for that front door to be opened when we knock, when we say, "Level the field of opportunity." I want to see Hispanic contractors and service providers part of every single major construction project. I want them involved in the Marquette interchange project, the UW additions and expansions, the hospital and public and private projects. I want to see in public and private projects, the Sone Companies, the Benavides Company, Rodriguez

Construction, and others. I want to see my Hispanic contractors participating because they're the best qualified. On top of giving you the best quality, cost-effective competitive services—on top of that—you can also count us in as minority contractors, as Hispanic contractors. That's what I want. We got where we are, we are achieving, we're absolutely progressing, because we have a strong work ethic, determination, tenacity, discipline, and we can give you the service you are looking for. And on top of it, icing on the cake, we're also Hispanic.

Minority inclusion programs have opened the doors for us, they've opened the doors, but those doors should have been open to us before. Absolutely. We wave the banner here; we champion our contractors and service providers; we provide opportunities for them. Being a member of the chamber doesn't mean that you're going to automatically get a contract on any project. We have a big spectrum here. Members can come in and review the plans, inspect the plans that are made available here, and if they feel they have the capacity, bid for them. That's the member's doing. I don't hold your hand and go with you. It's

Figure 8. María Monreal Cameron
featured on cover of section 2,
March 15, 2013, *Business Journal*.
Photo used with permission of
Milwaukee Business Journal.

impossible for me to do that for every single one of our contractors. You have to put in your two cents worth. If you're having difficulty, you know what, all of my Hispanic stars in the organization are all willing to take somebody under their wing; they're not adverse to that; they share the successes; they share their best practices. I can count on many stars of this organization who are Hispanic business owners, contractors, or service providers to help other members. All I have to do is say, "I have a person struggling here who could really use a little one-on-one. Is there any way you can fit a couple of sessions into your schedule?" They always say, "Absolutely, yes, tell me when," or "This is when I can meet." Those are the kinds of things we do to help ourselves. And, if a minority certification is going to give my people a hand up you know what, we're going to take advantage of it because that's why it's there.

Getting Active in Politics

I benefited from my husband's career and activities because he knew everybody; he was very involved politically. That's how I started, and then I worked at developing relationships later on that would benefit the Hispanic Chamber of Commerce. The chamber is nonprofit, and the chamber cannot endorse or support candidates or campaigns, but I, as an individual citizen, do support those people that I see as having a good strategy for the upward mobility of this community. I go toe-to-toe with the ones who I see aren't acting in the best interest of the community, too. I learned to nurture the early relationships that I made through Ed, and to communicate with elected officials regularly about our concerns.

For most of us, meeting an elected official is sometimes intimidating. We say, "*No, ¿cómo lo voy a conocer? no quiero que . . .* [No, How would I meet such a person? I wouldn't want . . .]." There's no way. That's why I love the annual Hispanic Chamber of Commerce banquet, because it's an opportunity for our Hispanic business and professional people to rub elbows with top elected officials from the state, city, and county, and to engage in conversation with them. To me, it's really, really important that we have that kind of setting where elected officials are approachable and accountable; we should do away with this mentality of being intimidated, that "Oh no, how can I? He's an elected official. How can I possibly go up to the mayor of the city of Milwaukee and introduce myself?" In fact, we need to do more of that. We need to get more politically involved so that our voices don't go unheard, so that they understand who we are, what we're about, and what we need.

This community has always been about a hand up. I don't want you to lower your standards. All I want for you to do is open the door of opportunity, take a minute to know who we are, what we're about, what we want, what our aspirations are, what our hopes are—that's what I want. We're here like any other immigrant population, working hard to prove ourselves. It's going to happen. The perspective I have is that I don't go in expecting anything, nothing—you don't owe me anything, but don't allow law enforcement to come and treat my community like second class citizens, don't bypass Hispanic contractors because they don't speak English. Our business people work with their hands and their heads; they'll give you the best product.

Helping Others Achieve

During my time with the HCC, the chamber has received many honors, and I, personally, have also received many awards.[2] Being recognized by the parent organization, the United States Hispanic Chamber of Commerce, as the best Hispanic chamber in this region for thirteen consecutive years, this year being the most recent year, is quite an acknowledgement.[3] I personally was included in the *Business Journal*'s list of high profile newsmakers over the past twenty-five years, and I was awarded the *Business Journal*'s Woman of Influence Award in 2005. Things like that humble me. I'm honored by them, and they move me to tears, no matter what the award or who gives it to me; I am honored by it. Everything, though, is secondary to the honorary doctorate that I received from Cardinal Stritch University for my nineteen years of service to this community—well that was just tremendous. Sometimes in life you find yourself thinking, "I'm given way too much, this is way too much for one person," and that really rang clear for me when I received the Honorary Doctorate in Humane Letters. Wow. All I could think about was myself as a child—a little *mocosa* [snivelly] with *trenzitas* [braids], pulling three little sisters on a coaster wagon to the A&P Food Store on National Avenue for groceries. I just thought to myself, "Who would have thought that this daughter of Mexican, hardworking, proud immigrants one day would be traveling these same streets as Doctor María Monreal Cameron?" It just blew me away. It moved me to tears. ¡Ay, chillona [oh, a crybaby] like you wouldn't believe! At the ceremony I looked out into the audience at my sisters and they were nodding and crying, too. Who would have thought? Only in America. I'm not using anything as a crutch, not using my beginnings or my environment—although it was all positive and I wouldn't be who I am if it weren't for all of that—but all of that notwithstanding, here was a moment in my career when I was actually acknowledged for the work. Not the work that I felt obligated to do, but the work that I wanted to do. This is my life, this is my passion, this is what I'm committed to.

Some of the most gratifying moments in my career are those unexpected acknowledgments that I've enabled someone else to achieve something. I've walked into El Rey Supermarket to have a young girl come up to me and say, "I'll be the first one in my family to graduate from college. *Gracias, señora.*" Those kinds of things make up for every exhausting, frustrating, challenging moment of this nineteen year career, hearing that person saying, "My business is thriving because of you," or "I'm graduating because of you," or "I just recently accepted another position."

To me, it doesn't matter what title you have, or money you have, or how you dress, or where you live. What matters is the compassion you have in your soul for your community. I have never ever forgotten the words of my mother: "Don't ever forget where you came from, don't ever forget your roots, and if you are going to return to this community to work or to help out do it because it's here, because of your people, not because you're looking for credit." She warned me not to look for aggrandizement or recompense, not to look to get paid back, because there is none. I have never forgotten that and my mother is gone over twenty years now. *Pero esos consejos me duran* [but that advice has stayed with me].

As a young girl listening to my mother tell me these things, I wondered, "Why is she telling me this?" I guess at the time I just thought I was going to make a lot of money, going to live in this big house and have things—I was young and didn't know many things about life then. I think I just heard it and expected it would go in one ear and out the other, never thinking that there was going to come a stage in my life when all those *consejos* would come back to mind. But they did, and then I knew that this is what Mamá Luz wanted. Anybody who comes in here, anybody, and I've taught this to my staff, gets treated with dignity and respect. It doesn't matter if he's the CEO of a major corporation, or if he's the factory worker from down the street; if he's looking for help and we can help him, he'll get it here. If we can't help, then we'll direct him to the resources or organizations that can, give him the address, telephone number, names he needs. I feel I am carrying on my mother's example. When people ask me who is your role model I tell them that it is my mother, who has been physically gone twenty-six years, but whose memory and instruction and guidance and good words of advice remain with me. She continues to guide and direct me, absolutely, there's no question about it.

Encouraging Education with Scholarships

We serve young people and the community through our Hispanic Chamber of Commerce of Wisconsin Education Fund/Philip Arreola Scholarship Program. With the help of the former police chief, Philip Arreola, a Mexican American, we established this fund in 1993. We have award cycles each and every year in

June, when we award three $10,000 scholarships and three $1,000 scholarships. The $10,000 scholarships are specifically designed for graduating high school seniors, and with that money we are telling them, "Don't let any grass grow under your feet, go right from high school to college." The $1,000 scholarships are for Hispanics already in the college system who may have taken time off from school but they're reenrolled and they have never applied for the scholarship as a graduating senior.

Every year the application process leaves us both frustrated and very optimistic. Frustrated because of the limited resources: we're a small nonprofit and we've awarded close to $450,000 in scholarships, many of them $10,000 scholarships.[4] Optimistic because you wouldn't believe the caliber of the applications we get in here, you wouldn't believe the talent that is out there. These are students who are only limited by the financial challenges they face. We get incredible applications, but we're limited to choosing just three. What we do then is we work to see if we can get some of the other applicants a scholarship through INROADS. We encourage all applicants to seek other kinds of financial help to get them into school, not to let their dreams die.

We don't have the resources to give each and every applicant a scholarship. Our focus is not on the highest-ranking students, the valedictorians; instead, our focus is on that next level, the "A–" or "B+" student actively engaged in good things in the community. The high achievers, they'll get courted, they will get help based on their academic rankings; we try to focus on that next level of students with promise. I have made sure that there are good people involved in the scholarship program, and good scholastic advisors involved, but I don't participate in the selection process, because I know too many people in the community directly. Since 1993, it's been just an incredible scholarship program bearing the name of Phillip Arreola, who gave that dream of mine wings. I love young people; I love their vision; I love their dreams; I love their aspirations; I love all of that so I always try to encourage it.

I will give advice as a mentor, but I think that a mentor and a role model are very different. If I'm going to mentor someone, I'm going to share what I have learned. I'm going to share best practices and proven strategies or show how I've done something. I think that people can draw strength from a mentoring relationship. A role model, to me, is on a higher level; my role model is my mother. I learned from her example. Your role model should be a real human person close to you, a sister, a father, a mother—that's who I think a role model should be. I think that that privilege should be afforded to people who really have a direct connection to the person. I like to mentor and to share my experiences, but my role models are people who are connected to me, people who have shared their human weaknesses and strengths with me.

The Annual Salute to Hispanic Women Events

Here at the HCC, I also launched the annual Salute to Hispanic Women Conference and Luncheon in 1989, to provide a venue to feature accomplished Latinas who could share their successes but also, and perhaps more importantly, to share their struggles and obstacles.[5] It became a site for Latinas to gather for discussion. It started out as a luncheon only, but then years later I incorporated a conference component. We have it every year the Saturday before Mother's Day in May. At the morning conference, we discuss issues and challenges facing Latinas—Latinas talking to Latinas. Then we follow-up with a luncheon and a featured Latina speaker. I think it's important for Latinas to let go of the things that keep us from advancing, and we have so much to share with each other—not just successes but also struggles and obstacles. I think it's a very important gathering, and particularly important to have this separate venue. Males do participate in it, they do attend, but the majority of the five hundred people that usually attend are women.

In 2001, our Salute to Hispanic Women Luncheon focused on the topic of the unspoken abuse, domestic violence. This is something that Latinas don't complain about, or take legal action against. Latinas go to their parish priest to discuss it and the parish priest blesses them and says, "This is your cross to bear." I wanted to explore it more. So one year I asked past victims and past survivors to speak. That opened up just an incredible, amazing outpouring at the conference, where every session was filled with the comments and questions of women who actually had the courage to come up to the microphone and share their stories. It brought many of us to tears to realize the domestic abuse that is tolerated. We don't talk about it; we don't air that dirty laundry. That's why I called it "the unspoken abuse." Many times it's more verbal than it is physical, it's more of a macho mentality infiltrating a lifestyle. At the end of that session, I announced that this was just the tip of the iceberg and that we were, in fact, going to spend a whole year on this issue. I formed together a task force to address this topic over the next year.

I committed to calling the Task Force on Family Violence, the Sojourner Truth House, the Milwaukee Woman's Center, and all the people who are actively engaged in this issue to be part of our Task Force on Domestic Violence in the Latino/a Community. We decided, also, to include survivors, the victims, and clergy, because they have to understand that they have to address this problem in a different way. I wanted to be all-inclusive. It was a wonderful Task Force. We met every single month for one year, and we ended it right before the next Salute to Hispanic Women. At the end, we called a community meeting and we invited the whole community, everybody. We had different groups from the

Task Force reporting on outcomes to the meeting, and proposing initiatives that we wanted to launch. For example, the Milwaukee Woman's Center at that time (it's no longer in existence because it merged with Community Advocates) was primarily aimed at providing services for African American and Anglo women, and they didn't have a bilingual resource center there to assist Spanish-speaking clients, and it wasn't a very welcoming environment for Spanish-speaking victims of domestic abuse (Latinas who brought their own food to the shelter often heard disparaging remarks about the food), so they added bilingual staff and resources. Then United Migrant Opportunity Services (UMOS) stepped up to the plate and committed to taking on this issue and developing, housing, and administering the Latina Resource Center, which is bilingually staffed. It's open to all women, but the focus is on Latina victims. They provide advisors, counselors, and resources; they even have a division where you can get business outfits to wear on a job interview.

Every year the Salute to Hispanic Women is on a different theme. This year it's going to be on mental illnesses. There was a woman at last year's conference who, in tears, spoke about how grateful she was for the conference, how she comes every year, how she learns so much. She asked us if we would address the topic of mental illness in the Hispanic community at a future conference. I asked her if she would be a part of the committee to plan it, and she said yes. So there was our theme for this next year. I try to listen to what the women themselves want; that's why a survey goes out at the end of the event asking participants what they would like to see featured in the future, or what's important to them or what's affecting their communities. No one can have all the answers, you just can't. Our survey helps us improve, because everything can be improved; it doesn't matter if you've been doing it for years, you can always be better.

Why My Parents Moved from Texas to Milwaukee in the 1940s

My older sister Juanita told me about these conversations between my parents, when they lived in Texas, about whether they would move to Wisconsin. Try to imagine this scene. Mother trying to persuade Daddy, you know, to move to Wisconsin. She says, "*Silvano, me dicen que las oportunidades en Wisconsin son mas grandes. Tenemos que buscar mas oportunidad pa' nuestros hijos*" [Silvano, they tell me that there are better opportunities in Wisconsin. We have to look for more opportunities for our children.]. Daddy looked at Mother and said, "Luz, it's cold in Wisconsin, there are no Mexicans in Wisconsin. It's not like it is here, although you know, the treatment of Mexicans in Texas is not the best, at least we know the place, we have the language. They say it's cold there.

Here, I have a good job with the railroad; you go and you pick vegetables. Life is difficult, but life is good." According to my sister, that's how the discussion went, but my mother would not give in. She insisted, "No. I don't want to stay here. I want to go north, because I keep hearing that there's more opportunity north." That's what was important to her. I can't help but wonder, would I have done it in her shoes?

Daddy and his brothers came at the same time, although Daddy settled in Milwaukee, and Tio Jeremino and Tio Fernando settled in Waukesha. There was a foundry there in Waukesha. They found work at Waukesha Foundry and General Malleable and that's where they settled. Our family, the Monreal family, was the only one that settled in Milwaukee.

My father was Silvano Monreal, and he always used Flores, because that was his mother's maiden name, so he always used that hyphenated name. My mother was María de la Luz, her maiden name was Velásquez. My grandmother was Irene Velásquez. Our homestead was at 621 South Sixth Street. This was before 1962 when we started the first Mexican restaurant, because when we started the restaurant then we moved from our homestead into the upper level of the restaurant. When we lived at 621, of course, we had a large family. A lot of pride was instilled in us. We had humble surroundings but we took care of them. My grandmother made sure that the stoops were swept daily, and to this day I follow that tradition at my home in the suburbs. My front stoop is always swept and my curb is always swept.

My grandmother also maintained an incredible garden at 621. She used to grow vegetables, herbs, and flowers; she had an incredible green thumb. We had this gorgeous magnolia tree in the front yard surrounded by rose bushes, surrounded by mum bushes. It was really spectacular.

The First Mexican Restaurant in Milwaukee

We moved in 1962 to 600 South Sixth Street, which was at the time a business building. My brother, encouraged by my mother—who had this strong entre-preneurial spirit—had decided to start the restaurant. My mother encouraged my brother to follow that dream, to go after it. They sold the homestead at 621, so that we, in fact, could buy the building at 600 South Sixth Street. The upstairs of the new building had been all medical offices—there has been a dentist and a family practitioner there—and it was renovated and remodeled so that we could live upstairs from the restaurant. That's where we lived for many, many years. We lived upstairs.

A while back someone who had known my mother said to me, "*Cómo te pareces a tu mama* [My, how you resemble your mother]." To me, God, that's the best compliment anybody can give me, to say that I resemble my mother. I'm sure that my story mimics other stories, and that others also put their mothers on a pedestal, but I don't know, to me my mother was really extra special, she really was. She knew what it meant to be in a strange city, with nobody to rely on, with kids that were young.

My brother Silvano Monreal—we called him Sal, was the one who had the dream of opening a restaurant, which he did in 1962, and we all worked in it. I had another brother, Frank, who already had a very successful business called Monreal's on Sixteenth and National, but it was a nightclub not a restaurant. Frank was already in that enterprise and it was all very successful, when Sal, who was younger than Frank and who worked at the Ladish Company, decided that we should open up a Mexican restaurant. At that time, there were two Mexican restaurants in Milwaukee: Texas Café on Fifth Street and Hernandez Café on South Sixth Street. There were only two others. It wasn't the commodity that it is now where you see Mexican restaurants on every corner. Sal said, "I think we can do this."

When the restaurant opened we were featured in an article in *The Milwaukee Journal*. It was a family-run enterprise and my brothers were the bartenders and hosts while we girls were the waitresses and kitchen helpers. Mother was in charge of the restaurant. Pretty soon word got out and Monreal's El Matador Restaurant became this incredible success. Of course, we lived right upstairs so Mother didn't have to go outside or anything to get to it. She would get up very early. She would never start her work in the restaurant without first going and hearing mass, and she would hear mass every single morning at the church. That's how it was.

My brother Sal actually went and he got the loan, oversaw the construction and remodeling, and then we opened. The first couple of years we had no outside employees because everything that was earned went right back into the restaurant, to pay all of the liabilities connected with it. If you have a business, you need insurance and utilities, you have all of those expenses connected with running a business. For the first couple of years there was no outside help. As the years went by, we started becoming more and more successful, and that's when we started employing the kitchen help, the bus boys, the dishwashers, the extra bartenders.

Working in a family business taught me about accountability, certainly, that expenses always had to be offset by the revenue. I learned the basic fundamentals of how a business operated: what has to be paid, the importance of having an accountant, the importance of having a lawyer, the importance of making sure that your credit was built and maintained at a very high level, those kind of things. When the grocery or the liquor store dropped off your order they weren't going to take your word for it that you were going to pay. You had to build a credit history with them. I also learned the importance of treating the customers with dignity and respect, even if they were 100 percent wrong; in a complaint, you knew to bite your tongue and do something to make it better. If, for example, a customer didn't like a dish, you asked if there was something else on the menu they would like. You accommodated the customer. To me, that was very, very important. Although what the customer says may not always be true, the customer's always right—that basic fundamental principle has stuck with me, that you learn to accommodate your customers, to please them, because your livelihood depends on that food check being paid. It was a very good experience.

I've always had an outgoing personality, and it was not strange for people to be waiting for a table to turn over so that I could wait on them. I knew most of my regular customers by name, and there were some who later became big names in the City of Milwaukee. For instance, Terry Henicke, who was heir apparent to Manpower International, worked his way through school as a bartender at the Matador. Richard Abdo, the retired chairman and CEO of WE Energies, came with his family every single Saturday, and I waited on them. There were also regular customers who were also just starting out in their careers, because a lot of professional people ate at Monreal's El Matador Restaurant. In those days, our customer base was not Mexican. If I want Mexican food I'll cook it in my kitchen. I don't need to go to a Mexican restaurant, unless there's a huge gathering or something. Our customer base was all Anglo, East Indian, and other ethnicities. We had very few regular Mexican customers, because, I think, Mexicans didn't need to go out to enjoy Mexican food. We know how to make it all. Nowadays, yes, Mexicans go to Mexican restaurants, but it's more for the convenience of not having to cook.

The Influence of Mexican Popular Culture

My mother, myself, and my three younger sisters often went to Don Carlito's Record Shop, across the street from Segovia's Grocery Store, to get the music of Trio Los Panchos, who were very popular, or Miguel Aveces Mejia or Lola Beltrán.[6] We would go there to pick up the latest 78 record of what was popular at the time—the old 78s, not this new technology. Those are the records you could get from Don Carlitos. His store also had *novelas*, magazines, and other publications, things like that, though we mostly went to Don Carlitos for our records.

I was taught to read in Spanish. They had these *novelas*, the magazines with huge, huge script. My grandmother was illiterate, she did not read, but she said to me, "I will teach you how to read," and I remember sitting with her, and I'd say "*pero Mamá Irene, usted no lee, con todo el respeto* [But Mamá Irene, with all respect, you don't read]," and she would answer me, "*Yo te ayudo, cuéntame, trata de leer lo que estas viendo* [I will help you, read to me, try to read what you see]." So I read to her, and if I had trouble with it, she would say "sound it out," and then she would correct my pronunciation. That's how I learned to read, by reading those *novelas*; that's how my grandmother, who was illiterate, taught me. She was taught how to sign her name, so she knew a little bit, but mostly she had a lot of patience with me, teaching me how to read. Spanish was our first language and learning to read it was not too hard; really Spanish is not a difficult language to maneuver. She would say, "*No hija, así no se dice, se dice así* [No, dear one, that's not how you say it, this is how you say it]," and she taught me a lot of patience. That's how I learned, from those *novelas* with pictures. Of course, once you can read Spanish it's easy to write it. The hardest thing for me to remember was that the letter "i" was always pronounced like the long "e" in English, and the letter "e" in Spanish was always pronounced like the short "e" in English, so those kinds of things I always remember.

In the late 1950s and early 1960s, we would go to the Mexican movies on Sunday afternoons at the Royal Theater on Sixth Street. Whatever they were showing at the Royal, that's what we would see. I think we saw every single Pedro Infante or Tony Aguilar movie we could. I loved to see these incredible-looking Mexicans singing atop their horses. We admired Miguel Aceves Mejia, Lola Beltran, Libertad La Marque, and all those Mexican actors. We would see whatever they were releasing at that time. I must have been between eight and ten years old when we went regularly. The movie that most impacted me was *Nosotros los pobres, ustedes los ricos*, with Pedro Infante. For some reason I love that movie and the story connected to it. Any movie with music in it, though, I adored. To me, that was fantastic. And it was always very crowded at The Royal because the Mexican community was growing.

Cultural Values

Our Lady of Guadalupe was the Parish we belonged to in our childhoods, and I continued to maintain a close relationship to the parish in adulthood, even when we lived in Greendale. The Parish was formerly on Third and Washington, then later it merged with Holy Trinity on Fourth and Bruce, where it is now. Even though I did not live in that area any longer, we went back for masses celebrated in memory of my family members. My mother was very active in the parish, and she was always organizing collections for the church: "The church needs a new furnace," or "the church needs a new refrigerator," and "I need donations from each one of you." We were active supporters of the Parish. I'm one of thirteen children, and there were a lot of Monreals around to help. We were very active in the parish's annual posada tradition, and in the celebration of the feast of Our Lady of Guadalupe. Those two events were very important to my mother. Of course, because Mamá Luz loved it, she got all of us involved, and so ours was often the house where the posada ended and the participants were welcomed in for food and celebration.

I remained active in the community because being Mexican, that part of me has always been strongly felt. I love everything that is Mexican. I love the folklore, music, food, traditions, and culture! To me, it's very important, yet due to my mother's influence, I am equally proud to be an American. My mother always said, "Nobody can take your roots away from you, but this is your country, so it's important that you understand how the government is run and its history, and it's important that you become proficient in the language because *si bien no te hace, mal tampoco.*" In other words, "It may not be helping you, but it's not going to hurt you either." Words of wisdom from so many years ago that truly resonate now, because I am fully bilingual, and you cannot believe how that has helped me as the president and CEO of this organization. It has helped me tremendously. It has set a comfort level in my everyday work, yet I still work constantly and try to better myself with my Spanish language. I read Spanish publications, listen to Spanish broadcasting, and view Spanish programming. I believe it is important to maintain the Spanish language in my life since it was something instilled in me since childhood. Spanish was significant in my upbringing and informs the values that I still cherish.

We also imbibed strong moral and religious convictions as children because religion played such an important part in our family. A rosary was said every single night in our home, before our altar with its fresh flowers, *veladoras* [candles], statue of Our Lady of Guadalupe, and statue of Mother's revered San Martín de Porras. That was one of the religious icons that she was extremely devoted to. In the lobby of the United Community Center today is a replica of my family's altar with the statues from our family altar.

We were also raised with an ethic of hard work—that was modeled for us—and we all worked in the family restaurant. My mother always said, "*pobres pero limpios* [poor but clean]," or "soap isn't expensive." Our house was always organized and clean. I remember my older brothers, when they would bring home the women that would ultimately become their wives, how amazed their future partners were about how clean our floors were, because every Saturday morning we—the girls—got down on our hands and knees and scrubbed the floor, taking up the old wax and putting down a new coat. We also washed and ironed. At very early ages we were taught how to cook, how to prepare meals.

At very early ages, we knew how to use the broom to clean the entrance to our house. The porch and the curb were swept every single morning. When it snowed, the boys made sure that the walks were clear. I remember we had a furnace that was coal fired, and I remember when Snyder Fuel would come and deliver the coal. In our culture, of course, the women were the ones who woke up early, and I remember helping my mom stoke the ashes and then start the fire in the furnace, and things like that to prepare for the day. I remember my mother making baskets and baskets of fresh tortillas, because tortillas and beans and rice were staples—that's what we ate each and every day. Before my mom would head out to work, there was always a huge basket of tortillas for the meals.

The Importance of Grandmother/Second Mother in Everyday Family Life

My mother was an only child, and when my daddy married my mother, a mother-in-law came with her, so there was always a maternal influence; even though Mother and Daddy always worked to keep body and soul together, there was always a maternal figure there in the form of my grandmother. She was Mamá Irene. She was our second mother. My mother was Mamá Luz, her name was María de Luz—she named me after her. But my grandmother was never *abuela* or *abuelita* nothing; she was always Mamá Irene. Her name was Irene; she was Mamá Irene, and they made sure, my two parents made sure, that all the respect and regard was given to her. She was a figure of authority in our upbringing so in essence we had three parents; we were blessed with three adults who were in charge, who oversaw everything.

From the time I was young, I remember that both my parents worked outside the home. My mother's very first job was washing dishes in a Chinese restaurant on Eleventh and Mitchell, what is now the Lopez Bakery. Upstairs there used to be a Chinese restaurant that you entered from the side stairs. My mother washed dishes there to supplement the family income. My mother didn't speak English, but you don't need to speak English to know how to wash dishes, you just wash dishes, so my mother worked there. She also worked in a tannery, at Law Tanning. In the cleaning division of that tannery there were a number of Spanish-speaking women. The majority of them were Puerto Rican women, and Mother, of course, made great friends. Although Mother was very reserved, very quiet, a very simple woman, she had this innate ability to draw others to her. Mother had a group of coworker friends when she worked at the tannery. Daddy started and retired from the old Grede Foundry on First and Greenfield—that's where Daddy worked. He was cupola tender, and he worked with hot metals and everything.

From "María" to "Mary Lou"

I went to school at Holy Trinity Catholic School. By this time, we had already experienced a little bit of English immersion with the older siblings, because, of course, they were out working and they would talk to each other in English, and we had a general idea of the English language although it wasn't the language that we used the majority of the time. We could understand it. I remember when my mother went to register me at Holy Trinity. At the time, the Principal of the school was Sister Mary Berchmans. My mother brought my birth certificate that stated that "María de la Luz Monreal" was my name. The Principal looked at it and said, "You are in the United States; she will not be called María de la Luz." She told my mother, "She will be called Mary Lou." All of my school records list me as Mary Lou because that's how she translated "María de la Luz" and that's how I was enrolled. My mother, having a high regard for people of the cloth— nuns and pastors—didn't argue with it. In school I was referred to as Mary and at home and outside of school it was María. My Spanish-speaking girlfriends called me María, but my English-speaking girlfriends all called me Mary. Of course, you use your school records to get your social security card so that's on my social security card, too. Since you use your social security card to get your license, that's how I'm listed on my license, too. I know that I'm María, and on my birth certificate and passport it says I'm María, but my school records and all of that say "Mary Lou."

That happened to many people: *Nicolás* became Nick, *José* became Joe, *Pablo* became Paul, *Francisco* became Frank, *Miguel* became Mike, *Silvano* became Sal, *María Elena* became Mary Helen or Mary Ellen. I mean it was not right. It could never happen now; it would never happen, now, because it certainly is an infringement on a legal document. It couldn't happen now. When I think about it now I wonder how they got away with that, but I don't think anyone back then said, "No, that's not my name." You just didn't argue with authority in those times, and certainly my mother, with her limited English, wasn't going to argue about it. She wasn't going to go toe-to-toe with this German nun at a time when there were not a lot of Mexican Americans enrolled in the school. You either sank or you swam. You had to jump in; it was all "come on get going, you need to learn this language," or you just kind of fell by the wayside. I can't say I felt discriminated against there or singled out, but I also made it a point to always excel in everything so that, of course, the ruler never came out for

Mary Lou Monreal. I didn't go into the closet; I didn't have to endure those punishments from the nuns in schools.

Encountering Discrimination in High School

I went to St. Joan Antida High School, a Catholic all-girl school. My mother was adamant that we continue having a Catholic education, and St. Joan Antida had just started up, run by Italian nuns for whom English was a second language. That was one of the reasons why my mother continued working for as long as she did at the tannery, because if you wanted to go to Catholic school there was tuition to pay and uniforms to buy, too. I was the first girl from our family to go to this private all-girls school named St. Joan Antida High School. I was followed by my other three sisters, Isabel, Guadalupe, and my little sister María Elena. We went to that school, and at that time there were only a few other Mexican American students there. The majority of students were Italian. Well, to me the Italian culture and the Mexican culture have a lot of similarities—even in the language there's a lot of similarities—so we quickly assimilated into the student body of Italian American girls. We did well there.

The nuns, although they were limited in their English, certainly gave us a very good secondary education, and I have to tell you that to this day some of the nuns who were my teachers continue teaching there. I was always very spirited, always very opinionated, always very inquisitive, so it was not uncommon to hear my name over the loud speaker, being paged to report to the principal's office for some small infraction. Typically, these involved questioning the curriculum. I would question things, especially in our religion classes. I asked, "Why should we believe this? I need to understand why." Well, they viewed that kind of question not as being inquisitive, but almost challenging, and I would be reprimanded for that.

I was reprimanded, for example, when we were in history class and they said Pancho Villa was a bandit and an outlaw. It was a statement that sort of shocked me, and I raised my hand and said, "That's not true. Do you consider Robin Hood an outlaw?" I remember the teacher's face when I asked that! Now, it was her turn to be shocked. I continued, "If you don't consider him an outlaw, why would you say that about Pancho Villa?" I was pretty forceful in simply saying, "I disagree. This is wrong." Then I heard over the loudspeaker, "Mary Lou Monreal report to the principal's."

Sister Alfreda, the principal of St. Joan Antida, and I became very close friends during those years—because we saw so much of each other! She was stubborn, and she, too, was opinionated, and she would always try to reason with me. In that case, she said, "This is what the book says." I answered, "But the book is wrong. How can we accept this? You don't know anything about Pancho Villa. You don't know what the revolution created, the upheaval, the fight against the bureaucracy and corruption and graft of government." I remember that I was always challenging the nuns. I was not at all following in my mother's example of being reserved and quiet. I was always very vocal.

This was true even among my friends. I had a good friend who was Italian, a very good friend who for some reason when we got into an argument in the gym, she called me a "spic." This was from my good close friend! I looked at her and I slapped her. I said, "You don't use that word to describe me. To me that's a very insulting, degrading word. I am not that, I am not that." Well, she pushed me back and slapped me, and then, of course, the nuns in their habits came to separate us and we were both taken to the principal's office.

Sister Alfreda said to me, "You don't fight, you don't fight!" I said, "Nobody is going to degrade me, or insult me by using those disparaging terms to describe my ethnicity. There are certain words that I do not accept, one of them is "spic" and the other one is "wetback." I will not accept those to refer to me." Sister Alfreda said, "No, but you have to learn that you have to turn the other cheek." I said, "When it comes to that, I will never turn the other cheek, because that's not who I am. I don't call her a 'dago.' I don't call her a 'mafia.' I don't call her anything like that, so, no." I added, "And I am not apologizing Sister for what I did. I stood up to a prejudicial kind of mentality. She deserves it, and I deserve an apology." She wouldn't apologize and so it was at a standstill. We all left and she and I were never close again.

In Charge of Younger Siblings

In the family ranking, Juanita, the oldest of the Monreals, was followed by seven boys, one after another. I was the first girl after those seven boys, and then came my sisters, and then Ricardo, who was between Lupe and Lena/Maria Elena, but he died when he was just an infant, you know, and Mother never wanted to talk about it. *Le pesaba mucho a Mamá, le dolia mucho* [It grieved Mother a great deal; it pained her], so we never kind of delved into what happened, how he died, but he died as an infant. The four of us girls had an incredibly close bond because we were very close in age.

Not counting my oldest sister Juanita, I was the oldest of the girls. Mamá Irene and Mamá Luz always called me "madrecita" because of that. I kind of road herd on the three younger ones, but we played together, too. We didn't really have outside influences or friends. There was no "let's go to the playground" moments because we never had bikes, or roller skates. We entertained each other. At one time I thought I would become a nun, so we would play mass and we would use these little candy wafers. We entertained ourselves very well. It also then fell upon me to make sure that they did all of their chores, to make sure that we hung up the laundry in the summertime, that we took it down when it was dry and folded it, and that we came home for lunch. I made sure that they all knew how to cook, clean, and iron, and all of that.

Women's and Girls' Chores

We learned housework from Mamá Irene and Mamá Luz. It was really on the shoulders of the women to keep the home fires burning. It truly was, from washing and cooking to everything else. My seven older brothers shoveled snow, but they did not have a lot of household chores. We more or less catered to the men because that was the culture. There are certain things in the Mexican culture that I think should be thrown to the wind—I truly, truly do. For men, why can't you pick up your plate and take it to sink? Why can't you wash dishes? Why can't you heat up your own tortillas? I remember early on that the weekends were just absolutely task-filled days: getting up early, cleaning, scrubbing floors, putting down wax. Mother used to sprinkle water over the week's laundry, which she then kept in huge plastic bags for us to iron—the shirts and the pants. We ironed everything, including the handkerchiefs, pillowcases. The four of us girls would take shifts at the ironing board, and iron everything, but everything. We put creases in the slacks, ironed shirts, just everything, and we used to take shifts, two shifts at a time until it was all done. It was a lot of laundry.

I remember once when my brother, who was six foot four, was complaining about the crease in his pants, because even *los pantalones de mezclilla* [blue jeans] had to have creases. I mean, it was incredible what we used to do. Well he was complaining that it wasn't right, that the crease wasn't right, and he was talking to one of my other sisters. I said, "Wait a minute; you know what, no, if you don't like it then you have to do it yourself." They were taught never to manhandle us, they could not touch us, they could not slap us, they could not pull our hair, they could not do any of that, so he went and complained to Mamá Luz. She said to him, "Hijo, you know, they've done all the ironing, *si no es a tu gusto* [if it's not to your liking], you need to do it yourself."

I think that my ranking in my family taught me that assertiveness, taught me that I needed to stand up for myself rather than give in or back down. In our culture, the men were the kings at home—they sat at the table first and they were served first, while we would heat up the tortillas, wait on them, and tend to their needs. They never changed a bed, ever, they never held a broom, et cetera. That responsibility and aura dominated in our house. I think that being the first girl in the family after so many boys taught me to be extremely assertive, which truly helped me. It truly has helped me a lot standing up to challenges, voicing opinions, being vocal, looking for justice on certain issues affecting this community. I think that ranking had a lot to do with it because from a young age, I would not back down.

Opposing Racism on the Airwaves

Nonetheless, I've made it my point to be flexible, to be understanding, to be a good listener, rather than hostile and combative. I made it my point. But when I believe in something I am assertive, and there is a distinction between being assertive and aggressive. As I said, I've always been able to set a comfort zone in my interactions with others. This is what you see, this professional woman. I never hesitate to smile. I don't come in demanding. I don't assume anybody owes us anything, but I do insist on the opportunity to plead my case and explain our struggles and challenges. I will show you how we can get from point A to point B with your help, and how opening up procurement procedures can be beneficial to all. That's me: assertive, comprehensive, flexible. I think everybody deserves to be listened to. I'm not a fire and brimstone kind of person. Our people put food on your table, clean your houses, clean your offices, and so deserve that opportunity, and deserve to be heard. Our beginnings are not any different than that of any other immigrant group, whether Chinese, Irish, German, or Polish. My approach is not protest but communicate. Let's talk. Let's get a plan on the table. Discuss what your approaches are going to be and follow through—don't let it die. I am absolutely for holding people accountable for the promises they make; that's what I want.

That was the approach I employed in the whole Belling controversy. Mark Belling, a local radio personality, made some extremely offensive remarks about Latinos on his radio program in 2004. What he did was absolutely unacceptable, and we wanted Clear Channel, the corporation that owns the station and employs this man, to know that it was not going to be tolerated. We asked them to sit down and talk about it, because we wanted to hear a resounding message from them that he would never use those words again. People said, "María, if you think they're going to do anything to him, you're wrong. He's money for that corporation." I said, "Let's sit down and we will discuss it." We wanted him suspended for two weeks without pay. He was suspended for one week without pay. If they didn't live up to the agreement we promised to send out a letter from the Hispanic Chamber to all their advertisers explaining our position. We also asked for Clear Channel to allow us a radio program—and not at two o'clock in the morning—that could start putting a positive face on the professionals in our community. That's how *El Valor Latino* was born on WISN Radio 1130

AM at 9:30 every Sunday morning. Perfecto Rivera hosts *Valor Latino,* where he interviews business owners, professionals, and people in the community who are making a difference. We asked for billboard space, too, not just for the Chamber but for the community, so that we could send out positive messages about this community. Every single request they responded to, and that was a big victory, because we insisted on communication. It was a resounding success in my book. The perspective of Hispanics emerged in that whole discussion in a very different light.

Much to my dismay, we received volumes of hate mail during that controversy. I knew that there was resentment, but I didn't know the depth of the hatred for Mexicans before that, because I rarely encountered overt prejudice. Some of them made me cry they were so horrible. Others, I just couldn't believe that someone ate with that mouth. It blew me away. I may have been in situations where I felt hostility from someone but it wasn't expressed verbally, so this was a shock. We handled it professionally, because people use responses to emails against the sender, so we handled those emails very professionally. That's when I realized that this world will never be rid of racism, ever. It was disquieting, uncomfortable, and hurtful to encounter that, because I am full-blooded Mexican. When you say, "Go back to where you came from," *this* is it, this is where I'm from, this is my country. The fact that I still speak my native tongue, the fact that I follow cultural tradition, that shouldn't detract from who I am but enhance who I am and what I have to offer. I am Mexican American. I'm an American citizen. I was born here. I wave the flag. But none of that strips away my pride of being Mexican in origin.

5. A Life Dedicated to Education

OLGA VALCOURT SCHWARTZ

Interviewed on Monday, June 21, 2010

College Student, Homemaker, Teacher,
Director of Bilingual Education, Volunteer

Educational Pursuits Brought Me to Milwaukee

I was born in Caguas, Puerto Rico, in 1935. I went to Catholic schools in Puerto Rico that were actually bilingual, because the teachers were nuns from schools in Baltimore. When I graduated from high school, my parents decided I could come to the United States to go to school, and so after some searching, I settled on Mount Mary College here in Milwaukee. I came to Milwaukee with my dad. He brought me. We didn't know a soul here, not one person in Milwaukee! When school began, I learned that there were three other students of Hispanic background: one was from Venezuela, and two were twins from Mexico. Needless to say, we became very good friends.

I graduated from Mount Mary with a bachelor's degree in education and a minor in mathematics. My intention, at the time, was to get a degree and go back to Puerto Rico and teach there, since I had a boyfriend there and I wanted to establish my life in Puerto Rico. But as life had it, in my junior year, I met a man from Milwaukee, Mr. Schwartz, and we got engaged. In my senior year we decided to get married, and one of my father's requests was that we marry in Puerto Rico. He wanted my husband-to-be to know where I came from, to know my background and culture before, as my Father said, I gave that all up to come to Milwaukee.

In addition to my undergraduate degree from Mount Mary, I went to UWM for my master's degree, while I was teaching and working. Then later, I got a grant from the Title VII program to go and get my PhD at UW-Milwaukee. I took a sabbatical of one year to get one year of my coursework in, and then I finished the coursework as a part-time student while I was back at work. I completed my coursework, but I couldn't do all the writing and research, and I left after three years in the doctoral program.

Becoming a Teacher

When Mr. Schwartz and I returned to Milwaukee as a married couple, my new husband was enrolled at Marquette, getting his final degree. He was Anglo, from a German background. My first five years of marriage I dedicated to having children. I had five children in six years. [*laughs*] I was a very good Catholic! [*laughs*] At that time, I didn't work outside the home. I was living in New Berlin, a suburb of Milwaukee. In my seventh year of marriage, I started working as a substitute teacher in the New Berlin public school system, at the elementary level. Then the next year we had trouble and I got a divorce.

I decided to teach full-time, and I moved to Milwaukee and I started teaching seventh grade at St. Peter and Paul Elementary School on the East Side here in Milwaukee. In the 1960s, while I was there I was recruited by the director of the Foreign Language Services in Milwaukee Public Schools to help them write a grant to begin the first bilingual program in the city of Milwaukee.

In 1966 I started at the Head Start program in Milwaukee, which was located at the old Guadalupe Church. We started the first bilingual Head Start program at Guadalupe. I was there for ten years, and our preschool grew to be filled with bilingual four-year-old children. We didn't have three-years-old, only four. After ten years with Head Start, I was recruited by the Milwaukee Public Schools in 1979 to be the supervisor for the Bilingual Program in the Milwaukee Public Schools. The program had previously started first in two schools: Vieau Elementary, which is one of the oldest schools in the city of Milwaukee (and it's still standing!), and South Division High School, which was the first bilingual high school in Milwaukee. We then kept expanding the program to the South Side and to the North Side. When I retired, I think we had over twenty schools participating in some kind of bilingual education and ESL programs.

From the Early Years of Bilingual Education to Multilingual Curriculums in Milwaukee

When we started in the Milwaukee Public Schools, it was not an easy situation. A lot of people resented bilingual education; they felt that we were taking classrooms away from schools to provide bilingual education to the kids I had taught in Head Start. I kept telling people: we worked so hard in Head Start with kids who came in with those bright eyes and dying to learn, and then they went to the public schools and there was nothing for them, because there was no language of any kind. That's why I decided to go work in the public schools at that time.

I had a lot of battles at MPS. Mr. Grudesnek, the director of foreign languages, was really a big help to the bilingual program. The community members were key, though. We had meetings at the Spanish Center, and at several different community organizations. We marched. Oh, there were lots of marches. There were lots of publications, too. I mean the paper at the University of Wisconsin-Milwaukee (UWM) was involved, too, in writing about these issues. Eventually, we progressed enough and then another problem arose, which was that the Anglo teachers complained they were hiring bilingual educators, but not Anglos, and that some of them were no longer able to continue working in the schools where they wanted to work. That was something. A lot of jealousy. It was especially intense at Kagel and Longfellow, which were schools on the South Side that had been mostly Anglo but where the Hispanic community was then moving. The teachers, supervisors, and parents had to deal with that. The parents were the number one helpers in expanding the language programs in Milwaukee.

My work life included meetings for all sorts of things, including writing grants and building bridges with other groups. I often collaborated with my Anglo colleagues to ensure that our efforts in the Bilingual Program were not misinterpreted and resented. We worked with the specialties in the areas of math and language arts and science, making sure that we had the correct curriculum and that we were not taking anything away. Of course, the number one priority was that the children learn English. I mean, a lot of people kept saying bilingual is Spanish; bilingual is not Spanish, bilingual is dual. Many of the children in our program did not have very good Spanish skills, because they came from very poor homes. They had a language, but it was not the correct Spanish language. We had to make sure that they learned English while they developed their Spanish skills at the same time. That was a lot of fun. It was a lot of fun. While I was working, I also supervised teachers from Mount Mary College. Now, I'm working with Alverno College and Cardinal Stritch College.

We worked on large federal grants, such as Title VII. I served as a reviewer for those grants, traveling to Washington to read and evaluate the proposals from all over the country. I also participated in the writing of the first bilingual books in the State of Wisconsin, used in many classrooms. In creating those books we learned from Miami-Dade County, and California. The books were published by McGraw Hill for our system—a bilingual series from kindergarten to grade six that included different cultural perspectives. It was very well received throughout the United States.

Before I retired we had started work on creating an American Indian school in MPS, working with the different tribes in Milwaukee on this, because there were several different native languages to consider. We went to the school board and we really waged a good fight to get a building for the school and start the project, but at that time, the City of Milwaukee wasn't quite ready. We had fought a lot for bilingual education in Spanish at the time, and we had been successful in getting bilingual education for Asian American students started, for Hmong and Laotians, and some of those programs still exist, but we didn't succeed with the American Indian school.

At the end of my career, Milwaukee Public Schools joined together the bilingual education program and the foreign language program to make sure that all languages were important. At one time there was a push to create a bilingual Chinese program, but we didn't have the proper teachers, with the right qualifications, at the time. In my twenty-four years with MPS I participated in everything that we did related to bilingual education. We also always made sure that Latinos/as were active in all areas of MPS, including the banking, education, and social areas, so that Hispanics had representation.

Language and Content Challenges in MPS

Before the bilingual program, MPS had an English as a second language Program (ESL), but they were not combining language instruction with content. They taught English and students learned English, but in the meantime, students were not learning math because it was only offered in English. If you could teach English and teach subjects in the language the student knows best, then students could fly. That was my belief then and I still believe that to this day, that language instruction should be included in subject areas and subject areas should be offered in both languages, if necessary. Otherwise, you have many so-called bilingual kids who are not good at English or good at Spanish, and you have to make sure that they have at least one language, well, both languages. Students learning ESL had to be integrated so that they could actually transfer those skills to every class.

Making sure that the culture was celebrated in the schools mattered to me, not only for Latinos but for all cultures. We wanted to make sure that the people were also learning about other cultures, because we had a two-way bilingual program here. Our logic was that if we are learning their language, they should learn ours and then that's a better mixture. We actually tried to do that and incorporate into the school events calendar celebrations such as *Cinco de Mayo* and others.

Spanglish was another issue. Someone would say, "Well, I'm speaking Spanish." No, you're not. You're speaking Spanglish, and you can't get a job where you have to write and talk to the public using a mixture of both that is not intelligible to anyone. I had a lot of problems with my colleagues at central office over these issues, because they did not see the necessity of this approach; instead they took the sink or swim approach to language acquisition, and some kids swam while others drowned. There were many dropouts.

To do something well, it costs. Until you have a healthy number of staff that can really deliver a program and you can see results, then it's not working in their eyes. I and many of my Hispanic colleagues felt that we had to do everything twice as good to be able to get our teachers prepared. I guess that's not only true for education, but for anything that we face in life, that we have to be twice as prepared. Despite all the headaches, we had fun. I had fun. Our staff consisted of me as director and three specialists, and additionally we had parent coordinators. We always felt that parents were an integral part of the team, and we had two parent coordinators on staff full-time: one Asian and one Hispanic. We also had another set of two parent coordinators on staff part-time to have that contact with the home and to help us promote the programs to both the administration and parents.

We also had to write a lot of grants; the program didn't come with the budget that it now has. Our staff specialists worked on grants, and we collaborated with Anglo staff members, because they had a lot of experience in the grant proposal process. They were very helpful. We had Title VII grants for a good ten years when I was there. What we had to do was make sure that when the grant ended, that the expenses of the program were integrated into the regular budget and the programs could continue, otherwise the programs would just disappear when the grant money ran out, which is what happened to many programs in the state of Wisconsin.

Teacher Training and Heritage Speakers

I worked closely with education departments at different universities to make sure that they were offering Bilingual Education training or ESL training or strong Foreign Language training, including teacher training programs at Mount Mary College, Alverno College, University of Wisconsin-Milwaukee, and Marquette University. Our biggest triumph, I think, if we had one, which I think we did, was working with universities to create programs for the heritage speakers. Back then there was an assumption that just because someone spoke Spanish that they didn't have to study Spanish. However, we had many Spanish-language candidates who spoke Spanish of the home rather than an educational Spanish or skilled Spanish, Spanish used in a professional setting. We had to make sure that future Hispanic bilingual teachers knew their Spanish well, plus their English, because that was one of the things that we had to prove to the public, that our teachers could teach both languages and do it well, and they had to learn the content areas. As a result of these needs, we worked with many professors and departments, including Dr. Toni Griego Jones, Dr. Ricardo Fernandez, and Dr. Salomon Flores, among others.

I think we need to start that language learning in the schools, when it's fun and when students are young. If we begin early, learning language doesn't have to be "you have to write a paper and get all these verbs right and stuff." Instead, when you teach language to younger people, you're in a situation where they want to talk, where they want to sing, where they want to play, and they're curious. I firmly believe in dual languages. I also believe in the continued education of the staff and teachers so that they don't just get a degree and stay home, but they still continue their own learning, perfecting their profession. In some districts, they pay you if you get additional training, but realistically you have to continue to stay one step ahead of the students and make sure that students get what is available.

Figure 9. News report of Olga Valcourt Schwartz's appointment to State Advisory Council in local community newspaper, the *Spanish Journal*. Latino/ Hispanic American Collection. Milwaukee County Historical Society. Photograph courtesy of the Milwaukee County Historical Society.

Community Service

I've been very active in the Latino/a community in Milwaukee. In 1987 I was honored as Hispanic Woman of the Year by the United Migrant Opportunity Services, Inc. and the Hispanic Chamber of Commerce of Wisconsin. I have participated in the Puerto Rican parades and was even the Marshal of the Parade one year. I was also active in Mexican Fiesta, taking part in committees to make sure that things ran smoothly. Among the many community organizations in Milwaukee where I have volunteered are the Spanish Center, the Great Milwaukee Chapter of the American Red Cross, and the Legal Aid Society of Milwaukee. Legal Aid helped lawyers take cases for economically challenged people, especially in the Hispanic community. In 2001, I received an Award for Professional Excellence from Mount Mary College. I also did a lot of translation work for schools like the Medical College, to help out by making information available in Spanish.

I belonged to an organization of professional women that was made up of women from all different classes, and in different fields—education, business, entrepreneurship, media. We focused on getting publicity for women's efforts. We were trying to build our own group of teachers with the skills for being good teachers but who also had the additional language skills. It wasn't just because you were Spanish that one could become a bilingual teacher; you had to be a good teacher with the language to become a bilingual teacher. We worked very hard with those schools to motivate the students, and to get the administration on our side because bilingual education was not cheap. It was a lot of training. We always had to get grants to get additional teachers, which cost the district.

I worked with several boards, too, of Hispanic organizations, such as Daycare, SER Jobs for Progress, and the United Community Center (UCC). I served different positions on the board of UCC for twenty-five years. A couple of years after I retired, my son joined the UCC board! When he was going to graduate school in Michigan, I kept saying to him, "Once you're out, you have to give back to the community." Now he is, on the Board of UCC. He looks at me at times as if to say, "Do I have to?" And I always give him that look back that signals, "Oh, yes. Uh-huh!"

I love working in the community. I love working with the students; that was always my priority. Since I was little, I always wanted to be a teacher. But times are changing now, and that thirst to become a bilingual teacher or a foreign language teacher, well, it's not there much. People take it for granted. They forgot how much we had to work, going to the capitol in Madison to get special provisional licenses to get people hired into the system. Unfortunately, this is true not only in Milwaukee, Wisconsin, but nationally.

For a time, I was an officer in NABE, which is the National Association for Bilingual Education, located in Washington, DC. At another time I was the president of the Wisconsin Association for Bilingual Education (WIABE). In my professional career I received several honors. For example, in the 1970s, *The Milwaukee Journal* published a piece on movers and shakers titled "Seventy for the Seventies" and included me in the list of prominent individuals. Sometime later I received the Madonna Medal from Mount Mary College.[1]

More recently, I've helped the School Sisters of Notre Dame with the Catholic, girls' middle school they created over near Greenfield. That school is now about seven years in operation. The Sisters came to me because they wanted to start with the fifth and sixth grade, and get kids from our schools, the public schools. Although we would be losing students, we wanted to make sure that if kids go from here to there, that they have a good school, and it is a good school. Now they're up to eighth grade. The girls are going to very good high schools, just like UCC students: they are going to Dominican, Marquette, Divine Savior, and others. They have to pay tuition at those high schools, but they are going because academically they are doing well.

The United Community Center

I worked with the United Community Center (UCC) for twenty-five years, and I really enjoyed it because it was progress. When I joined the UCC they had just moved to their current location on Ninth Street, and it was just a small building on the corner across the plaza. They asked me to be on the Board, which grew over the years. We did a lot of fundraising, and we saw that the money was used for progress for the Hispanic community. Then we started Bruce Guadalupe Elementary School. Oh, that was a doozey. But we started it and then I wanted to add the preschool, which was a whole other thing because Wisconsin doesn't pay for preschool children, so funding would have to come from community organizations for the program. Usually, that means going to organizations different than the ones that like to fund public schools. We had to make sure that we had enough funding to get the three- and four-year-old kids in the community center. I remember getting the books, getting toys, ordering all those supplies, and getting the teachers to meet for development. Now it's one of the largest early childhood programs, and it's doing very well. It has continuous funding. Next we opened a middle school, on the other side—it's in another building. When we started the school, we received funds from Milwaukee Public Schools, through the Choice program, but now they are independent of MPS. Now the schools are paid for by grants and tuition. Students wear uniforms. They have rules, and it's very, very well run.

We also created activity rooms for senior citizens at UCC, because we wanted to try some programs bringing together senior citizens with early childhood kids. You know, involving *la abuelita* and *la tía*, and they came and they read books—those that could read. Now we have a separate space for senior citizens, a day care for senior citizens, and now a senior citizen building called "Olga Village" in my honor. Honestly, I'm very, very proud. I recently told the director to save me a room, because I'm going to need one pretty soon! To build the senior citizens' residence we partnered with the Medical College, HUD, and others. You have to collaborate to do things. All of that came out of the daycare for seniors, then the lunch program for seniors at the UCC, and from there things expanded and evolved. When you are working hard and you are asking people for money, you want to make sure you show what you're doing, and when you see the things that are happening with that money, then you know that the effort and expense was worthwhile.

From the beginning, the work with UCC was a vision. Creating all the schools, and the senior citizen center—it was all a vision. We started with what used to be a gymnasium at the other location; Cesar Babón was the one who started UCC in the previous location. Then they moved to Ninth Street and the gym, because boxing is very big in the United Community Center. They have actually had a couple of champs that went to the Olympics and other prestigious games. Now they have English as a second language classes for parents. They have dancing groups for salsa. They have activities to attract not just the kids but the whole family. They have the Arts Center and Gallery, and they're exposing the kids from a young age to art. When did our kids go to art exhibits, or museums, or to an opera? That little bit is good; you don't have to have it every week, but exposing them to art is good.

The UCC always had a good board. To this day they do as well, making sure that all Latinos are included. That was very intelligent on their part. They included key people from the different areas that would be necessary to build. We had people from business and banking, people from the Medical College, parents, and educators. When you put it all together, you're not just working for one faction, but everybody has to come together for one vision. That's what happened. We also had good directors, people who were open to the board's decisions and to the community. We just grew; we just kept expanding and expanding. Now there is the restaurant there, and children in Bruce Guadalupe Elementary have a Mexican mariachi group. They travel all over with the band. The next project will hopefully be a high school so that the kids that are graduating from the middle school can continue there. UCC now takes up two blocks that used to be homes. Every time we bought one, we said, "Now what are we going to put here?" But it has expanded very well and they keep it very well. I mean, you know, there's no graffiti, the interiors are extremely tasteful.

I have worked with many organizations, including beginners started by community people. Some of them didn't have experience, and sometimes they failed because they didn't actually have the training to run all aspects of an organization and attract money. When they fail, people say, "Well that doesn't work." But they were all good, young people who started a lot of groups and organizations that were for the benefit of the community. Some were for employment, for employees who needed help. Some were for assistance with the law. But they were all small. In contrast, the vision, my vision for UCC, is still very, very big, and the director, Ricardo Díaz, has a big vision for the center.

Raising Children to Attend College

In the meantime, I had five children of my own to educate! I was very, very lucky: all of my children graduated from high school, went to college, and got master's degrees. Raising five children while working full-time was very interesting. My children were small when I started working. The ones at kindergarten age went to school here at Maryland Avenue School, while the last two, the youngest ones, went with me to the Head Start program at Guadalupe Center the first year, and they loved it. They just loved it, and, of course, the children loved them. Then they started going to regular school and we studied together. I don't remember if I had a car at that time, I don't think I had a car, but we used to go to the library together to study. I also had the help of many people who would babysit at night while I went to meetings, like those Title I meetings that lasted until one o'clock in the morning. The kids were very helpful, too. The fields they chose for themselves were very interesting. By the time all of my kids were in college, I had been in education for over thirty-some years and I decided that it was time to stay home. I retired at sixty-two from work, but not from education because I continued to do a lot of volunteer work. For example, I volunteered in my grandchildren's schools making sure they learned Spanish. I was there for the culture programs and the grandmother's programs, but our programs were always in Spanish. I wanted to make sure that they learned Spanish.

When people ask me, "How many children do you have?" I say, "I have five of my own, twelve grandchildren, and thousands in the public schools!" Because I just love them, and I still love them now, years later, married with their own children, grown. One thing I kept saying to our parents and to our young teachers is that if we promote education among children from their infancy, if we have them saying, "I'm going to college when I grow up," or "I want to be this when I grow up," then they will succeed. But when you don't talk about it and there's no desire, then they don't continue. I saw a lot of young people that I thought had great promise at South Division High School, but when they got to be a junior or senior, they just gave up on school, or they had to go to work, or they had other priorities. I saw a lot of talent—not wasted, but not fulfilled.

When my kids were little, it wasn't "if you're going to college," it was "where you're going to college." Thank God that my family, my sisters, came to the States, too, from Puerto Rico and that their children also have all gone to college. It's been true for all my family. My dad never went to college. My dad was a pattern maker/garage owner in Puerto Rico. He had some land, but we were not a rich family. We were, I suppose, what you call here middle class, but limited, and my dad told us, "I will not leave you any inheritance, but I can give you an education." In our family there was a big emphasis on education. There were five of us and we kept saying, "We're not going to get anything from Dad, so we better learn!" He would pay for our educations. My older sister had studied first in Puerto Rico and then had gone to Cleveland, and she got her degree in medical technology. I was the second child, and I came here to Milwaukee. The third child was my brother, Gallego, who went to California and then returned to the island. That was very interesting, because he wanted to study hydraulic and mechanical engineering. He went to California, was there for two weeks, and got so homesick that he sold his books and everything and came home. My father said, "I always said you can get *an* education, not *many* educations." My brother stayed in the family business and my other siblings stayed home, too, in Puerto Rico, and married Hispanic men or women. They went to the University of Puerto Rico, and to the Catholic universities and engineering schools on the island and they got a good education.

Getting a college education is a matter of promoting those goals at a very young age. There are many good universities in Puerto Rico now so this is available anywhere. I always told our teachers to emphasize not "when" but "where" in talking with students about college, building that expectation, that sense of "when I grew up, I'm going to be this." I don't care how many years away it is or how many it takes to finish, but if that seed is in you, you know that you can do something.

My College Experience in the 1950s

For myself, I chose Mount Mary College. The first thing I liked about it was that it was run by the Sisters of Notre Dame, the same order that ran the elementary and secondary schools that I attended. Second, I liked that it was a girls' school, an all-girls school. What I didn't know was that it was so cold here in Milwaukee!

That I did not know. My first year was very shaky, because I was homesick. I was very homesick, but the nuns helped me, and friends helped, and I made it.

At a mixer between Mount Mary and Marquette, I met my husband. Marquette men used to come over once a month or so for dances. That's how I met Jerry and his family, and it was a very interesting thing, because when I came to Milwaukee, my dad brought me and then he left me. I didn't have anybody in Milwaukee. No. In fact, I still don't have anybody in Milwaukee except my children. You know how you have cousins, people move here after you? Well, I still don't have that, nobody from home here. My sister who moved to the U.S. is in Illinois, but everybody else is in Puerto Rico.

When my dad left me here, he left me in the care of the Dean of Women at Mount Mary, Sister Mary Selene, who was a wonderful woman. My dad said, "She's all yours. You take care of her for these four years. You have my permission with her, and if you say, 'no,' to her, it's no." And that's how she was. She took care of me and I had to get permission from her for things. For example, for dating, you had to ask permission. Mount Mary was very, very strict in that, but that was good. It was a good education. In fact, I sent my oldest daughter to Mount Mary, too, the one that is a teacher. My other children went away to school.

I went home every summer. Every summer. The first year I went home for Christmas because I was so homesick. But then the following year and after, I always spent the holiday with other students, and I went to Wausau and Michigan. Then I got engaged while I was at Mount Mary and married the semester after in Puerto Rico.

Considering Career Options as a Young Woman

In college we started a group that continued to meet after we all graduated, a group of women who would meet to talk about the future—it started as a place to discuss what we would all do when we finished school, besides get married. For us, that was a big question then: "What are you going to do? Where are you going to work? Are you going to work?" That was the other one: "Are you going to work?" We started early to think about those questions. It was a girls club in college, very informal. We used to meet on weekends and go out to eat or something, and then talk about goals and the future and courses and whether any of us were having problem with this or that and how we might solve those problems. It was very informal but I thought it was very, very real, because we didn't have anything to profit from it except our own education. After all, nobody was going to pay us for it; we were paying them, to go to school, and so we talked to our professors about these issues, too.

I remember when I came to Mount Mary, I didn't come for education; I came for math because math was very important at that time. I remember hearing a talk in my sophomore year about the possibilities for a woman in the area of math. The speaker was a company representative, and it was a Career Day event, and I remember that man saying—and our classes were small, maybe ten or fifteen students per class—"Well, math is very important for engineering, for every class of banking, and for sales, but to be honest with you, women that apply for those careers are not rated as highly as candidates because eventually their plan is to get married and have children." Honest to God! I thought, "He's in my college, telling me that I'm going to school so that I cannot get a job." Because I'm going to get married and have children! Afterwards, I said to him, "You know, that was the most illogical, heart-breaking presentation." Then I changed. I changed my major. I went into education. Because I didn't have a future in math. I told him, and I'll never forget it, "If you go to another women's college, don't say that." His response was, "I'm telling you the truth."

That was the way things were then. I don't think it was intended to be discriminatory, it just wasn't expected, whereas education was supposed to be a women's job. You could always get hired as a teacher. So I changed. There were only fifteen in that class, and I think most of the other students were preparing for occupational therapy. You always had to know numbers; math was important and some stayed in math, but I was the one that changed right away because it was my second year. I think teachers today have to motivate students to infiltrate every profession available, because that's the only way that women are going to make a big difference. You have opportunities now that were not there before; I always tell students in education that you're in the right field in education, because you will be teaching all your life. You'll be teaching your children. You'll be teaching your colleagues. You'll be teaching your family. You'll be teaching yourself. But when you go to another field where there are fewer of us, then you have an advantage. If you are really an educator, then stay in education, because we need good educators, but I encourage them to consider other fields.

Perceptions of Puerto Ricans in 1950s

As a foreign student, it was pretty assertive of me to say what I did to that guest speaker (on careers in math), because that's what I was: I was a foreign student at Mount Mary, even though I was from Puerto Rico, a territory of the U.S.! Anybody that came from outside of the mainland was a foreign student back then. I remember that well. I graduated from Mount Mary in 1956, and I recall another moment that really, really hurt, because I was younger then: it was when President Truman was in office. There were a group of pro-Independence

Puerto Ricans including a woman named Lolita Lebrón, who attacked Congress and killed a couple of people. I remember being in a class, I think it was social studies or world something, and a nun coming in and saying, "Some Puerto Ricans, some Puerto Ricans got into Congress and killed some people." When she said "Puerto Ricans," she was saying me, and I felt like I was on the spot, and I didn't know who Lolita Lebrón was or any of those in politics; I was only seventeen or eighteen years old. But that really, really made me feel bad, because they were from Puerto Rico. There were so few of us there, so it wasn't anything about how other students or teachers viewed us, but just how that news made me feel. I know now that Lolita Lebrón paid her debt, went to prison as a woman, for killing. She's been free from jail for years and she's still active in politics in Puerto Rico. I saw her on a news program, commenting on the money situation in Puerto Rico; she's an older woman now and she was commenting on the government bankruptcy situation.

From Outspoken Teenager to Assertive Adult

I was what they called a "loudmouth" in high school, but I wasn't really a loudmouth, I just always made my point known—if I agreed or didn't agree and why, because too many people say, "I don't agree," but don't say why. Some people can be outspoken and don't say anything. I know a lot of people that criticize this or that, but they didn't vote. They didn't do the thing that gives you permission to be criticizing. You vote and then you get up and complain. That's who I was and my daughters take after me, they're outspoken, but differently from me because they aren't in the same position as I was here in Milwaukee.

In a way, I was involved in breaking the tradition of what a public school is for and how it should be. Any foreigner, as they called us, that came here went to a regular classroom, and either they made it or didn't make it. Language learning classrooms did not exist.

Current Challenges in Public Education

Milwaukee Public Schools have been much in the news. For many years, the school boards in MPS have been very political, but this is even more so now. The District has been losing so many students to the Choice Program, or to different programs that take students away from the public schools. That means the district doesn't get the money for those students, and the teacher-student ratios in MPS are getting larger, and there is less money for materials, less money for teacher education. I think it's very political; they even wanted the mayor to take over the school system, but he's not an educator. Yet, other people are very good educators, but they are not mayors. You have to somehow balance who's running our schools, and it's going to get tough.

Right now, this year, MPS put 428 teachers on layoff at the end of the school year! The majority, well really all of them, were less than three years in the system. That's very hard because we have a very strong union in Milwaukee, with strong seniority protections. This means that the newer teachers will lose their jobs, because they don't have seniority, but at the same time, these are the teachers that are getting some of the best preparation in education, because of the universities shaping up. It is very hard. It's been very, very hard.

It's going to be very hard to attract students at the college level to go into education. Already, I don't think we have as many in education as there used to be. The interest in careers in education has fallen off, and I think that's because of salaries. When you compare the salary that a young man or woman with four years of college commands as a teacher with the salary of another person who went into a technology or business field after the same four years in college, well, there's no comparison. I think that teachers should be rewarded. I think that some of them are not good, and we should be able to help them or eliminate them, but those that are very good should be rewarded, because they don't make enough in salary.

I've seen many good candidates in education, including during one class I taught at UWM in the education department. I taught that course, and it was an exploration of the theories, logics, and beliefs in education. We read history of education, the changes in education, for example, the many times that teaching of math changed in educational systems—we're going to do the metric system, then we're not going to do the metric system, or the teaching of reading, including the "whole language" movement, sign language, and then the emphasis on phonics—all that. One method is not the only one; you have to know the children and then bring in what you need, put together methods. It was interesting. There were many people who didn't believe that they should have one system, so it was a fun course for teachers in training. That was an interesting time because education was not a side issue, it was front and center. For example, if you wanted to be a nurse, you had to take some education courses, because you had to have an integrated approach to the work and to your own education. I enjoyed it very much.

Few Women in Central Leadership of Schools

As director of the bilingual program, I shed many tears. I'm an emotional person. Going to budget meetings and staff allocation meetings and integrating the program into individual schools was all challenging. I was also a woman among colleagues that were mostly men at the central office. They were not only men, they were older men who had been there for many years. I often heard, "My, my, that didn't exist before," or "according to the rules," but I kept saying, "rules change, that's why we have them. Students change. Needs change. Directors change." It was a tough battle trying to make your voice heard among so many men, but men dominated in the administration in many public schools in the United States. It's still male dominated. It's getting better, but the positions that count, from where the money trickles down and everything, I think they're still male dominated.

They looked at me and saw a woman, and I have to say, I always tried to be charismatic and politically savvy. I've always thought, I know I'm in the minority here; I can't go against every one of them. I knew that. I also said, "I'm sorry, I'm very emotional." Many times I broke down into tears and called them and I said, "I'm sorry. But I'm here, I'm here to stay and so, like it or not, we're going to work together, because I'm not going away." I had to fight to make sure—because it wouldn't just be me that would be gone, it would be the program—that the positions were there and that the respect for the positions was there. That's what I wanted, respect, because I had as much education, probably more, than they had, and I knew what I was talking about. They couldn't do my job. But I could do theirs. I always felt that. I could do their job, because I knew what they did. I had the potential and the education. But they couldn't do my job.

We had women supervisors in our program, but in the 1960s and 1970s, when I was there, we didn't have many women in the administration. Now there's more, but I still think that there are more men. When you are in a position like I was, you try to get allies from other minority groups. I started when there were more newly hired Afro-Americans, because there had been a movement that spurred that hiring and opening those positions and everything.

There were some good and some bad superintendents, as far as understanding our program and the populations we served. But today I'm happy with what they're doing. My successor there has been honored, and continued the work. They did a lot with the regular programs, and I think the bilingual, ESL, and language programs are in good positions now.

Working with Parents and Communities as an Educator

One of the activists for bilingual education was Tony Baez, who was then a teacher in MPS; he's from the same town that I am from: Caguas. I first met Tony Baez when I applied for the position and arrived at my interview with a committee from the parent's group. The parents' group always interviewed candidates for the position, too. They had a vote. They were not the only ones with a vote, but they had a vote and they included parents and activists.

I remember walking in and introducing myself as "Olga Valcourt Schwartz," and Tony Baez looking at me and mistaking me for a white person.

I said, "*Mira Tony Baez, yo soy puertorriqueña. Y yo soy de tu barrio* [Look, Tony Baez, I'm Puerto Rican. And I'm from your neighborhood]."

He said, "Are you?! Are you Joaquin's sister?!" You see, he had gone to school with my brother.

I said, "Yes, I'm Joaquin's sister!" And we both laughed.

The activists, and we had a lot of them, were very, very strong and they were, they actually were part of why we have the organizations we have now, community organizations like the Spanish Center, UCC, *Casa Esperanza*, and SER.[2] Not only did they make the voices heard of people who couldn't speak before or weren't heard—poor people, but they took on the government and its agencies. I've always said that's not something you can do unless you have the community behind you. The activists were very strong, but they sometimes made me so angry, because they needed to get this and needed to get that and how they went after what they wanted, well, that wasn't how you got it. You have to use different tactics. But they were great help. The children and the families were great.

We had to do some work on training staff for when children and parents came to register to know a little bit of history and culture that not everybody knows. We had families with four or five children arriving to register, to fill out registration forms. In the Hispanic countries, you have your name, your father's last name, your mother's last name. You might have three or four names. My name was Olga Valcourt Muñoz. So the person registering you puts down the last name Muñoz, which is my mother's last name, when it should have been Valcourt. But someone else might put down my brother's name as Valcourt, and then someone will ask, "But did you all have the same father?" And the parents, offended, answer, "*Seguro, ¿qué quiere usted*? [Of course! What are you suggesting?]" It's all a matter of culture and tactics. We worked with that department, too. We worked on that throughout the whole system, not just getting teachers and educating teachers, but also getting people who were sensitive. A lot of change and exchange was necessary, showing this is how it's done and this is not how it's done, and it's not that the parents are always right, but you have to have respect for the parents.

There were always also internal politics among Latinos/as. The truth was that there were more Mexicans than Puerto Ricans. I mean the statistics show that Mexicans came first to the population in Milwaukee. Puerto Ricans came later. There was always a great, not a division, but something there that caused problems. It was the passport, the visas. Puerto Ricans did not need to have any papers to come to the United States. Mexicans had to have the visas or the passports, and that was always something that was causing problems, because when you register a child in school you have to go to very different departments, you had to go to the clinic to get vaccinations and this is what it is and you go to the welfare office and this is where you get some money and so on, just to get them started. If they didn't have papers, well, that was a problem. Milwaukee Public Schools had a policy, and I don't know if they still do, but we never could ask for passports—never—for registering children for school. You came and you got registered. We worked to establish friends in all those different programs, to help parents and families. That way we could call and say, "Hi! I'm going to send this family, and they need this and this, so they can be registered in school." Heck, otherwise, you stand in lines forever and ever.

Now more than ever, I think that there are more professionals in Milwaukee that are Hispanic who understand these issues. I am not sure how many of them come from other places, but we now have an association of Hispanic lawyers, an association of professional women, and others. They are breaking the glass ceiling. Sometimes you just crack it, but many people can get in between those cracks. I see that happening. That's great. It's an *orgullo* [point of pride] for me, to see Latinos moving forward, not as fast as we would like, but moving.

Faith and Church

I sent my children to Catholic schools because, well, we've been always Catholic, and the schools were very close to where I lived. My children went to St. Peter and Paul's school on the East Side, where I've always lived in Milwaukee, and the school was on the corner. I could drop them and then come and get them very easily. It was actually the most accessible school to me.

I went to Catholic schools for my entire education, from elementary through college. We were very religious. My father talked a very good story about Catholics. He used to say, "I am a Catholic. I was born in the Church, I got married in Church, and I'm going to be dying in the Church. In the meantime, I don't visit Church that much." That was my father. I mean, he would tell us that! What kind of a thing was that to say when here we were going every Sunday?! But he was a good father. He was a good father. My mother died when I was three; my father remarried and he married a woman from Spain. I have two stepbrothers and a sister. There were five of us. I had a good childhood.

I, we, still go to Church. When I got divorced, that was a long time ago, and at that time, I remember a divorced person was not welcome. It was not okay. As I said, my kids were little then; my oldest was eight and now she's fifty-two—so that was quite a while ago. But I mean at that time, I had to—again, that was the thing then—I had to go to classes and everything in the Church. It was part of reconciliation. At that time, I just wanted to make sure that I as a person had not done anything wrong. The process makes you feel like you broke something. I remember one of my kids coming home from school then—they were still taught by nuns then in Catholic schools—and the nun who was my child's teacher in religion class, Sister Theodora, said to my child, in the class, "Your mother cannot receive communion because she's divorced." My daughter was in second grade! Can you imagine? My daughter came home and she told me and I thought, "What?! Sister Theodora said that in front of the class?!" I said, "Good." I went to Sister Theodora's class and I said, "Sister, I'm a believer in God, I'm a believer in forgiveness. You are a human being. You're a teacher. You are not to tell my children if I can go to heaven or hell. You're here to teach my children to have faith." She said, "Well, you know, the religious laws." I said, "I know the religious laws now, but they have changed, and they're still changing." And I added, "You don't tell my children, you educate my child. You don't tell them where I'm going to go eventually—if that will be hell or heaven." Poor Theodora. She was a good teacher, but she had a rough voice.

For me, I know I'm not bad. I know my God. I believe that he's just. I know that if I am not deliberately doing bad, that God is just. But if I know I'm doing something bad, then I know it's bad. I've had a lot of good education in my life. I think you have to have some beliefs in order to be a teacher. I've always said that teachers have to believe that children are born good. You have to know that that kid wasn't born bad, or swearing, or hating. He learned that from home or from the neighborhood. You have to have some belief that you can make a difference. If not, why teach?

The same thing is true in life, if you know that you're going to a position where it's not going to be smooth, you have to have the *pantalones* to go through it knowing that you're going to have a lot of tension, but you do that because you're doing something right, something good, something necessary. Is it going to be tough? Of course it's going to be tough. To get things done, it's not always smooth because people do not easily change the beliefs they've held for so long, that they were raised on, or the ways they do things, how it's been, you do it the way it was always done, that type of thing. Changing makes you more tolerant.

Encountering Racism

People ask me whether I was discriminated against when I came to Milwaukee, and I have to say I wasn't, as a person, because, for one, I come from a lighter-skinned family, and second, I married an Anglo man and moved to New Berlin. My children are all light-skinned with blue eyes. Plus, I didn't live right on the South Side where many Latinos were settling. I was not discriminated against as a person in my daily life, per se, but in my professional life these things come in and matter, who you are—there, I've always said, I'm discriminated against twice, for being a Latina and a woman. My children have not felt that daily discrimination, either, yet they are very much involved in community issues, not so much because of their ethnicity as because of their sensibility about making a difference.

I have many friends who tell me, "Oh, Arizona? They should go back to where they came from," referring to the current controversy about Latinos/as in Arizona.[3] Yes, I have friends like that. I say, "Well where, where did they come from? That land used to be theirs." They look at me. Then I say, "Where did your parents come from?" Usually, people say they're from a German background or a Polish background, and then I ask them why they don't go back to where their parents, grandparents, or great-grandparents came from.

Unfortunately, that sentiment is very present today; racism is coming back. Otherwise, Arizona wouldn't be now resorting to laws and arrests of people "suspected" of being here without documents. Latinos/as in Arizona are not criminals, but Arizona is making them feel like criminals. There are many Latinos/as who have been there for ages—the grandparents, and the parents, and the generations. They say, well, "*Yo nací aquí, mis hijos todos se crearon aquí!* [I was born here, my children were all raised here!]." I feel that racism is coming back, especially in jobs and hiring because the majority population feels that it has too many graduates and too few jobs for them: we're creating highly educated people when jobs and businesses are being cut.

On Perseverance

When I divorced, I did go back to Puerto Rico. My oldest was eight and the baby was two. When I divorced, and even to get to the divorce, I consulted with many priests here and people I knew from Mount Mary, trying to work out what was going to happen, because at that time divorce, well, I was the first one divorced in my family. I called my dad and I said, "I can't do it." He said, "Okay, you make up your mind if your marriage is broken." He added, "If you want to come home, you are welcome to because this is your house, but it's not to be jumping back and forth between here and your husband." He made that clear from the very beginning.

I decided and he came and picked me up with the five kids and our poodle. We went back home to Puerto Rico. He bought me a house there and many friends gave me things for the kids, like the cribs that they were not using. The kids were fine. My oldest one went right to school. However, it wasn't just me that needed taking care of, it was also my five children and I myself felt it wasn't fair for my dad to be taking over that responsibility, of taking care of six people. I had a degree. I could work. My husband was here, in Milwaukee. He was young. He was the same age as I. So I decided that the only way I was going to raise my family was to go back to Milwaukee, to make sure that my former husband faced his responsibility, and I faced mine. Because I had the children, not my dad.

My dad said, "Think it over. If that's your decision, I'll back you up. I'll help you go back, get you a place to stay." When my daughter finished the school year, my dad helped us return to Milwaukee, told me to let him know if anything went wrong and went home. I was back on the East Side. Right away I got a job teaching at St. Peter and Paul. I found a young lady I knew who was in college to live with us while she went to school, and she helped me with the kids, while I was teaching. Later I went to work at Head Start. Monetarily, I made it with what I was earning, and with my former husband's help. I needed to do that. I had the opportunity to go home, and I did—for about six months, but I knew that that was not the right or fair way to do it.

Over the years many people have asked me, "How did you do it?" I tell you, there were many times when I felt lonely, or overworked, but then I also had all these opportunities to work for Head Start, to get my master's degree, then continue and go into the PhD program. When you have motivation and the kids are good it all works out.

6. My Group of Mexican *Comadres* Made All the Difference

RAMONA ARSINIEGA

Interviewed on Monday, December 1, 2008

Homemaker, Assembly Worker, Cake Decorator, Lathe Operator

A Transnational Marriage

I came to Milwaukee in May 1956. The reason for my move was that I had met and married an American citizen in Mexico, Jesús Arsiniega. My husband Jesús was born in Fresno, California, and then as a child he moved with his parents to Minneapolis, and then from Minneapolis they moved here to Milwaukee. They were migrant workers, so they followed the migrant circuit. They went to Monterrey when they were retired. Well, really they were repatriated in the early 1950s with their belongings. They were originally from Durango. Well, Jesús went back to Mexico with his parents, because he was the youngest, and he stayed there for a time, but then he began to migrate back and forth, spending some time here in Milwaukee then returning to Mexico for a time, always with permission.

It was because of a bad toothache that I met my husband! One of my molars had been causing pain but there wasn't any dentist in my town, which was very small and only had about 500 households. My mom said, "Well, go to Torreón to see the dentist there." Torreón was right next to a town called Gomez Palacio, which was right next to Lerdo, so all three were near each other. My dad's sister, my aunt, lived in Torreón, and I went to stay with her and then got myself, very quickly, to the dentist.

The next day we all went to a dance in nearby Lerdo, where Jesús happened to be vacationing, and Jesús and I both wound up at the same dance in Lerdo. That's where we got to know each other. We dated for fifteen days and then we married! He went to the town where I lived and he told me that he was going to ask for my hand in marriage, as is the custom there, but my mom became so very, very mad about it.

"What are you doing getting married!?" she scolded me and continued, "You just met him!" She asked me, "Do you want to get married?"

Very timidly and fearfully I answered, "Yes."

Then my mom said, "Well then, we're going to do it right now. We'll get the judge here to marry you two and off you go with him!" She brought the judge and he married us.

Then my dad said, "Well, we're Catholics and I want her to be married in the Church, too!" In my small town, there was a Church but no priest. The priest only came to our town every three months. Between the priest's visits, there were only rosaries—no masses—said every day by the women of the town, who took turns leading the prayers. My dad decided that my older brother would go with us and watch over me until we were married in the Church. My brother traveled with us to Monterrey and within fifteen days of meeting we were married, after paying for the wedding banns and all. The priest was a good friend of Jesús's parents, who lived in Monterrey—that's where they had retired—and so he married us.

After we were married in 1951, I lived in Monterrey for five years while Jesús went to Milwaukee to work and traveled back to Monterrey when he could. I did not want to move here. No, I did not. I would say, "Oh, no, I don't want to live so far away from my parents." My parents, in any case, lived in a town far from Monterrey. My three oldest children were all born in Mexico. When I came here, I had three more children here.

Here in Milwaukee, Jesús worked at the Albert Troester Tannery. Then he moved to the Oilgear Company where he worked for about twenty years. When he was getting ready to retire he kept saying, "Let's go back to Mexico. Let's go to Mexico," and so we did. We had only been in Mexico a short time when he became sick, and then two years later he was dead. Now I travel between Mexico and Milwaukee regularly but mostly I'm here, here in Milwaukee.

Migrating with a Women's Network in Place

I was finally convinced to move here when two women who are now my dear *comadres*[1] arrived to stay at the house where I was living in Monterrey. Gudelia Talavera and Avelia Talavera stayed with us in Monterrey while they arranged their passports to go to the U.S. Because their paperwork took some time, they were with us for three months and I spent much time with them. We became fast friends. After that I said, "Well, now I'll go to Milwaukee, too, because Avelia and Gudelia are going there!"

"Well," I said to Jesús, "Now I want to go to Milwaukee with you because Avelia and Gudelia are leaving for Milwaukee."

He said, "Good, then make the arrangements." I did.

They were going to Milwaukee because an uncle of one of their husbands, Jose Zaragoza, who is also father of Nacho Zaragoza, was helping them arrange it. When I decided to go, I made all the arrangements very quickly. Because Jesús was a citizen of the U.S., I just had to go and ask and they gave me the visa. I didn't have to wait at all. Because their dad was a citizen, the children didn't need papers. That's how I crossed the border in 1956 with my three children. Then at the age of eighteen the three of them all became U.S. citizens.

Nowadays I tell Avelia and Gudelia, "You two are to blame for my being here!" Oh, how they laugh about that. For me, it was important to know that I would have comadres here. I thought that if I came here I would be too alone, without anyone and without any family. They became my family here. Jesús had a brother and a sister here but I didn't know them well. Actually, I didn't know them at all before we arrived. While Jesús worked in Milwaukee he stayed with them at first, then later rented a room where he lived alone.

When we came to the U.S. we came by train. Because I was traveling with three small children who were so much work and would have to change trains, my mother-in-law came with me, and Jesús agreed to meet us at the train transfer point. "I'll meet you in St. Louis," he said, and he did. From there, we traveled north to Milwaukee with him.

During the five years before our arrival here, Jesús traveled between Milwaukee and Monterrey—usually staying for three months at a time in each place—and we communicated by letters. I lived in his parent's house with him when he was in Monterrey, and when he returned to Milwaukee I went to stay with my parents in my small town. That's where two of my children were born, in my town of Carrillo, Chihuahua. That's where they were born, with just a nurse to assist. If women today knew how we had children back then, at home, they'd be surprised.

Here in Milwaukee, I don't even remember anymore where the first house was where we lived, but later we moved into a house on Virginia Street, after Bruce Street. It was a house with two bedrooms, a kitchen, and a small living room. There was no bathtub or shower so we had to bathe in a big tin tub, and there was no hot water in the house. We lived there for two years. Then we moved into our house on Scott Street, and I felt so rich because now we had heat, a water heater, and four rooms! The kids would just huddle up around the heater they were so cold!

I arrived here with many illusions about life in the United States, because in Mexico people said, "Oh, in the United States you'll have everything, everything." Even so, I wasn't interested in moving here until I knew that Avelia and Gudelia would be here. But I had illusions, nonetheless, and when I arrived to discover that we didn't even have hot water in our house—well, that was hard. I thought that houses in the U.S. just had buttons to push for everything, but we were worse off than in my small town in Mexico. We were a little taken in by the fact that people often came back to visit in Mexico with brand-new cars, and we didn't realize then that they were all financed and they owed lots of money for them. For these reasons, I was never bowled over by the U.S. I felt I had had a better life in Mexico, with my family, and that here I was poor. We didn't lack for anything here, though, and my kids are better off today than we were when I arrived, but that would also be true in Mexico. Mexico isn't the backward place that many people imagine.

Acclimating to Life in Milwaukee: Mexican and U.S. Foods

On Virginia Street, I think the house we lived in had six units and the other tenants were older and different ethnicities, like Polish, but we were very near to the Mexican store on Fifth Street. I was just so happy to be near the Mexican store run by Segovia. Mrs. Segovia had a helper, but she ran that store and she was always there. I tell you, at that time I was so young that she looked so much older to me but in reality she probably wasn't all that old, just mature! Age is all in your perspective, no? My kids remember calling me "viejita" [little old woman] back when I was thirty, and nowadays they wonder how they could have thought I was old at that age! In any case, I bought everything at Segovia's—tortillas, chile, bread, everything, everything. Later, Segovia's became Martinez's grocery store.

In those years I did not like American food. I cooked our meals exactly as we had had them in Mexico, exactly the same food. It took me about three years to get used to eating American food. I remember the first time Jesús took me to eat Chinese food, at a new restaurant that opened up—"let's go," he said—it just made me sick, but nowadays I absolutely love it! Back then, though, I could not even eat a sandwich because I couldn't stomach it. I was so accustomed to the fresh food we had back home where we would get fresh eggs from the henhouse, and my mom had dairy cows for fresh milk and she made cheese, and there was a bakery that made fresh bread every day. We had a large house there and while it was only adobe it was very pleasant. Jesús, however, was familiar with American food. He would buy his ham, and his bologna, and other things. "How can you eat that!?" I'd say. Our kids quickly adapted to American food.

Before that, though, they were accustomed to eating rice, beans, sautéed meat, enchiladas, tacos—well, everything that one would make really—and they still prefer Mexican food over American.

Here in Milwaukee, Jesús worked and I stayed at home with our small children. I would wake up every day and make breakfast for everyone, pack Jesús a lunch, and yell at the kids because they were always driving me crazy. Sometimes I would cry, well, because we were so poor. The kids never missed Mexico; they adapted to Milwaukee very quickly. In Mexico they loved to wander around outside on their own—well, there was lots of space for wandering there, and so here they wanted to do the same but that wasn't possible. They were always getting into other people's yards and one of the neighbor ladies would come and tell me, "Hey, your kids are over here in my yard!" But I didn't even understand her well because I didn't know English. I would scold the kids, but they were little savages! [*laughs*] They loved to run off into the neighborhood. There was a factory nearby that had a pretty little garden at the entrance and the security guard there regularly stopped over to tell me that the kids were over there, and that they were even picking the flowers! I had to tell Jesús so he could go find out what the man was saying, because I couldn't understand him. Gradually, the kids learned that they couldn't wander around like that.

We didn't always have health insurance in those early years. When my daughter was born in Mount Sinai Hospital, I think they charged us $200 for the delivery. They must have moved me around to ten different beds then! [*laughs*] For $200 it was good, and I stayed there for three days—that was how long they kept you back then. The doctor charged us $40 for the delivery. We had the money to pay for it because Jesús received some kind of payment when he lost his job, but later on when he started working in the tannery and then at Oilgear, we always had health insurance, but not dental insurance. For dental, we went to the free clinic.

Making Friends and Learning in Adult English Classes

I went to school to learn English, and that's where I met other Mexican women in the neighborhood, including Amalia Delgadillo and a woman named Connie. Amalia and I were recently arrived so we would get together. I think Amalia arrived in 1957 and I arrived in 1956. We walked to English classes together all the time because we lived near each other. She lived on Sixth Street, near Carmen Arsiniega, and I lived just a little further—if you kept on walking and then took a turn on Virginia, there I lived. Off we went, according to them, to learn English, and for me it was great fun! "Oh, my, it's my turn to go to school!" I said. We went to school in the late afternoon or early evenings. Jesús stayed with the children, caring for the children while I went to school where a group of us gathered. We went three times a week and there were about twenty students in the class—both men and women. Just the other day, we were reminiscing about that, especially one very handsome young fellow in that class! [*laughs*] The classes were in our neighborhood school, Vieau Elementary, which was right there near Memo Topitzes's store—just on the corner there. That's also the school where the children went.

We took English classes at Vieau for a year, then I moved and then Amalia moved, too. In my new neighborhood, I went to English classes at Walker School, which was nearby. I went there for a while but I didn't really like the teacher, who was a little flaky. [*laughs*] All the teachers in English classes were Americans who taught there at the school in the daytime. I really enjoyed English classes because I wanted to learn and I enjoyed learning but, honestly, while I understand much I do not speak English very often. It's that I was—how can I describe it?—willing to let others do the talking. If I was with Jesús, I'd say, "You speak," or "You do this for me." All the time! When the kids grew older I would say to them—either "my son," or "my daugher," depending on who it was—"Take me to this appointment with the doctor and you speak to him." That's how one never learns to speak English!

My kids ask me, "Mom, why didn't you teach yourself English?" I tell them the truth, "Because I was accustomed to relying on your father for help with language, and he was also so good about it." Then later, I continued to rely on my children. I spoke to my children in Spanish and they spoke with Jesús in English. That's how they learned both languages, so I tell them, "Well, look, I may not have learned English but you sure learned Spanish!" [*laughs*] I tell you my kids became good translators: they'd be talking to me in Spanish and if Jesús said something in English, they'd continue seamlessly in English. That's how it was easy for me to live here but I didn't learn well, I didn't learn how to speak English as well as I should have.

Enjoying Ethnic Traditions and Entertainment

When my older kids were mature enough to watch over the younger ones, Jesús and I became involved with the International Institute.[2] We were invited to join by a friend of Jesús's and we met every month at the International Institute building. It was an adult organization, so the kids didn't participate in it. They did festivals and celebrations there, and we joined. It was a big group. We met every month. We organized ethnic celebrations and parties—we'd take food and have a dance. We had one every month. It wasn't just Mexicans, either, there were Cubans and other Latino/a races involved. That's where I met many

Cubans, who at that time were arriving in the U.S. There were also many other Latinos involved, Argentines and others—that's why it was called the International Institute! We joined in and participated in all the celebrations of festivals and national holidays.

The celebration of Mexican Independence Day on September 16 was already in place when I arrived in Milwaukee. I can't remember the hall where that dance was usually held, but the community celebration was already established—and that was separate from the International Institute—and it often featured the wonderful music of La Orquesta Martinez.

Another entertainment for us was the movies. There was a movie theater on Sixth Street that screened Mexican films featuring Jorge Negrete, Pedro Infante, Cantinflas and others on the weekends. Jesús and I often went on the weekends, because they showed those films on Saturdays and Sundays, but we rarely took the kids. Instead, we'd take the kids to the American movie theater—usually, we dropped them off at the American theater on Mitchell Street and they went in together. At that time it was so nice that we could do that. Jesús would take the kids and he would ask at the ticket office what time the movie ended so that he could come back to pick them up. Then he would leave them there all comfortably set up, and the theater would allow him to enter to pick up the kids when the move was done. Meanwhile, we went to the Mexican movies. Occasionally, when one of our kids was an infant or very little, we'd take them to the Mexican movie with us. They would let us enter with a child if the child didn't cry or create a disturbance.

For Mexican music we listened to Dante Navarro's program, every Saturday, which was very well-known at that time. I never missed a show! [*laughs*] It was the only program I listed to!

All of these things, and having my comadres nearby, and also having Carmen Arsiniega nearby—Carmen was married to my husband's brother Victor but I didn't get to know her until I arrived here in Milwaukee—these all made my early years here in Milwaukee good. I wasn't very preoccupied with material things because, as I said, I came from a small town where we had a good life. I had never experienced or seen poverty. Yet, we didn't have running water in my town. No. The train would deliver a tank of water to our town and the kids would cart containers of water back to their family homes. I think, too, that I was unfamiliar with living in a city so there's a lot here that I didn't notice. I missed, I really missed Mexico, but I was happy here.

I never stopped missing Mexico, either. All my life here I've missed Mexico. All my life. Carmen would say to me, "Ay, you've been here already for so many years and still you pine for Mexico!" I would tell her, "Yes, well, I can't forget."

Even today, I am still more at home, more comfortable in Mexico, because I feel it is my land.

In those early years, I did all my shopping within walking distance of our home, or I would wait until Jesús got home so that he could take us. He had a car—an old one, but a car. That's how I got around, but I never went anywhere alone. Never. I was and still am a scaredy cat. I don't like to go anywhere alone. Jesús was always the adventurous one. Oh, yes! He was always saying, "Yes, yes, let's go, let's do that" and I was the voice of "No, no."

Jesús often took us to the Milwaukee County Museum and to the Zoo and to the lake—places that weren't expensive to visit, but they were all new to me and they were memorable. The one day that we all did something together as a family was on payday. The first thing Jesús would say on payday was, "I'm taking you all out for ice cream." Uuuuy, we were all delighted to go out for an ice cream cone! [*laughs*] We still remember that fondly, the ice cream cone on payday. We didn't go out to dinner much because it was expensive to take the whole family out to dinner.

Class Bonds and Ethnic Tensions in South Side Neighborhood

Jesús once had an accident at the tannery; his hand got caught in some machinery and he couldn't work. "Oh, my goodness," we thought, "what will we do now?" He couldn't work and so he applied for public aid. They told us we had to get rid of our telephone and our car, and then we filled out the papers and waited to hear. After eight days, they said, no, we didn't qualify for aid because it was a work injury. "Ay," said Jesús, 'the only time I ask for help in my life, and with six kids, and they didn't grant it!" They told him that because it was a work accident that he could fight it and get paid, but Jesús said, "How am I going to fight them? They'll take away my job and then what?" Poor thing. He put on a metal brace, went back to work, and told them he'd do whatever they had. They put him back to work sweeping and cleaning the machines, because he couldn't do his regular job with his hand injured.

The woman who owned our little corner grocery store—around the corner from Scott Street—told us, "Don't worry, don't worry. I know that Jesús pays his bills but that he's injured now, so just take whatever you need and I'll put it on your tab." We were always sending the kids there, to Sofi's store, for bread or milk, or whatever we needed at the moment, and when the accident happened it was so kind of her to extend us that credit—even for meat! That store had everything. There was another store down the street, but that man would've never given us

Figure 10. Ramona
Arsiniega (left) with sister-
in-law Carmen. February
1968. Photo used with
permission of author.

credit! When Jesús finally got paid again we paid Sofi. That was a sad time. No
matter. We managed to survive it, and we are grateful that we always had work.

Not long after we had first moved into that neighborhood, one of our neighbors stopped to see us and he told Jesús, "You know that Crutza [another neighbor lady] is collecting signatures because she doesn't want Mexicans living in this
neighborhood. I've told her I won't sign that, and I went to the other neighbors
to tell them that they shouldn't sign it, either." His name was Richard and he
was a very nice man. There were no Mexicans then in that neighborhood, only
Polish people—and now it's all Asian. Crutza often yelled at my children and,
later, one of her kids fought with one of my kids and she came to yell at me for
that, but my friend Clara sorted her out. Clara was quite a fighter; she didn't let
people take advantage of her. Jesús was the same way; when his Polish coworkers

gave him grief at work about being a Mexican and called him "wetback," he'd ask them what river they swam to get here!

Factory Work for Women

My first job was with the Mary Lester Company. I think they made uniforms. I found it in the paper and I told Jesús that I thought I could work. I proposed to him that since he was working in the evenings, or second shift, that I could work in the daytime. He said, "Mona, it's not easy, it's not easy. You think it's easy." I told him, "I know how to sew, and look, in the paper it says they need people." Well, he took me there and right away they told me to come in the next day, which I did, but I only worked there that one day!

It was a sewing job and I didn't like it at all so I didn't return. It was mostly American women there but there was one Mexican woman—who I later got to know and we became the best of friends: Clara. There I was working the whole day, and I had noticed her, but she didn't speak to me so I thought that she didn't know Spanish. When I left work that day to catch the bus she caught the same bus. It was on the bus that she said to me, in Spanish, "Oh, you live this way?" I said, "Oh, my goodness! Why didn't you speak to me all day?!" She answered, "Well, I thought you didn't want to talk. You didn't look to me like you wanted to talk." I had thought the same about her! Then she sat with me and she got off at my stop and she said, "I'm going to go with you to see where you live." [*laughs*]

The next day I didn't return to that job, but after quitting time Clara showed up at my house and asked, "What happened? Why didn't you return?" I told her that I hadn't liked the job, so while we never worked together, from that day forward we became friends. Clara didn't stay at that job long, either. In fact, she moved around quite a bit on jobs. Later she would laugh and remember that first time she came to my door. My kids were little then and they would all run to the door when someone was there. When Clara arrived, the whole bunch were there and yelling, "Mom, a lady is here for you! A lady is here for you!" [*laughs*] When I opened the door she said, "Ay, one, two, three, four! You have four kids!" "Yes," I said, "I have many," as I invited her to sit down. A while later, my youngest, who was still in the cradle, started crying and Clara jumped up and said, "Ay, and you have another one back there!" [*laughs*] Oh, how we laughed together. After that Clara stopped by every day. We were friends for forty years, until she died.

I lasted a little longer at my next job, which was with Western Leather. I had spotted the job in the newspaper, too. I worked there for about five years, making leather cases for radios. I was in the gluing section and other women did the sewing. We made all kinds of cases, purses, and bags of leather. The workforce was half women and half men. At Western Leather, I had a Cuban friend whose husband had been a lawyer and there she was working in a factory. They arrived here with nothing. She didn't last long there. I also met my friend Lola there.

Next I worked at Grebes, a job I found out about through a friend of my Jesús whose wife worked at Grebes. I stayed there for about three years but at Grebes it was mostly women. The only two men there were the supervisor and the baker. I was in the Cake Department at Grebes where we decorated the already baked cakes.

Later, it was my comadre Avelia who told me about the job at Starline, where she was working. She invited me to work there. She said, "They're hiring and they pay really well!" I was excited to apply, but I told her to let me talk it over with Jesús. By then the kids were all in school so Jesús could leave for work as soon as they came home from school, and then I would get home just a little bit later. I was traveling by bus then, and Jesús couldn't come and pick me up because he had to be there when the kids got home. Avelia recommended me for the job. I worked for twenty years until I retired and started dividing my time between Mexico and the U.S.

At Starline we were lathe operators. One of the men would set up my machine, well, all the men set up the machines and the women would simply run them. They gave us a course in how to run the machine. They taught us how to use the micrometer and other instruments to measure the pieces and ensure the machine was properly shaping the pieces, but if the machine wasn't working right then I couldn't fix it. That was what the men did. Starline was mostly a male workforce; there were only about ten women working there, no more. They had about fifty employees and there were four of us Mexicanas there. Sometimes they hired extra temporary help, too. The men and women had separate lunchrooms there, so we got along fine—we were like a family—but we had our separate spaces.

At Starline we made faucet handles and I worked, standing up, on a lathe. I was satisfied there. The company treated us well. The supervisor was very nice, always making sure that everything was okay. They never scolded me for doing bad work and they never did anything bad to me. I was very comfortable working there. The owners of the company were very good to us. When I told them that I would be leaving work and dividing my time between Mexico and the U.S., they ordered catering and closed the plant for two hours to give me a bon voyage party. Yes, they were very good to us. They told me, "Whenever you want to return, your job is here for you." I was already more than fifty years old and I never returned. Avelia, however, continues to work there. Reina also worked there and also Rosa, though Rosa didn't stay long because she didn't like it so much. At every job, I always had Mexican or Latina friends. I would often run into them around town and we were friendly, but I socialized mainly with my little group of Mexican women friends: Avelia, Gudelia, Reina, Clara, Amalia, and Rosa. We all worked outside of the home.

Working Outside the Home:
More Income but Double Duty

Jesús never minded my working. When I would complain of being tired, Jesús would remind me, "You work because you want to, because you want to have more money." I answered, "Well, that's true." But no, there was never any problem about my working.

I didn't drive but I got to work at Starline by carpooling with my comadres *Mexicanas*. Actually, our husbands took turns driving us. One week Jesús took us–and we picked up Reina and Avelia and the three of us went to work together—then the next week Reina's husband José would take us, then the next week Miguel, Avelia's husband, would take us, and even Pedro, Rosa's husband, drove us to work sometimes. The men all took turns transporting us to and from work. Later, when the kids started driving, we got the kids to take turns driving us. "Oh, how we hated that trip," my kids say now! Well, it was far from our home, way out there on Burleigh. Jesús would take the bus or, in the summer, ride the bicycle to work so that the kids would have the car to take me to work.

I liked to earn my own money. If I wasn't earning my own money I couldn't get things that I wanted, because we couldn't afford them, but once I started working I also contributed to the household by buying all of our groceries. That was me. I took on that obligation. I told Jesús, "I'll buy the groceries and you pay everything else." That's how I had so much left over for myself! [*laughs*] My daughters tell me now that they always saw me with money in my pocket, and I tell them, "Yes, but only after I started working." Jesús didn't take notice. He just paid all the bills and bought the kids their clothes, but he didn't buy my clothes anymore. When I was working, I bought my own clothes and whatever else I wanted—that's why I loved to work! After I stopped working and retired, then I only had social security—but it was my social security. I had earned it.

The only bad thing about working was that I had more work, because my work outside the home was in addition to the household work. I had two jobs. I would get home from work and start cooking for the next day, while I heated up the food for that day's dinner. We all got home at the same time and I raised my kids to expect a home-cooked meal every day so that took time, which was why I was always cooking a day in advance. It was hard, yes, but, of course, when you're young you don't even feel all that work. Now, I couldn't do that.

Even my daughters now say, "Mom, how did you do that? You were always cooking!" I tell them, "Well, of course, I had to feed six." They have the option of getting take-out now. My daughters have many more conveniences in their lives today, for example, disposable diapers. Back then I had a bucket full of diapers to wash every day, and without a dryer at home, or even a hot water heater in that first place. In my hometown in Mexico, we had to boil the water over a wood fire. We always kept hot water for dishes and washing. But in Monterrey, Mexico, we had hot water in the house. The most difficult time was when I first arrived here, because the house we rented for about $40 a month didn't have hot water. I was used to keeping a big pan full of water on the stove, but it was a lot of work. Those diapers especially because they had to be soaked first, then washed in hot water with soap. After we bought a dryer, I thought the work was a snap. Forty dollars a month seems inexpensive but that was what Jesús made in a week.

Choosing Not to Drive to Limit Work

I did learn to drive back then when I was working and Jesús was alive, but when I went to take my driver's test I was really nervous and I didn't pass it, and then I didn't want to go back. Jesús would tell me, "Mona, you drive very well." I remember that one time I was so angry with Jesús for being drunk when he was supposed to drive us to work that I just took the car and went to pick up Avelia. "Let's go," I said. Avelia answered, "Ay, Mona, you're driving!" Yes, I was. I took the car. I knew how to drive, but I never got the license. Later, in Mexico after Jesús died, I called a school and they came to show me again how to drive. Well, the man took me out in the car and then he said, "What am I going to show you if you already know how to drive?" I had to get my license there, and I did, though I'm afraid to drive there because the traffic is like Chicago.

Here, I don't drive either. My girls say, "Don't underestimate yourself, Mom, you can still get the license and drive." Yet I tell them, "No, because if I do then you'll have me running here and there picking up the kids, or getting this or that thing." No. No. I'm glad I don't have the license. I have helped them quite a bit with the children, though. I have. When I came here, I didn't have any help. If only I had had a relative here when I came, but no, no one. I really missed that. I cried so much when I came here; I wanted to go back to Mexico right away.

Getting together with Avelia and Gudelia Talavera made a difference. We saw each other nearly every day because we lived in the same neighborhood. We would often go to Mitchell Park—that was our outing. We'd put the kids in a wagon, and take bologna sandwiches and Kool-Aid and head to the park! [*laughs*] There we were, the three of us pregnant and with a wagon full of children at Mitchell Park. None of us were working yet, then, so we could go. Later, we all started working around the same time, too. We were always close friends, and always together.

When I started working I was very comfortable working. I tell my daughters now that when I went to work I felt like I was getting a rest after being with all the children—it was a rest for me from the children. An eight-hour rest. It meant so much to me. Since Jesús was there taking care of them when I was gone, I had no worries about them. I really liked working.

I didn't encounter any discrimination at work but I did come across it when I went to the eye doctor once. He was speaking very rapidly and I asked him to slow down, and he said, "Oh how I struggle with these Latinos; I don't know why they come to see me." Then he continued on and said some other offensive things. It was horrible. My daughter was waiting for me outside the office and I called to her, and left that office in tears. "What happened, Mom?" she asked. I told her what he had said. My daughter said, "You should have left that office!" That was the only time that something like that made me cry.

Marriage Difficulties and Illness

There was a time when Jesús and I nearly divorced. Our oldest was sixteen years old then. Jesús was fighting a lot, just a lot of fighting, and he was drinking too much. On the weekends he wouldn't even come home. He wouldn't talk to anyone about it. He denied it. He had started to say things to me and one thing led to another and well, I just couldn't take it anymore. Jesús then left the house and lived elsewhere for about a month. I told the kids, "I'm going to leave him. I can't be with him anymore." We even went to court and started the divorce proceedings. It was a difficult time because the children were all still young, and there I was alone with them. I called my brother in Monterrey—he had some stores there—and he said to me, "Look, if you need money, I'll send you money." He sent me the money to go see an attorney, and told me to get the divorce and come back to Mexico, but in the end we dropped the divorce. Jesús became ill and he wound up in the hospital, and so I brought him home again. That put an end to the divorce. We continued together—fighting, but together until he died.

His illness brought us back together because, well, I had compassion for him, and he was my husband. He got sick and then confined to the hospital before they brought him back home to me again. He continued on with his fighting and drinking, but now it was less, now he couldn't do as much. As my kids were getting older they often said to me, "Well, leave him Mom, leave him. Why do you put up with him?" because he drank so very much. In those years I often cried. Yes. Turns out it was the death of him, because he developed a liver illness, cirrhosis, and died.

I guess I didn't just cry to myself about it. I went out to try and get some help because I thought, well, I thought I just couldn't do that to the kids: their father drunk, and me crying all the time and making myself sick. I decided that I had to be strong. First, I went to the priest. Next I went to a counselor. They all said the same thing: it's a lost cause. My doctor told me, "Either you put up with him or you leave him—those are the only two solutions here." It affected my health, too—not drastically, but it did though I was strong. We lived like that until the illness changed him.

Then it was too late. Even after he was diagnosed, he kept on drinking—less—but still drinking. We lived together another eight or ten years with his sickness. I dropped the divorce because it didn't seem to matter anymore. Then he wanted to go to Mexico and okay, we pack up and head to Mexico, with him already very sick. He died in McAllen, Texas. They operated on him but there just wasn't anything they could do anymore.

Social Norms about Divorce

During that time I felt so alone. If my parents had been here, or brothers, or someone who could have supported me through that then maybe I would have acted differently. But I thought to myself, "How am I going to raise these kids here on my own?" The kids were already adolescents, and despite everything, they still respected Jesús. I worried about what would happen to the kids if he wasn't there, if they would get involved in bad things. I didn't think I should raise them here by myself; I felt that I needed support to do that. What would I do without him? I know it's bad to think that way but that's how I felt. If I had had a profession where I earned enough to support my children then it would have been a different story. I wouldn't have second-guessed myself. That matters. But I didn't earn enough to support my family.

My family supported me from afar. They learned how Jesús treated me and they didn't think I deserved that. If they had been here, I don't think they would have said, "You have to stay with him because you're married." No. No. No. My mom used to tell me, way before Jesús treated me that way, "My daughter, if your husband treats you badly there is no reason why you have to endure it. No. Remember, you weren't born with him. If you left us, who are your parents, why should you feel compelled to stay with a man who treats you badly?" She was very much in agreement with women taking care of themselves and the availability of divorce. She was the first to speak out for that. My family was not critical of divorce, no, and even less so today. I have four children who have been divorced! No, my mom was not one to insist on staying in marriage. Instead, she said, "Good for you, daughter, that you don't put up with that."

There were people, however, who would criticize you for divorce. Even parents who would say to their children, "That's what marriage is; you have to endure it." That's wrongheaded, because if you aren't going to live happily then why are you here? This is changing in Mexico, too. It isn't like it was back when my daughters were kids; there are a lot more divorced people in Mexico. You don't hear that "divorce is bad" so much anymore. If you can't stand it or you're not happy or you're treated badly in your marriage, why stay?

Transnational Lives, Even in Retirement

When the kids were small, we went to Mexico every year in the summer. Jesús took us and we stayed for about fifteen days or two weeks. That's why my kids know so much about Mexico. Jesús and I always took our vacations at the same time and we all drove down there together—six kids and all! It wasn't easy traveling in the car with six kids, but if we were going to Mexico then I hardly noticed. The first year here we didn't go, but the second year and every year after that we went to Mexico in the summer. We would go despite the many mechanical problems we had with our old car. Once we had an old station wagon, so that we could all fit, and it had a big hole in the floor. Jesús had to scold the kids not to throw paper out of that hole while we were traveling! My family in Mexico was more or less living well and they all had their new Volkswagens. Well, here we arrive in our old, broken-down station wagon. My brother grabs the front fender, and he says, "What a sight! Look at the messed up shape of this car!" [*laughs*] They would say to me, "Why do you come visit every year, Mona, when by the looks of it you can't afford it?" [*laughs*] But we went, and we always went to stay at my mother's house. My brothers were all crazy about my kids—because they were the first nieces and nephews in the family—and they'd take them out on trips and adventures. My kids loved to go to Monterrey. They still do. Now, I take my grandchildren every summer for vacation in Mexico and they spend the summer there.

In Mexico, my daughters often overheard one of my sisters saying that she didn't get together with a former friend anymore because the friend had divorced. My girls couldn't understand that and they asked about it a lot, what that meant. I just said that that's how they are there—but not anymore. There it is the same as here, exactly the same as here. The only difference is that there is still a fiction that in Mexico it's different. But no, there's divorce and everything else. The one thing, the one custom that still remains there is that children still generally live at home until they are married—unless they go off to university or go to study in another country. I see this among my neighbors in Mexico, where my son lives. That's why my daughter likes me to take her daughter to Mexico: "So that," my daughter says, "she'll take on the Mexican custom of living at home until she marries." I think the ship may have sailed on that one already! My granddaughter is already thinking about where she'll go away to university.

Those trips were memorable. We took our sandwiches and bread in the car, and off we went. I have to give Jesús credit for that, for taking us every year. Later, when the kids were older, they'd drive us and Jesús would stay, saying "I'm not going. I'm too tired. You all go." We all went and Jesús stayed here. We never missed a summer. Never. That trip gave me life! All year I looked forward to my vacation so that I could go to Mexico. I always returned from there very happy.

Nowadays I still keep in touch with my Mexican comadres. Of course, some have passed on: Reina died, Clara died, and Carmen died. I tell my daughters, "Now, my comadres are beginning to leave me behind, alone." Yet just the other day I got a message from Avelia that she's here in town—she's sometimes here and sometimes in San Antonio. Rosa doesn't live here anymore; she went to Texas, too, but she visits every year. Gudelia is the one I see least often lately. So we don't all get together and visit like we used to earlier in our lives, but we still know how to keep in touch and talk. Oh yes, we still do that.

7. It's the Hispanic Community That Keeps Us in Business

OLIVIA VILLARREAL

Interviewed on December 1, 2009

Homemaker, Bookkeeper, Business Manager, Store Owner

Immigrating to Milwaukee as a Child

I was born in Mexico in 1949, in the town of Agualeguas, in the state of Nuevo Leon, a place that is southwest of Monterrey. I am the third oldest of nine children. There were six of us when we migrated to Wisconsin in 1957 to join my father, Sijifredo Gomez. He arranged our papers, making it possible for us to immigrate here legally—all six of us children and my mother, Demetria Gomez. I don't know how he did it, but I admire him greatly for it. It was quite an accomplishment, because he had to visit various offices and he spoke very little English—he had only finished the sixth grade—and there was no help in the 1950s when he was doing this, so I admire his accomplishment. He had been here since the 1940s, and had traveled back-and-forth between Mexico and Milwaukee since then, because this was the industrial belt of the Midwest, so he went back-and-forth. I owe what I have in brains, determination, and intelligence to him!

During that back-and-forth, my parents were separated for times, but that's how he supported us, from industrial work in Wisconsin. After he brought us all here, he worked for Grede Foundries in Waukesha for almost thirty years, before it closed down. Then he worked for us here at Supermercado El Rey for a time because he was older by then, and in all that time all he had known was those foundries. There weren't many openings for a sixty-year-old man.

My mom was primarily a homemaker. In the summer times we would all work in the farm fields in Palmyra, at Kincaid Farms. We would all go out there, and the oldest would stay home and take care of the younger kids. So in the summer times, my mother worked in the fields; otherwise she was a stay-at-home mom.

Education in a One-Room Schoolhouse in Waukesha

I went to school in Mexico for kindergarten and first grade. I was only seven years old when we moved to the Waukesha area, to Mukwonago actually, which at that time was called Heaven City. We went to a one-room schoolhouse for the first semester—myself, my younger brother, and my two older sisters. Our school was first through sixth grade in six rows of desks. The four of us went to school in that one room, which was good for us because we were all in the same classroom. We were just in different rows. We were all together; we weren't separated. There was no coddling in that school; you went right in and you learned. There were no Hispanics, and there was no bilingual program in existence. I mean, I can imagine this poor teacher wondering, "What am I going to do with these kids? Where do I start?"

The good thing is that though we didn't know English we had already learned math and science. Mathematics was the universal language, the bridge, and we knew math. We knew how to do that. In Mexico in those days—I don't know how they do it now, but back then we were so much more advanced than here, because in Mexico they had to get as much into those kids as they could before they left school to go out and work. In Mexico at the time children left school earlier than here so they were only in school for a limited number of years. For myself, I had already been through half of first grade in Mexico, which would have been third-grade math here, for example. In that one-room schoolhouse in Mukwonago they kept us busy with workbooks and such, which we could do with no problem. They kept us busy with stuff like that while we learned English by playing with the other children and learning vocabulary—"this is a desk, this is a chair," that kind of thing.

In our Mukwonago school, there were about thirty-five or forty kids in that one-room schoolhouse. I think there were two teachers. That was the last year of the one-room schoolhouse; they did away with it after that year. In 1958, my dad moved us into Waukesha and we went to Saint Joseph school there, which was almost harsher than the one-room schoolhouse because it was very demanding—very straightforward, again—no coddling, very "get right to it." In those days, of course, it was all taught by nuns. We were made to learn. By our second year in school we were fluent in English. We were thrown into the mix and we just had to learn. We were the only Spanish-speaking kids at Saint Joseph. It was not until our second year at Saint Joseph that we met other Hispanic children, who had been born here. They could speak Spanish but they weren't really allowed to speak Spanish to us; they really needed to speak English to us.

Now we were each in our separate classrooms. At first, the school considered that maybe they should put us all in one grade because we didn't speak very good English, but then they nixed that idea and instead put us into our respective classrooms, the grades where we belonged. That was good of the nuns to do that, because they forced us to work at our level. It was all about "get to work," and "be done." Our family still belongs to that parish.

When my father first got to Waukesha that's the parish where he worshipped and that's the school that he knew. He really didn't know the school system at all, so it wasn't so much that he wanted us to have a Catholic education as that was the school he knew. After a few years we moved to the neighborhood of White Rock Elementary School, a Waukesha Public School. In fact, the school was right in front of our new home. He moved us there for the convenience of walking to school instead of the longer walk we had to the parochial school.

Later, White Rock Elementary became the first bilingual school in Waukesha. It's kind of like the "South Side" of Waukesha,[1] where all the Hispanics tend to live, but in the 1950s we were kind of the only Hispanics in that neighborhood, and in that school. Well, I think there were maybe two other families that were Hispanic, but I think their children were born in Texas, and they were bilingual because they were Texan not Mexican. Most of the other families in Waukesha were from Texas. My dad worked at Grede Foundry there in Waukesha while my mom kept house and raised the kids. They had three more children, born here; after we moved to the Waukesha area we became a family of nine.

A Big Working Family That Pooled All Income

We first came to the U.S. by car. In those days the back seat was huge and my dad packed us in. Those cars were just huge—with no seat belts. Here in Waukesha we used that car on Sundays for family outings, too. My father always believed that Sunday was the family day, and he'd pack us all into that car and take us to the Zoo, or to Holy Hill, or a picnic in the park. Sundays were family days. Actually—and this is funny—it wasn't just family day because we often took along neighbors. I have the pictures of those outings with neighbors along. Our house in front of White Rock Elementary was next to two apartment houses, where some families from Texas and Puerto Rico lived. We'd always have those kids with us, too! It was never just our family. We have so many pictures with our neighbors on outings. There were nine of us kids, six born in Mexico and three born here, so lots of friends, and we always had neighbors on outings with us. There were always packs of us kids together—it was not just a family, it was always groups of kids. We also played with neighbors at Frame Park, just down the street from where we lived.

We never went back to the town in Mexico where I came from because, well, there was no money for those kinds of trips. There was always an abundance associated with our Wisconsin outings, but traveling to Mexico? No, there was no money for that. We could just barely make it. My father always had two or three jobs. He would work at Grede, and then he would have a Saturday job, too, working during the day, and then in the evening he'd have something else to do. He would always have two or three jobs. Always. As soon as we all hit fourteen or fifteen years of age then we would all work also, and we gave all our money— other than ten or fifteen bucks we kept for ourselves, that's all we kept—to the family to support us. It was never that we went to work and the check was all ours—never, never. We never looked at it that way. We didn't know any different. For us, that's how it was supposed to be. It was just natural that you went to work and you worked to contribute to covering the household expenses. Other than those few years that we rented, my father always owned a home, and he never took welfare. He never took help from anybody. As many of us as there was and he never took help from anybody. He was a very proud man.

I was fifteen when I started working, doing odds and ends at a restaurant. You didn't get normal jobs until you were sixteen. I also worked at a grocery store [*laughs*], and now I am back at a grocery store! My sisters worked at stores, too. My older sister worked at a hospital, and then at a bank. When I married I worked at a mortgage company, and then at a bank, too. We all graduated from restaurants to stores to office jobs.

Figure 11. Olivia Villarreal on her wedding day, getting kissed by her mother. Photo used with permission of Olivia Villarreal.

No Opportunity for College

There was no money for college then. At Waukesha High School my guidance counselor was always trying to prime me for college: he always had me in his office working for him and his secretary. He had me all ready, but the scholarships were $500 in the 1960s. What could you do with $500? My dad said, "Sweetie, what are you going to do? $500 is going to buy you your books, then there's no money." So there was no college. There weren't student loans or grants, nothing like that in the early 1960s. When I told my counselor that I couldn't accept the scholarship, he was so disappointed and he became very mad. He was just downright mad and nasty. He said, "Fine, go get married, have twenty kids, live like your parents." I said to him, "Well, thank you anyway." I never went back to his office again. He never spoke to me again. It was the end of the school year anyway.

When he said that to me, well, I felt like I had let him down. I felt like I had let myself down. I was very angry at my father, because I didn't know any better. I wanted to go to school. I wanted to go to college. I had straight As all through grade school and high school. I was in the Honors Society. It didn't mean anything to anybody except myself. Nobody was there over my head saying, "You had better bring home As," or "You had better do well in school." It was just something in me that I wanted to do. It was just a matter of pride for myself, that I could do it. It was very hard for me, because in the Waukesha Public Schools there were levels: you're either an "A" group, a "B" group, or a "C" group. You were assigned a group depending on your grades, and those are your classmates. That's the part of high school I didn't like. I was the only Hispanic in my "A" group, which was a group made up of people with money. I was the only Hispanic in that group and all my friends were in the "C" group. In my "A" lunch group I had very few friends, because this was a group where they all lived on the side of town where there was money to be had. It was a very uncomfortable situation. My friends who were Hispanic were not in the same class and sometimes it was no fault of their own. I hated high school, I really did.

I will never go back for a high school reunion there because I was made to feel like I was inferior, not because I couldn't do the work or keep up with them academically, but because I was Hispanic, I didn't have the money that they had, and I couldn't dress like they could dress. I had my nice clothes, but I didn't have a new outfit every week. We had a set amount of money for clothes at the beginning of our school year and that was it. I couldn't go to dances or other high school events, because I was working or helping with my siblings. School dances were open to everybody, but students kind of stuck to their little groups in private parties, too. You get stuck into a group depending on your grades, and those are your classmates. That's the part of high school I didn't like, because it was each and every class.

I pushed myself in high school. I guess I just thought, "Why not, if I could?" If I read something and I didn't get it, why not read it again? Why settle? I didn't find a reason to settle. If I got a "B" I would think, "Well, why did I do that?" I would go back and reanalyze things. I do those kind of things, and I'm not the only one in my family who does. Other people in my family say, "Okay, something went wrong, let's analyze this." I guess that's how we are. I guess it's just part of me. I wasn't a bookworm or anything like that, it's just that I'm sort of a perfectionist: Why isn't this done the correct way? If you do things correctly, and do the best that you can, and if it doesn't work out, well okay, but if you do the best that you can, you're probably going to get it right. I guess I've always done it that way, without relying on anybody looking over my shoulder to push me because when that external help stops pushing you, you're going to screw up! [*laughs*] I'm not like that.

Hispanic Student Graduation Rates—Then and Now

I was very disappointed in Waukesha High School because when I graduated there were only five of us Hispanics in the graduating class of 1968, and twenty years later when my daughter graduated from there it was basically the same. In her graduating class in Waukesha there were only another five Hispanic kids. A lot of kids were kind of falling off the edges, and it didn't look like Waukesha Public Schools were doing such a great job of retaining Hispanic children in the school system. By the time of my daughter's graduation, 25 percent of Waukesha was Hispanic. There should have been at least a hundred young people graduating with her, because she had a class of almost five hundred graduating. There should have been a hundred Hispanics graduating with her, not five or six. Where are they? I was so disappointed. They were not doing a good job of retaining children in high school, or graduating them.

My children did not take bilingual education; because of our business, I was never worried that my children wouldn't continue speaking Spanish. I know that my brother and sisters do have that problem with their children, but since our business serves a Hispanic population and my parents only speak Spanish I knew that my children would still have that link. Spanish was built into our family life and business. I wouldn't have been so confident any other way! Both of my daughters married Anglo men, and their husbands speak Spanish. They learned it here in the stores.

Juggling School, Work, and a New Business in the 1970s

I have four children. I started with a boy and I ended with a boy; the two girls are in the middle. I did marry young, at nineteen, and I stayed at home for about a year. Then I went to work for Associated Mortgage. Then I became ill, and I stayed at home again for a time before I went out again and got a job working for what is now our banker, Associated Commerce. Back then it was Bank of Commerce, before they were bought out by Associated Bank, becoming Associated Commerce. I started in bookkeeping and then they transferred me to auditing, and then they said, "We think you need to go to school." I said, "Sure, I can go to school." I started taking accounting courses at MATC to get my Associate Degree but then lo and behold, we started the grocery store business in 1978. As a young woman, I was going to school, I was working at Associated, and we were starting up our grocery store business at the same time!

It all worked out surprisingly well, because you don't understand accounting until you work it, so it helped us to set up everything. I mean when I look at some of our original documents now, documents and forms that I set up, I think, "I did this! This is pretty cool!" I don't know if I'm as good anymore, but this February, 2009, it will be thirty-two years since we started our grocery store business: Supermercado El Rey. Working in the real world while going to school for a real-world skill, and while actually starting up the business, it just all clicked at the same time. It was just kismet. It really was. It all came together.[2]

We had some challenges but mainly these involved our child care because we had no daycare. I remember that we began our business two years before Head Start began. Then when it started we were able to get our three-year-old into Head Start, and we had at least three hours that we could come here and work on the business. We also had help from my mother-in-law, and a babysitter who came to help us out. My poor daughter had so many different caretakers!

Building a Family Business

As each of my children finished school, they all came back to the business. Ernesto Junior is the plant manager and his wife, Yolanda, does the bookkeeping for that plant. Since we have four stores now, Anna and her husband Chad manage El Rey Food Mart at Thirteenth and Burnham Street. Elizabeth's husband, Nelson, who graduated with her from Marquette University, is a manager of the store at Cesar E. Chavez, along with our youngest son, Marcos.

We also have a real estate holding company that owns all the properties where our businesses are located. Elizabeth does all the books for the real estate holding company.[3]

The El Rey Plaza store on Thirty-Fifth and Burnham is run by my sister Criselda and her husband, Heriberto Villarreal, who is also my husband's brother, and their family. There are two brothers and two sisters who started this business together. So everybody's in the business!

All of my children were exposed to the business from a young age. If I had it to do again, I would shoot them out to other directions, but they themselves chose to come back here. When our tortilla plant manager left fifteen or sixteen years ago—just took off, my oldest son said, "Well, let me stand in, let me just help you there." He had just graduated from Carroll College, and he was just helping out here. He asked his dad for a chance, and he stayed there! Ernesto Jr. has made the plant grow, and he's changed out the machinery so many times. He just has a natural ability with it. At the plant we make chips, tostadas, and tamales, but the tortillas are the main product. We make tortillas for all of Wisconsin and all restaurants in Wisconsin. We sell wholesale to all stores in Wisconsin and some northern Illinois stores; we do that, too.

Ours is a state-approved plant, and we have a seal that means the state inspector is present five days a week, including Saturday and Sunday because then they can charge you time and half. [*laughs*] We pay the State Inspector because that's not free. Two days a week he takes off in the middle of the week, and comes in on Saturday and Sunday to make sure that no funny businesses goes on during the weekends. Our *tortilleria* [tortilla factory] is a Wisconsin state-approved plant.

Shared Histories and Courtship

Ernesto, my husband, and I met through our families. Our parents knew each other from Mexico. His dad came here in the mid-1960s and then he brought his family, whereas my dad brought us all here in the 1950s. His dad brought his family a little later in life. At family gatherings they always need to talk about the old country. [*laughs*] Ernesto and I were born in the same town, we're actually from the same town in Mexico, and we left it at the same time except that we moved here to the United States and Ernesto's dad moved them to another town in Mexico first, then later moved them here to Milwaukee in the 1960s. Our parents knew each other as young adults, in their teens and their twenties. When they knew that we were all up here, then they reconnected. Ernesto and I were teens when we first met; I was fifteen.

We dated for four years before we married, all through high school. I was going to Waukesha High School and Ernesto went to Boys Tech here in Milwaukee. He went to Vieau School through the eighth grade, and then he went to Boys

Tech for high school, and then he worked second shift at a job in Cedarburg. He had a hard life. His dad worked at a tannery here in the Menomonee River Valley in town and he became ill, so while Ernesto was in high school he started working a second shift job. When his dad became ill, he became disabled, but there was no disability in those days. Ernesto became the sole support of his family.

I saw him on Saturday and Sunday only, and usually just Sunday, because Saturday I would work. It was just the weekends we would see each other. During the week we just communicated by phone. He'd call me whenever he could on his ten minute break from work in the evenings. Eventually, I knew that I was going to marry him, and one year after I graduated from high school, we married. Our families were okay with it because to them it was the normal progression of life for a young woman. In those days, that is what was supposed to happen: you went to school then you got married.

The Early Years of Grocery Store Business

By that time, Ernesto's family had established a little grocery store on Third Street to supplement their income. It was a little mom-and-pop grocery store there on Third Street. His mom ran it and his dad, who couldn't leave the house, could help. It didn't require any hard physical work—not like the tannery, which was very hard for his dad. He started the grocery store business, actually. That's where the idea came from. Ernesto's dad was just a wonderfully gentle man. The grocery store was in the front of the building and their living quarters were in the back so they were always there. Somebody might be knocking at an off hour saying, "I ran out of milk," well there he goes, opening the door for them, getting them their milk, so it was just like being in Mexico. They enjoyed it, and he enjoyed it, because then he felt useful, that he was doing something. He never lost his pride in work and it was very good for him.

When we first married we had no plan of starting a business—no, not at all. We just had our heads down to the work. Ernesto continued working at Mercury Marine, and then when Mercury Marine was going to move—I think to Fond du Lac—he switched to Milwaukee Valve, which was on Lincoln. Then his brother opened a little corner grocery store right across from where we are today on Sixteenth Street, but it was going under and he was going to shut it down—just bad management and bad bookkeeping—when he and Ernesto decided to work it together, and we decided to help them out. They decided to work at the store part time; they weren't going to quit their jobs. Then I started doing the book work for them, and I kind of held the reins on the checkbook, like: "Okay, we only have so much money, guys, so we can only do this much." That's how we started. It was just kind of a mom-and-pop store run by the four of us: two moms and two pops. We all kept our day jobs, and little by little, one by one, we left those jobs as our grocery business grew. We then started the *tortilleria*, first in that little space across the street side by side with our first grocery, and then later we moved it into its own space on the other side of the street. Even later, we created a new grocery store space on the other side of the street, too.

One by one, we left our regular jobs to dedicate ourselves to the store and the growing business, but really there was no grand plan. We just kept working and then all of a sudden we looked behind us and thought, "Wow, what happened here!?" We were just very determined. I think it was a combination of hard work and being at the right place at the right time, because there were other little stores at the same time—we weren't the only ones—but we were just very determined. I also think that the sense of family that we brought to the business, that it wasn't just one of us but four of us involved, made a difference. Then there was our having left our other jobs—I mean we had to make it work, because how were we supposed to eat? We had to make it work, there was no going back anymore.

Building a Business

I think I left my other job when we were two years into our grocery store business project. We had already moved across the street on Sixteenth, which was only possible because the banker who gave us the loan to move into the building across the street did so because my sister and I worked at the bank, at Associated Bank. That was the only reason they gave us the loan. They took a chance on us. Even if the building was worth the loan, banks still weren't going to give us the loan, but they gave us the loan because we had been employees there for a while. I had been there for six years and my sister had been there for ten years. They knew our character, our reliability. Lending was different then. As I said, even if the building we proposed to buy was worth the loan, banks still would not have taken a chance on us. We still had an uphill battle because we didn't have any business knowledge, and we didn't have anything to show. All we had was this dream that this was going to work, that we were going to make it work. So we did.

We have always had to work double, triple, and quadruple times to prove ourselves in this business. It wasn't just handed to us. We've had to prove ourselves, again and again, to bankers, and to the city, and to others. We have to deal with the city in everything because we're subject to inspections and regulations. For example, this building, I mean, this is jumping way ahead in time, but this building is made entirely of brick outside, while across the corner from us, the brand new shopping center is made of block. They got away with it; we couldn't. We asked, "Can we make the part of the building that's not visible to the public with block?" They said, "No. We want it all in brick." They dictated what needed to be done. Nothing has ever been easy for us, nothing. We have had to jump through many hoops.

Another example of this is the one time that we exported tortillas to Germany. A business there was interested in our product; they were the first ones to bring Mexican food products into Germany. In fact, they built a whole project around us, and they had billboards all over Germany announcing, "Nachos are coming, Nachos are coming." For four years, we exported flour and corn tortillas, nachos, and nacho cheese to them. At the Department of Commerce, the only person who could help me was here in downtown Milwaukee, and that person could stamp my papers that the product was really made here in Milwaukee. Other than that, I had to come up with all the paperwork. I had to figure out how to complete all the paperwork, how to get the containers here and there, where to get frozen containers, because the product had to be frozen in order to get it across the ocean on a ship. I had to do it all myself. I don't know how long it took. I learned about international shipping and all. Plus I had to deal with the food regulations of the European Union.

In fact, we stopped exporting because a new law went into effect when the Euro changed that was to the advantage of a competitor. That's when we stopped. One of our competitors that distributes tortillas nationwide built a *tortilleria* over there with a partner in Germany, and the new law said if the product can be found in the country then you can't import it anymore. Our competitor partnered with somebody in Germany. We started that business for them! It was a four-year run and I learned a lot.

Pricing our product for export was outrageous because of the shipping. Then, additionally, only certain products can be imported over there. We had to make modifications to our product to meet their standards, too. For instance, our cheese supplier uses an additive for color because cheese is naturally white, not yellow. Well, we had to get them to stop that and use nettle seed instead to make it yellow—and they could only use a certain percentage of nettle seed, too—otherwise it's illegal to import it into Germany, because they only allow certain products as additives to food. There I was, working on formulas when I'm not a chemist. I had to. Nowadays, I know much more about anything that has to do with government regulations, city regulations, state regulations, because we've always had to do it double, triple, quadruple times.

My children know this. My children know that everything has to be done the correct way, that way you never have to look behind you, and you never have to worry that this will be uncovered because in the first place, there's too many of us. If you lie about something how are you going to cover it up? It's impossible. If you do everything correctly, or do as much as you can then that works. If the inspector says that's black and you see it white, well make it black because that's what he's telling you, that's how it's got to be. Every time they come, they change their mind about something. One inspector tells us, "Okay, it's grandfathered in on this rule, we'll skip it." The next guy comes and says, "Oh, no, I want that fixed." Okay let's go get the other one and have them talk to each other. If it was only a matter of bringing in product and selling it to the customer, it would be wonderful, but there's all this other stuff that goes on that people don't realize.

We try. I don't know that we are that good at it, but we've been able to build and run the business. I suspect that there are other people who are *much* better at it, but we've been able to do it. I'm hoping that my children don't get discouraged. Ernesto and I are a little tougher, because we've lived through a lot, we've seen worse situations and we've been able to supersede them so we're just hoping that our children, who have seen some of the difficulties involved already, aren't discouraged by this whole thing. We may have been boiling inside, but we just went on, because the authority always has the upper hand. We learned to roll with the punches. We didn't have a choice. We had to succeed.[4]

Raising Children While Building a Business

For me the most difficult part of the business wasn't the business, it was leaving my children so much. This is an emotional topic for me. My children nearly raised themselves, and they did a damn good job of it! Some of my brothers and sisters criticize me for giving my children so much, but I really think this business is theirs, because they earned it in all the time that I was away from them. For so long, for five or six years we didn't even take a day off, and we had no vacations because we had to be here at all times, whole shifts, and so my kids had to do a lot of things for themselves. I often forgot to pick the kids up from Brownies—I can't even tell you how many times. It was a problem until we built a house right next to the grade school for the two little ones, and I could open the door and say, "Bye now, and you know where the door is to get back." But it gets old for them, too. When they were in high school, I missed so much of them growing up. I don't remember when they learned how to read, for instance. I missed a lot and I'm so glad that they have the opportunity now to stay home a lot with their children. The girls can spend a lot of time with their children, they can go to the school, and spend days helping out at school with their kids. I never had that opportunity. I had to be at work. But I'm glad they have that opportunity. For me, that's the hardest part of having been in this business for thirty-two years: that my children raised themselves. Yet, like

Figure 12. Olivia and Ernesto Villarreal. Photo used with permission of Olivia Villarreal.

I said, I am so fortunate that they did such a wonderful job, because every one of them, all four of them did a wonderful job. I couldn't be prouder of them. They are all very accomplished.

When we finally took our first family vacation, Ernesto and I and all the kids went to Disney World! Doesn't everybody? Well, we got there and they just didn't know what to do. They weren't used to being out in the sun, and neither was I, and we got sun burnt. We just weren't used to being outside for so long. It was wonderful. Well then we made a habit of going on vacation, and then I did what my parents had always done, which was to take along the kids' friends. All of our vacations after that included friends or cousins. It wasn't just my four kids, it was six kids or more on our vacations. They all have fun memories of those trips, and my nieces and nephews who spent time with us on vacation also have fun memories of those trips, so that's kind of nice. That's a nice payback.

Lessons Learned about Work from Family

When I started dating Ernesto, my sister Cris was already married to his brother Beto. She's four years older than I am. She is the oldest, and they were a little more mature. When you're the oldest girl in a Hispanic family, you're almost like the mom—really you're the second mom. In addition to being her sister, I am her business partner. Yes. We're very close. We relate to each other very well. We're good with each other. Because of our shared experience in business, there are many things that we can only talk about with each other. When we compare war stories, we let it all out and then we can say, "Okay, we feel better now." [*laughs*] We both know that what's between us doesn't go any further, because nobody is going to feel what we feel. I'm glad that I have her. I'm certain that she is also glad that she has me.

She also had the same dreams as I did. She wished she could have gone on to school, too, but she never had the opportunity. Instead, she was the head bookkeeper at Associated Bank for many years, almost ten or fifteen years before she left. She was the last one of us to leave her regular day job for the family grocery store business. Yes, she was the last one to leave the day job for good. I guess you could say she was our collateral on the loan: "Okay, if you guys don't pay we keep Cris here forever." [*laughs*]

When we were growing up we all worked, but we didn't work in the same places, none of us worked together. We were all pretty independent. We all found our own jobs, and we were all in different schools most of the time because we're two years apart. The four older ones were in the same school, and then the next two were in the same school, and then the younger ones, the ones that were born here, well, we had no inkling of what the heck they did. They were all in their own world. It was just a zoo in that house all the time. A friend of ours, an attorney friend, once asked us, "How did you guys eat during the holidays?" We answered, "Oh, just up and down the stairs there; we just each took a stair!" [*laughs*]

From my dad I learned that nothing is free. If you want something, you have to work for it. He never said it. He never lectured us. He just did it. I learned from observing him and how hard he worked. It wasn't until we were older that we got it. When you're young you're just thinking to yourself, "Where is he?" But the older we got the more we thought, "How the heck did he do it?" When we started having our own families, then we began to wonder how he did it, because we could hardly do it and we only had two children at that time! How did he do it? Then we figured: okay, he had his Grede Foundry job, which was very hard for him, and then he found a job at night, and then a farm job during the weekends. I remember in the winter times, it was just miserable. He used to work at a mink farm, you know, outside in the Wisconsin winter. That would have been hard for him. When that job finished up, well then he'd find something else. I remember him rubbing liniment in his legs and on his arms when he came home, but he never said, "Oh my God, I'm tired." He just rubbed in his liniment and had his supper. We would ask, "Where's Dad?" And the answer was, "Oh, he's at the mink farm," or "Oh, he's over at the other job." I learned from him that hard work is all. He was very proud.

From my mom I learned the importance of patience. Patience. She showed tremendous patience in having all of us, and in just being by my dad's side all the time. She had patience beyond what I would call reasonable, because I don't think I could be that patient. Sometimes, I'd criticize her and say, "Speak, woman!" [*laughs*] because I never shut up, but her response was, "It's okay. It'll get better" and she'd walk away. She would never get upset. If my dad spent money on something silly for us, or whatever, she'd just say, "Oh my goodness. Okay, never mind," and she'd go on to the next project or the next thing. If I said, "But Mom he bought something for the car that's useless," she'd just shrug it off. She just had such patience. I guess now that I think about it, you would have to have a lot of patience in her shoes because, first of all, my dad was always working, and second of all, she had to put up with all nine of us. She had to have a lot of patience. I think that maybe one or two of us got that from her, but it wasn't me.

My oldest sister, well, she's just like me. There's six girls in the family and three of us, my sister and I included, are just like my dad. We are his spitting image: our mouth is always running off, we're always up to something, and we're always working. We got flack for that all the time, from our other brothers and sisters: "Shut up!" [*laughs*] I think, though, that those qualities have helped me in business. I really do. Well, sometimes they'll get me in trouble, I know that's true, but they also help, especially that perseverance part of it, the having to go on and come up with something because there is no choice. My dad knew, too, that he had no choice. He brought us into this world and he had to continue with us. He had to educate us the best that he could, and feed us, and put a roof over our head, and there was no going back. The perseverance and the hard work was there because there was no going back.

As an adult, I was in a lot of the Church groups at Saint Joe's. I was very active in my parish; knew everything going on in the parish. In fact, one of my license plates used to say "Committee," because I was a committee of one [*laughs*], because no one else would join, so I said, "Fine, I will do it." I was the vice president of the Parish Council, then the president for two terms, and secretary for two terms. I was on every committee available, it seemed, for about ten years, but then I just had to step back and let others take over. I was mainly involved in the church because of my children's activities and family. My kids were growing up in that area, and I wanted to show them that they have to be a part of a community, and that was my main focus until I got too involved and I decided to step back. My kids were in their high school years then, and I wanted to be there. I had already missed their little years.

Women in the Retail Grocery Business

Our business, Supermercado El Rey, will stay here in Milwaukee. The people are loyal here, and the community is here. As hard as it is to work with the city here, we've noticed that it's even harder in other cities. This is where the people are and the need is. There aren't enough people to maintain a grocery store this size anywhere else—we've done the studies. We have looked at the county census data, and county traffic data, and this is where our people are. It's nice that we have Anglos coming to shop here, but it's the Hispanic community that keeps us in business. That's a fact of life.

In terms of developing women as leaders in this industry: I would if I could find more women willing to work in this area. I don't find that. The three or four women who are working here at Supermercado El Rey have been with me since high school. They went through college, and they stayed here. Most others will finish high school and take other jobs. They think that this is a man's world. It is not. I feel that a woman can do a much better job than a man can, but I have not been able to retain any women in leadership positions. I can't just pull or pluck somebody off the street and put her in a command post. In order to command some kind of respect, she needs to go through the ranks so she understands all the aspects of the business. I have not been able to find that. The three young ladies that are with me have been here since high school, and they know everything about this business. I depend on them so much because they are my eyes, ears, and hands downstairs [on the store floor]. They have been through everything, they know everything. I'm fortunate that once they were done with college they stayed, that somebody else did not sway them to leave here, because they were asked, "Why would you stay at Supermercado El Rey? You can find a much better job somewhere else." Even when the pay scale was the same, they were trying to pull them out of here, to go somewhere else, and at least I was able to keep these young women. I would like more people on the floor with their capabilities. I'm holding onto them up here in the business office, but I would like to see women with their capabilities out on the floor—not just in this one but in all four of our stores. I would like to have women like that working here, but so far they have not and that's disappointing. Industry gatherings and marketing associations are maybe twenty percent women, the rest are just men. I really don't see why that's the case when we're the ones who do the shopping and the cooking most of the time. Why? I don't get it. I don't get that part. The men think they're the marketers.

Overall, being part of owning the largest Hispanic markets in Wisconsin has been very hard work for me and my family. We have enjoyed, tremendously, the process of building this business to where we are today, and I am very proud of my part as a Hispanic woman in its founding and growth. We Hispanic women are a determined bunch.

8. You Have to Believe It and You Have to Do It

DAISY CUBÍAS

Interviewed on June 25, 2010

Retail Clerk, Humanitarian Aid Activist, Translator,
Provider Service Specialist, Immigrant Services Specialist,
Education Administration, Parent Counselor,
Aide to Mayor, Poet, and Writer

From El Salvador to New York in the 1960s

In 1965, I came from El Salvador, Central America, to the United States, to New York City. I came as a student to learn English, go back to my country, and continue working with the statistical census, because that's where I used to work. As I was learning the U.S. system, I met some people at the university, at the library, and one guy in particular—Benjamin from Switzerland—asked me, "Are you from El Salvador?" I said, "Yeah." He said, "You must know about *La Matanza*." I said, "What are you talking about?" He said, "*La Matanza*, when they killed all those people in El Salvador, in 1932."[1] I said, "You're crazy. I never heard about it." Then he took me by the hand, took me to the library and we started reading about it and I was just . . . in shock. Before that I only knew my country as a nice place, with ancient peoples and history. After that, I thought, "I'm never going back to that place. I just cannot go back to a place like that."

That's also when I became more involved in learning the history of my birthplace, because in my country, if you don't get involved, you are safe. If you say something, you are not safe. Back home, every time I saw something, my grandfather would say, "It's okay, don't worry about it." My uncle had disappeared a couple of years before I came to this country. He disappeared. We didn't know where he was but nobody said anything. I used to go out to the countryside, and one day I saw a little *ranchito*, a little hut with people living there, and the next day it wasn't there. I asked my grandfather what happened to the people in that place, because there used to be a little girl there who I played with sometimes. My grandfather told me that the owner didn't want them here anymore, and he brought tractors and smashed the house. That's when I started questioning, "Why?" I was a little girl then and it wasn't until I came here to the U.S. that I found out why.

That new knowledge was just a shock; it was just . . . it, I was crying, because I couldn't believe how they could have done that. This person from Switzerland said to me, "Well they have done in America the same thing with the African Americans." I said, "I know." Because I had learned, by then, about slavery in the U.S., though it wasn't much studied at that time. That's when I became more involved in things that concerned me. I should have been involved earlier, but I wasn't. That's when it all started.

In El Salvador, before I came to the U.S., we heard about things going on, but the only thing I knew was that there were underground whispers of revolution. At the university where I took classes we would sometimes sneak topics or events into our class discussions, but we weren't really learning what was going on around the world, or around us. One day our sociology class was discussing the idea of socialism. We heard people talking just outside the classroom and then the teachers immediately got quiet. Why? Because we shouldn't even be mentioning Marxism, or anything related to it. In the 1950s when Fidel Castro came down from the mountains, I was a girl and thought him handsome, but I didn't understand that his struggle was about the big difference between the poor and the rich. It was not until I came to the U.S. that I was able to speak up, ask questions, and get answers. Over there you couldn't. It had always been a military government in El Salvador, and was when I came to the U.S., too.

Divorce and Relocation to Milwaukee in the 1970s

In New York, I got married in 1968. My husband was transferred to Chicago in 1970. By that time I had my little boy. He was born in 1970. I hated Chicago so much, I'm sorry. I refused to live in Chicago, and I lived in Milwaukee instead, while my husband went to work in Chicago. That's when I became a Milwaukeean, and I just love it. People are nice; it's a small town, but a big town—that's what it's all about.

My husband was a photographer. I used to work in retail and I met him there. He was a really big man with some connections that later became of concern to me, but at the time I didn't know any better. He had a limousine coming to pick me up and take me places, and it was fun, until I found out what it was all about—then it got scary. In 1976 I left him. My little boy was six years old.

Finally, in 1981 I got divorced, and it took a long time to get the divorce, but finally we made a deal: he kept all the money and I kept my son, Daniel. [*laughs*] It was a good deal! [*laughs*] My son is a journalist and a fantastic person who graduated from UW Madison.

Loss of Family in War in El Salvador and Immigration of Family to the United States

I travel a lot. I go everywhere. Every year I go someplace out of the country, but my life is here in Milwaukee. My home is here in Milwaukee. My sister María is here. She came over from El Salvador later, and my mother is here, too. They came here in 1982, because my brother and sister were killed in El Salvador, in the war. El Salvador is kind of . . . distant, my country, because I don't have a country. The U.S. is my home, where I live. I go all over, but I come back here, always.

Before she moved here, my sister came to New York to see me once. Then, later, in the 1970s, she came here on her own and stayed. She married and has her own family. I wanted my brother and sister to come here, too, and they said, "No. We cannot leave the country. This is our country." They refused to come, then later they were killed—no, they really weren't killed. They were kidnapped, tortured, and murdered by the government.

My brother Rodolfo was a teacher. In El Salvador, almost all the farmers, the landless *campesinos*, don't know how to read and write. My brother taught his regular class during the day, and then on Saturday and Sunday, with the help of my sister, taught campesinos how to read and write. They built a church where they taught. They didn't have paper and pencils, and they would use a stick to write the ABC's on the ground and everybody practiced that way. The government told him he shouldn't do that, that they weren't paying him to do that and that he was to teach in the school and not teach campesino adults. The government arrested him, beat him, and left him for dead. Then when he got better, he continued teaching adult campesinos. So they killed him.

My younger sister Delmy's husband, José, my brother-in-law, saw that and he decided to continue my brother's work. He was also kidnapped, tortured, and left for dead. At that time, Delmy thought it was time for her to get out. Since I am an American citizen, I sent all the paperwork asking to bring my sister and my mother. The day they were going to leave they got up really early in the morning. They had all the paperwork ready, except a birth certificate. They had to go to a little town to get it. Delmy left while my mother stayed at my aunt's house with Delmy's son Edwin, a toddler, when they all heard the machine guns—"toon, toon, toon." That was my sister and her husband being killed by soldiers. They attacked in front and in back of the truck they were riding in. They just machine-gunned them down. Just like that.

That's how my mother, Luz, knew who killed them. She decided to come here, and to bring my sister's and my brother's children. According to the lawyer in the U.S., the nephews and nieces did not qualify for me to bring them—they weren't close enough relatives. I met with everybody and their mother, from congressmen to senators, trying to find a way to bring the kids. A congressman I spoke to, who is now deceased, told me that if the kids came to this country without documents, they could apply for political asylum. So they went to Mexico, and from Mexico they came here and they applied for political visas, but they only came because they had to. My mother was sixty years old. My sister's son Edwin was two years old and my brother's children were two, four, and seven years

Figure 13. 1963 photo of Daisy Cubías, on far right, at her grandfather's farm house in San Vicente province, El Salvador, with sisters Maria (kneeling) and Delmy, brother Rodolfo (standing), and mother Luz. Photo used with permission of Daisy Cubías.

old. My brother's wife had left him earlier and they were completely without parents. Four children without parents. My mother, at sixty, was raising the four children alone in that country! They came here, with the help of many, many friends in the process—that's how they got here, but it was a long process and it was really scary.

When the kids came here, they lived with my sister, because my sister had a big house. I didn't have a house; I had an apartment. My mom and my sister and I raised the kids together. On Sundays we usually took them out to church and we did something fun. My sister took them to school and fed them on a daily basis. We worked together to pay for the food and everything. It was very hard, but we managed. When you have to meet a challenge, it's incredible what you can accomplish. Sometimes when I'm feeling lazy and just sitting around I say to myself, "Excuse me? I used to go to school while I was raising a son." How did I do it? I don't know. It's very hard, but you do it. When there is a need, you do it. Once they were safe in this country, they applied for political visas.

Activism against War

I often took some of the kids to demonstrations with me, and they got to know what was going on with the U.S. involvement in El Salvador. The U.S. made mistakes getting into those countries, helping to kill the people and using our taxpayer money to do it. The kids got a good education from us. People don't understand that most of the victims of war are children. They don't understand what we are doing to children and their future by supporting war. How can we manipulate children to hate each other and to hate other human beings? I don't understand that; it's horrible.

I don't believe in war. We shouldn't be in war. Why? It's just fighting over land or beliefs. Over the centuries, we have killed millions of people in the name of God and democracy. I've spent half of my life fighting against war. From 1983 to 1990, I also worked on aid to Nicaragua. I spent all the summers down there, working with kids—I still have sketches from the kids. We used poetry therapy and art therapy to work through the traumas of war. Yes. The most horrible thing is to see a little boy or a little girl who can hardly hold a pencil, but they can draw a house and a plane throwing bombs. It's all they know. How can we as grown-ups manipulate children's minds in these ways? It's just horrible. The worst part is that people don't want to give up their power. They become accustomed to that power, and then it's so hard to give it up, especially if you use it to exploit people and get rich in the process.

Through the Ecumenical Refugee Council in Milwaukee, I started working with the refugee camps for Salvadorans in Nicaragua. At the time, I went there every chance I got, to help. Every vacation I spent in Nicaragua working with the people and the kids. We also sent books and shoes and everything we could find. Many Milwaukee hospitals donated blankets, medicines, and more.[2] We used to have parties just to repackage the medicine in bottles. It was a lot of work, but things got better, and the war stopped though it's not over. It's still very hard. People are still healing from all that; many problems remain. It will take decades.[3]

First Milwaukee Job as a Retail Clerk

When we moved to Milwaukee in the 1970s, I came with my then husband, his three children, and my little boy. He had just been born. I think we arrived in February. I went to the supermarket one day, the A&P Food Store, with my baby and the manager said, "What's a pretty girl doing here buying groceries when you should be working?" I said, "I just came from New York and I don't have a job." He asked me, "Do you want a job?" I said, "Sure." He told me to return for work as a cashier the next morning at ten o'clock, and I filed my job application during my first lunch hour! I've been very lucky all my life that way. [*laughs*] I've never had to look for a job. Every job I ever got, it was offered to me.

I worked at A&P Food Store from 1970 to 1976. First, I was a cashier, then I was an assistant manager, then I was a nonfood manager. In the last position, I went all over the Milwaukee area making sure the nonfood shelves were full and that we had a good inventory. Back then, A&P Food Store was the biggest chain in Milwaukee. It was crazy busy, but it was also fun.

Faith, Religion, and Justice

I left my first job here in Milwaukee because I was going through the divorce and I left my husband and went to Miami for three months, before coming back to Milwaukee. He was a privileged man who had the law in his hands and I didn't have anything. I didn't even speak English that well. So the court made me stay here and gave him visitation with our son Daniel, even though I did not get child support. But I prayed a lot that somehow I was going to be okay. I believe in God; I don't believe in a religion, I believe in God. It doesn't matter what word you use—whether it's God or Allah or Buddha or whatever you want to call it, but there is something powerful up there that helps you if you really believe. You don't have to go to church. In fact, I've given up on church because I've seen too much injustice and misuse of religion that it's horrible—and it's a big business. My mother says I'm going straight to hell for that, but I say it's okay.

I was raised Catholic and I went to church at the time. We raised the kids in the Church. If you were to talk to my nephews and nieces, you'd learn that the reason they celebrated their First Communions was because I took them. Every

Sunday we took them, because I think people have to have something. People can change their minds later—it's their decision.

I stopped going to church. Well, actually, I go to church even though I'm not in the Church, because my mom remains in the Church—she's ninety-one now—and I used to take her to mass. Earlier in life I took the kids to church because they were upset at God a lot for taking their parents. Then maybe about ten years ago, I started questioning the Church, and I had some big fights with the priests and everybody, because I wanted to know why women could not be priests. That just brought up so many questions for me, and I didn't get the right answers. Then this scandal happened, I mean, we're human beings but when somebody abuses a child and a child suffers at their hands, I cannot accept that. Then denying it, too. I mean that's just so hard for me. Like I said, I believe in God. I believe some things that are good, but when I see the Pope riding in that crystal bubble and spending millions on a tour of Colombia, Nicaragua, and Cuba when people in some of these countries are starving, that's too much for me.

Raising Humanitarian Aid for Nicaragua during the U.S.-Funded Contra War

I was very active in the Ecumenical Refugee Council for a long time, but I left it quite a while back, because after Mrs. Chamorro was elected to the Presidency in Nicaragua, we could no longer send aid. We were forced to pull out, and I had been active in the group primarily to get aid to Nicaragua. We used to ship containers full of medicine to the country. Every month we used to send not one, not two, but tons of medicine and humanitarian aid. Then after the elections that brought Mrs. Chamorro to power, the new government started asking for us to pay to bring donations into the country.

Before the elections we worked very hard to get aid to Nicaragua. After she was elected, we sent the first shipment to the kids that we supported there in the orphanage named *Kilometro 10 ½*. It was all materials for the orphanage, but customs said, "Pay us and I will let your container go through." We explained that this was a donation, and we could not pay them. They went through it and they said a toothbrush was not medical aid, toothpaste was not medical aid, et cetera. They went through every item and said we had to pay import duties. We told them that if we had to pay $5,000 to get things through customs that were a gift to Nicaragua, then we didn't want to do that. We stopped the shipments. Since then, we don't send aid shipments there anymore.

We also can no longer send things to hospitals that we used to help there, including Berta Calderon Hospital, Children's Hospital, and the Military Hospital. We used to send lots of donated items there, not for sale. We also pulled out our volunteers. We had kept a house there, rented, for volunteers from Milwaukee: physical therapists, nurses, teachers, and others went. We paid for their food and provided a place to stay, room and board, and they worked for free. Volunteers went for periods of three months at a time, or six months. Some people stayed years. Suddenly, after the election, they wanted us to pay for the humanitarian aid we were providing. We just couldn't do that. We said, "No." That was the end of the medical aid to Nicaragua, even though the people there still need it.

Then the group kind of disappeared, because you know how we are in America—I say "we are" because we are, myself included: if it's not in the news, it doesn't exist; if it's not on television, it went away. If somebody tells you it's a democracy, you believe it's a democracy, even though it's still the same thing. Since Mrs. Chamorro was supposed to be the democratic savior of Nicaragua, interest in aid to Nicaragua dropped off. Nobody wanted to give us money for aid, nobody wanted to attend the fundraisers, so what were we going to do? The group just kind of dispersed because there was nothing we could do.

A few years ago I had the privilege of meeting Nicaraguan poets and one of them was the former government minister, Father Ernesto Cardenal, and we have become friends. Actually, I had met him during different trips to Nicaragua, but it wasn't until two years ago that we really talked. I had always dreamed of bringing him here to speak and read, and it finally happened. I was his chauffeur for ten days during his visit here. We drove to Chicago, to Madison, to Waukesha. Every day we drove. He told me whatever I asked, and he told me about the needs in Nicaragua. It was just sad, so sad, because the need is still there. Father Cardenal gave me a list of things they needed, but now that they want us to pay for everything going in to the country we could only send money for them to buy it there. We used to have a warehouse where we kept all the things we collected to send, but we gave it up. After 1990, we couldn't do it anymore because the cost was ridiculous.

Wisconsin remains a sister state to Nicaragua, but Milwaukee dissolved our sister city relationship with Ticuantepe because nobody was doing anything to maintain it. When I came to work in the Mayor's Office, we still had some kind of relationship, but no new projects because their government changed. I was the Sister City Coordinator for the city at the Mayor's Office, and about five years ago we had to dissolve all the sister city relationships because they weren't working. At the time, some in the community were upset, but nobody was doing anything. There's no reason to have something on the books that doesn't exist. We dissolved our relationships with many sister cities.

I used to go to Nicaragua maybe three or four times a year when I was working with the medical aid group. We partnered with the INSBI, the Ministry of

Health and Social Services, in the 1980s, up until 1990. The last time I was there was in 1990 for the election. I haven't gone back since then.

Serving as an Election Observer in Nicaragua

As an election observer, we were assigned to a voting place. Usually three or four people from different countries were at one location to make sure there was not any conflict, people maintained lines to vote, and nobody was buying votes. We also watched out that people were not telling others who to vote for, or what to vote for, or anything like that. We just observed. We could not interfere. Then after they finished voting, the observers made sure that the voting box was locked, that it wasn't overstuffed or dumped into the garbage and filled with something else, that it went to the right place. Whatever happened in the transportation, we didn't know, but we knew up to the placement of the locked box on a truck to wherever it's going to be opened and counted. After that, we didn't have any knowledge. Then at the end, President Carter was there for the counting, the final count to make sure. But what can one man do? Or a couple of people from the international community? People vote with their stomach. When they are hungry, they vote with their stomach. If they offer you bread, when you haven't seen bread for weeks, what do you do? Your children are asking for food. That's what happened in Nicaragua in 1990. Nicaraguans voted with their stomachs and the United States got the president they wanted.

A Grandfather Who Provided Education and Encouragement

I was about seven years old when I started writing poetry. I was always inquisitive about reading. I loved to read. I read everything I could find. My grandfather told me that I was too little to read some books so I started reading his copy of *El Paraíso Perdido* behind closed doors, when he wasn't there. I read Dante and discovered it was a long poem. I was amazed by how he did that. Later, I started reading the classics, and I fell in love with Pablo Neruda, Gabriela Mistral, Rubén Darío, Alfredo Espino from my country, and all those great writers. Reading inspired me to start writing.

Every time I thought I should write, though, it didn't work. For example, I was trying today, but the right brain doesn't fire up when I want it to. That's why I have paper and pencil everywhere, because I'm a paper and pencil person, for those moments when a poem whispers to me. You never know what is going to inspire you. You see an old lady walking around with a walker and you see her shadow and it's four legs. And you think to yourself, "This woman was a young girl at one point, dancing in the streets, who knows." Or you see someone begging for food and know that there is a story behind every person before, at some point, something went wrong.

My grandfather raised me as his own child. He wanted a grandson, so I wasn't raised as a typical Latin American woman; I was kind of raised as a boy, riding horses and going to school. My grandfather was very smart, very well read. He lived in a small village and he was so good with people. If you needed something you went to him, Don Chon, for whatever you needed. The people in the next small town, it was like a small city, liked him so much that they elected him mayor and he wasn't even on the ballot. They wrote him in. He was elected mayor of San Lorenzo even though he didn't live there. [*laughs*] I thought it was amazing. Then I realized, okay, everybody respected him, you don't fool around with Don Chon's children, I mean. No you don't. I learned to read, I learned to question, I learned all kinds of stuff from him.

He told me—and I even wrote a poem about it later, "One day, when you are in a different place you can question things." That's what I realized when I came to America, that now, oh my God, I can question things and I can get answers. Over there, you couldn't. You didn't ask questions. You just kept to yourself and you'd be okay. That was back then, at that time. It was hard, but that's when I started writing, because my grandfather said, "Write it down. Write it down, put it some place." Since then I've also always kept my papers. That was him: Write it down. Write it down. Write it down. Everything I wrote down, everything. It's incredible what you come up with when you're paying attention like that.

I learned from my grandfather that you have to treat people with respect and dignity, the same way you want to be treated. He told me, and I never, ever, ever will forget this, "*Ten cuidado de los pies que pisas hoy, porque pueden ser los pies del culo que tienes que besar mañana.*" [*laughs*] Yes, be careful of the feet you step on today, because they could be the feet attached to the ass that you have to kiss tomorrow. I always live by that because it's the truth. Yes. He added, "It's dirty, but that's the way life is. Yes." My grandfather also reminded me that no matter who you are, you are there because you had your opportunity, but many people don't.

He was the mayor, but he was also a campesino. He had land and he raised corn, chickens, and all kinds of stuff. He was a farmer. He had a very good piece of land. We had our own home. We never went hungry. We had mangos, papayas, pineapples, oranges, and lemons. I have never been poor. I've always had a place to live. I've been very lucky that way. My problem was that when I grew up, the kids I saw or played with one week, they weren't there the next week, and that's why I started asking questions. Why?

When I talked to my grandfather about going to New York, he said, "Do what you feel is right."

Building Community through Poetry

I have a book I'm working on called "Why?" It includes poems such as "Why Women Wear High Heels," "Why People Drink," "Why Men Wear Moustaches," "Why People Get Married," "Why Men Leave the Toilet Seat Up" and "Why Women Wear Bras," and a whole bunch of other "whys." Every country I go to, I ask people these questions, and believe it or not, it's almost the same answer. [*laughs*] I asked people in Perú, Bolivia, Colombia, Panamá, Puerto Rico, Cuba, even Spain. If I meet a familia with a person sitting and they say hello, I might ask them, "I see you have a moustache. Why do you wear a moustache?" It's always the same thing! Everywhere all the same answer! It's incredible that we have so much in common.

I enjoy working with children. In the past, I led a poetry therapy class here in the public schools for three weeks. We did the poetry therapy with seven-, eight-, and nine-year-old kids. The kids already knew how to write at that age. At the end of the course we put all the poems together in a booklet for them. One little girl started writing this very dark stuff and by the second week in this session, I spoke with the teacher about it. The teacher didn't see anything wrong with it, but I insisted and the child was referred to a social worker. In the third week, the little girl was still writing the same kind of poems, voicing the same scary feelings about being hurt while nobody cares and being afraid to say anything because everybody is going to get hurt. It was horrible. Later the social worker came over and thanked me for referring her, because it turned out that she was being abused by her mother's boyfriend, and she was scared because she was told not to tell the mom. Poetry therapy and art therapy work, but you have to have a long time for them. Sometimes you can see it right away, but sometimes you cannot. In the refugee camps we saw this, too. In the refugee camps, after they killed Monseñor Romero in 1982, everybody who believed in the cause named their children Óscar. In the camp, if you called Óscar, four or five hands went up. But it was very sad, too, because these were little kids of seven and nine years old [who painted] horrible things.

Educating People about El Salvador through Poetry and Fiction

I found my poems from 1963. [*laughs*] I was in El Salvador then. I also found poems from 1966–1968, when I was in New York. These mention Central Park and all this stuff and the pain of being alone in a country when you don't speak the language. Writing is a lonely sport, but it's also so nice, because as I've said before—actually as we Latin Americans say: you don't need therapy, you just write poetry.

Children of War is the first book. It's a children's book, and it was published by Jobs and Peace, not a big publisher or anything. We printed about one thousand copies and it sold like hotcakes because it was a fundraiser for Nicaragua. It was five dollars a copy. We had a big reception and everybody bought it. I don't know where the copies are now, but they are all over and people still use it. Last year the University of Michigan sent me excerpts that they wanted to use. I said, "Go ahead and use it." Two years ago, I was invited by Professor Sosa from Alaska to visit the University of Alaska at Fairbanks for a week. I've never been to Alaska so I said yes! They paid for my travel and even gave me a big check. I went for a week. I talked with the students of the university. I went to high schools. We did a big reception with the faculty. Then we did another meeting with the women. It was exciting. I didn't want to come back, it was so much fun. There were a lot of Latinos there from all over the U.S. They also had kids from all over Latin America there. Many Salvadorans. Cubans. Mexicans. Puerto Ricans. They are all there because they are making very good money.

When the book *El viaje de los gorriones* [Journey of the sparrows] came out—a collaboration between my girlfriend Fran Buss and I about Salvadorans leaving El Salvador—I also did some readings in several places. *El viaje de los gorriones* won the International Women for Peace and Freedom Award and the National Library Association Award. It's a collaboration, with Fran Buss as the main writer. Together, we interviewed many Salvadorans in 1989 and 1990. We went to Chicago, Madison, and migrant camps. We talked to them and we based the characters in the book on those conversations. I helped her with translation and shared some of my experiences with kids that inform the fiction. We started with an eight-hundred-page book, and kept cutting it down together—down, down, down, until it became a book for teenagers, for middle schoolers. That was a hit. It was published in Spain and it was published in Germany. Now it's everywhere, in hardcopy and softcopy, and in three different covers. It was made into a play in Chicago, too, about ten or fifteen years ago, sponsored by *La Raza Newspaper*, with a Cuban director. Then it also became part of the curriculum for middle schools in Boston, Washington, DC, Oakland, Baltimore, and in Pennsylvania, too—based on the book. It was exciting to see my work in a play and it led to me also visiting schools to talk about Salvadorans, something I still do.

Some of my poems are included in the first, second, and third collections of creative writing edited by Oscar Mireles titled *I Didn't Know There Were Latino/as in Wisconsin*. I'm on the cover of the second one. My friend, who was selected the Poet Laureate of Milwaukee this year, Brenda Cardenas, put together a collection titled *Between the Heart and the Land: Latina Poets in the Midwest* (2001) and included some of my poems in that book.

From Humanitarian Aid to Mayor's Assistant

I've had many jobs. I've worked for the City of Milwaukee, Milwaukee County, and the State of Wisconsin.

My job is assistant to the mayor of the city of Milwaukee.[4] I began in 2000 with another mayor, Mayor Norquist, whom I met when he was in the State Assembly. At that time there was an embargo against Nicaragua, and the group I was working with wanted to send aid to Nicaragua. I asked Congressman Jim Moody, a really nice man, for help, and he said that if we wanted to send medicine to Nicaragua we should talk to John Norquist.

"Oh, you have to meet John," he said, "he's a nice guy." Jim tells me that ten or twelve guys are going on a Sister State delegation from Madison to Nicaragua, including John Norquist. "I'm going to introduce you to John," Jim says. "Oh, I know him already," I said, "I worked on his campaign, and I'd met him before he was married." Jim says, "Let's go talk to him."

Well, we went to meet with him. I said, "John, can you do me a favor?" At that time if you were going to be in Nicaragua for three days you were allowed twenty-five pounds on the plane. So I asked him, "Can you give me twenty pounds of your suitcase for medicine?" He said, "You have that much medicine?" I said, "I have tons." He said, "I don't want to promise, but I'm going to ask everybody in the delegation to see if they can do that." "Thank you," I said. Two days later he called me. He said, "You know what? We got it. Everybody in the delegation is going to bring a *mochila* [backpack] with their clothes in it and the suitcase will be full of medicine, the whole twenty-five pounds." When they got to Nicaragua, they were waiting for them and those medical supplies. That was the whole thing then, we had to find ways to break through the embargo, because the U.S. Government didn't want to help Nicaraguans. We couldn't send medicine, but they were a diplomatic delegation and so they could carry in anything.[5] That's how we did it. We sent medicine. I was so impressed! Since then, we became friends. Norquist said, "Well, you guys are doing a good job." He helped us a lot in those efforts; he came to fundraisers and helped us.

Then when he got into problems with one of the female staffers, I wasn't a part of it. The following week I get this call from his Chief of Staff. "We want to ask you a couple of questions," he says, "Come on over." I went. They asked me about the Hispanic community and how to improve relations, because their relations went down the drain when the affair with the staffer became known. We sat for an hour. Then the Chief of the Staff said, "You're hired." "For what?" I asked. "To work for John," he answered. I said, "I'm not looking for a job. I have my job." At the time I was the eighth-grade administrator for Bruce Guadalupe Middle School. I added, "I don't want that job." He said, "Well, why not?" So I said I would think about it. "When are you starting?" he continued, "You can start tomorrow." I told him, "No, my kids have to graduate."

Wasn't that horrible? Anybody else would be saying, "Yes, yes, yes," and I'm saying no! But it was May and my students were going to be graduating in June. "If you can wait until then," I said. Well, he looked at me like "Who do you think you are?" But he's the chief of the staff and the boss is over there. I said, "Okay, the kids' graduation is in June. I'm going to start in June if you want me to." We negotiated salary and everything. That's how I started.

I have worked for some of the most interesting men in Milwaukee: John Norquist, Walter Sava, and Dr. Howard Fuller. [*laughs*] White, Latino, and African-American—and I get along with all of them. When they see me, they give me a hug, because I do my work. I do my best no matter what it is. You can talk to Howard tomorrow, and he'll tell you, "Oh, yes, she was a good worker." The same thing with Norquist and Walter. They're my friends.

Work as an Immigrant Services Specialist

In the 1980s, I worked at Children's Hospital, where I was recruited by Dr. Tom Schlenker. The HMOs had arrived in town at that point and I went to work in customer care. I got promoted four times in three years and became a Provider Service Specialist. That meant that I sat with doctors to find out how much they were going to charge for their services, then I would write it down in a contract for the hospital. I had never done that before in my life, but I learned quickly. I was in charge of visiting every doctor and every dentist of the HMO, and writing up the contracts for Children's Hospital. Then they sold to another company.

That's when my friend Irma Guerra told me about the state job, which at first I didn't want because I would have to travel and my son was still young. But she said I would only have to travel two days a week, so I said all right. I got that job, because Irma Guerra asked me to work for them, under Governor Tommy Thompson. At the State of Wisconsin, I was the Immigrant Services Specialist. In the 1980s a law went into effect that anybody who came to the U.S. before a particular age could apply for residency. My job was to go out to the migrant camps and find out if these people were here before that date. If they had been working with a Wisconsin employer, then they could apply for residency. Many people were residents and they didn't even know it because the employers never told them. I found so many problems. Being bilingual helped me a lot in that job. I had a state car, because I would have to travel all over the state, and I did that for a year. It was exciting but the winters are horrible here for driving.

I visited Black River Forest, Wisconsin, during that year where all the people, the sheriff, everyone in town is white. I arrived there in the middle of the afternoon and I walked into a restaurant. All these faces turn around to look at me. The sheriff wasn't there but all of a sudden I see the sheriff coming down the road. Then I ordered food. I think they couldn't figure out if I was Indian, illegal, or what. So the sheriff comes over and he says, "Ma'am, somebody called that you're driving that car." I said, "Yeah, that's my car." "How did you get it?" he asked. "I work for the state," I answered. "Are you sure?" he says. I said, "Yes!" He didn't believe me so he asked me for all kinds of identification, because, I mean, who gets there with a state car? They thought I was crazy, and there I am in the middle of nowhere. He let me go but he still looked at me suspiciously! [*laughs*] Until I opened my mouth, they thought I was Native American. They were used to seeing Latino men working in the Christmas tree fields in that area, but the Latino men never left town. They only went to the grocery store to buy food, and they never went to the restaurants to eat with the white people. And here I was, a Latina, going everywhere, and remember it's expensive to stay in the hotel and all that. To them I was suspicious, driving a car from the state. There were lots of farmers in the area. It was very interesting.

The Latino migrant workers lived there in their own camps, provided by the employer. Most are from Mexico, and they work in Wisconsin every season. I talked to them. I did a very good survey of about seventeen pages long. I reported to the state. For every person that applied for residency, the state received money, because it was a service for them. I found an old man, he was like seventy something, and he came every year, crossing the border like he was undocumented when, in fact, he was a legal resident. I said to him, "*Señor*, you're a legal resident. Look at this paper; it says you're a legal resident." He was very surprised, and even more surprised when I told him that he could take a plane here, that he could travel here sitting down on a plane, and that the employer had to pay him minimum wage. "I can take a plane!?" he marveled. Yes, yes, I ran into those things. Oh, the employer never wants to tell them that because then they lose money. They were treating those workers like everybody's undocumented. That's what big business is. Though they are required to do certain things, the Anglo employers exploit the Mexican workers. On that job, I went to all kinds of *fincas* [farms], saw *vacas* [cows] and *lecherías* [dairy farms], and pine gardens, everything. Those are areas where the work is all done by brown hands, brown sweat. Yes. I went everywhere in the state and I got my education in that year.

Working for Milwaukee County

After that job I was so tired from all the traveling and I needed to be nearer to my son. That's when I switched jobs to work with Howard Fuller. His wife worked for the state, in the same building and I got to know her. One day she mentioned that her husband was looking for somebody with bilingual skills for a South Side youth initiative. She said, "You're always telling me that you are tired of traveling. Maybe you want to talk to my husband?" I said, "Why not?" I got the job.

The Youth Service Initiative was a program to spread information about county services on the South Side and generate greater participation from the area in county business. Howard wanted the South Side communities to be more active, because they had not participated much in providing county services. I was the bridge between the county and the South Side; I spread the word about the services the county could provide and the monies and the contracts. Before that, the people in power didn't tell us how to access those services or how to do business with the county. Howard thought it was important to build access to youth services in particular—all the youth services. We rented a room at UCC, where I had an office, and I had another office downtown. We talked to every agency on the South Side, and more, telling them about the contracts out there and how to apply. We had all the directors of county areas come in and talk about the services that the county provided, and contracted for, that weren't going to the big agencies. This made it possible for South Side providers to apply to provide services to the county. My job was to let everybody in the community, from all the neighborhoods, know about the services and access to provider relationships, and to work with agency directors to apply. We worked on ways the county could provide the "how-to" information, including sitting down one-on-one to write proposals. That's what I did. Exciting. I worked like a crazy person. I was so busy. That's also how I met many, many people.

Working for the Education Trust to Build Parent Participation in K–12 Schools

That job was funded by a one-year contract. After that year, I ran into Oscar Mireles, who was the assistant director for the United Community Center (UCC). He told me about a new project that he thought I would be good at. The Greater Milwaukee Education Trust and the MMAC, Milwaukee Metropolitan Association of Commerce, had opened an agency called the Education Trust. They received funds from the Edna McConnell Clark Foundation in New York to come up with a pilot program for Milwaukee Public Schools (MPS). I went and talked to them and they asked me to work for them and, again, we negotiated salary. The pilot program was to get more education for the parents to get involved in MPS. That was a good idea. We had two coordinators to help do it. It was so successful. We started with two schools: one on the North Side and one on the South Side.[6]

I worked for them for ten years, and in eighteen schools. Ten years working on getting parents involved in education in MPS, from 1990 to 2000. It's a good idea: educating the parents. MPS didn't want to give us access because they said all their own information is confidential. We had to fight, but Howard was there, who had happened to be my boss in the County, and now he was MPS Superintendent. We went to Howard and said, "Howard, we need the okay." He had to fight with the union, because the union said that the teachers have the right to close the door if they want to. I said, "No, the classroom isn't a secret." My job was to get more parents involved and I created Parent Centers. We came up with the idea that the parents are the best customers. You treat them with dignity and respect, no matter what. I did the research before and knew that if parents dressed nice when they went to the school, the school officials paid attention to them, but if they went in everyday clothes, they made them wait.

The Edna McConnell Clark Foundation provided funds for the program and they gave funds to MPS, too, for extra things. We also raised money locally from foundations such as the Helen Bader Foundation, and others. We set up Parent Centers where parents visit, have a cup of coffee, talk. Each center had a coordinator. We paid parents to be there, to learn. We taught classes in English as a second language, flower arrangement, cooking, preparing for the citizenship test—everything. The program was a big success. We presented on it all over the United States. We went to Boston, New Mexico, San Antonio, Oakland, and San Diego to do workshops on how to get parents involved. It was so good. It made the front page of *The Milwaukee Journal*. We made the national news, too.

We also trained parents about how to talk with the teacher. In Latin America, the teachers, the priest, everybody official is held in high esteem. Whatever they say is okay. Here, we had to teach our parents to question education. We also taught English as a second language. If someone asked the kids, "Did you do your homework?" the kids didn't really know what they were saying, but if the kids saw the parents learning English, then that made a difference. My niece, Lucy, also taught English as a second language in the evenings and afternoons.

The Parent Centers got so big that we had hundreds of books in Spanish and in English. We even made it educational for the teachers, teaching Spanish for education, so they could at least say, "*Señora, ¿como está usted* [Ma'am, how are you]?" Teachers came to the center during their lunch hour and we sat down with the parents. We did not allow them to sit with other teachers; they had to sit with parents, and they talked. We also did ethnic festivals with food. Teachers learned about the different ethnicities, and they learned the difference between Puerto Rican Spanish, Mexican Spanish, the regional differences, as well as how parents viewed the teachers and vice versa.

We did home visits to the parents in the summer. If your son was going to our school in the fall we went to your home in the summer to welcome you to join in the Parent Center. We also got the schools to do a welcoming party for the parents and students at the start of the school year. They had never done that before. The teachers made hot dogs for the parents and everybody who came, and they gave tours of the school, especially the high schools and middle schools, because the kids got lost when they went there. Since they'd never been in a school where they had to change classes before, the first day of classes were often complete chaos. In that job, all of my ideas could grow. Research on the topic also grew.

Something else I did during that program was to send the parents of high school students to training to become teachers' aides. Fifteen years later, I still have ten parents working at MPS! Those parents would never ever even have applied, if not for that program. Most teachers, however, didn't have an aide, and when they needed to leave the classroom, they would call me to get a parent to watch the classroom. This is how the parents gained experience in class management. I was then able to take trained teachers' aides from among the parents to the principals when openings arose. The principals were so good because they already knew the parents, and they gave them the job.

The program was created because Milwaukee was changing, our Latino population was growing, and the school system didn't know how to deal with kids from these different backgrounds, mostly Spanish-speaking families. There was no communication. The kids were failing. The Edna McConnell Clark Foundation, in New York, knew that when you have parent involvement the kids do better in school. They were doing an experiment here. They gave a couple hundred thousand to MPS and they gave us only a hundred thousand, but we also raised additional money because the MMAC saw this as an investment in Milwaukee's future employees. One funny thing was that in that program we were among the first people to have cellular phones, because nobody had cell service then. [*laughs*] We were back and forth all over the city. We went to everything. Everybody thought I worked for MPS. I was there for ten years and I got to know everybody there. We were doing a good job. One year at South Division High School, I had 2,500 hours of volunteer time logged in just one month. Two thousand five hundred hours! One of my volunteers was a Mexican man who didn't speak English at all and didn't know how to read and write, but he had a child in school and he was in a wheelchair. Do you know what his job was? He would roam the halls checking on kids, getting them to class on time. He'd say, "Antonio, you better go to your class, I'm going to tell your mom." Or "Roberto, to your class." He knew all the kids. They're from the neighborhood. The kids respected him and they listened to him. If he caught a kid in the hallway,

"Hey, what are you doing out? To the classroom!" That was his job. He loved it. Then he would have a cup of coffee and talk with everyone. If a student wasn't in school, he went to the phone in the office, to find out how come that student didn't get to school. If the student didn't have a phone, I would take one of the parents with me to go knock on the door.

The schools then allocated funds for the Parent Center, but the teacher's union got very upset because they said we were interfering. The grant eventually came to an end and MPS continued Parent Centers in a couple of schools for a while longer before they ended the program altogether. I left that post in 2000. Now some principals are asking me to go back, saying we need Parent Centers. I told them that ten years before.

At that time, I ran into Walter Sava at a party and he told me about the job at Bruce Guadalupe as an administrator, which I took. I worked for Walter Sava when he was the UCC Director, and I was the Bruce Guadalupe eighth-grade administrator. At that time, in 2000, they were building the new Middle School building on Sixth Street, and that's why Walter was upset at me when I left after nine months. Walter Sava said to me, "I've built your office. You already chose the colors! And you want to leave me?!" That's when Mayor John Norquist was offering me the job as his assistant. "Walter, somebody has to do it," I countered, "We need representation." Walter answered, "I never want to talk to you!" He didn't talk to me for a couple of weeks. He was so upset that I was leaving. Now, we are very good friends.

I've never had jobs that keep me in one place. Even with A&P Food Store I was responsible for about fourteen stores. I never sat at my desk in one place. I think I would go crazy in that kind of job. Instead, I always went out and about, and it was exciting. I always loved my job. Every job I ever did, I loved it. The best part about every one of my jobs is that I had the freedom to do things. For example, when John Norquist gave me this job, I told him what I wanted and what I was going to do. I wrote a job description based on what I felt the community needed. No question about it, I like that very much.

Recognitions and Awards

Most of my jobs have been very blessed because of the people I work with. I think they think I know how to do my job. I always do my best, I go the extra mile and that's what they want. You go the extra mile and see. It matters.

I have received many awards over the years, including the Employee of the Year for the State of Wisconsin under Tommy Thompson, the Virginia Hart Award,[7] the Future Milwaukeean Award. My son says, "Mom, put it on the wall." I say, "Put it in a box." I have several boxes with all kinds of plaques and things in them, but a really special award was a recent one from the *Milwaukee Business Journal*: Woman of Influence. They gave me the award last week. I don't usually like awards; there are people doing better work, but this one included an awards ceremony at the Midwest Convention Center with several hundred people in attendance! They also put my picture on the cover of the *Milwaukee Business Journal* and interviewed me. The best part was that the award wasn't for my work but for my community involvement and my writing. I just thought, "Oh, that's good." I was surprised to get flowers congratulating me from many people and companies.

On Wednesday, we had a cabinet meeting and all the appointed people were there, including the chief of police, the fire chief, all the directors. I announced that I needed to leave to attend a women's event and someone said, "No, don't go yet." Okay, I waited. Then Mayor Barrett said, "Now the meeting is over but before we go, we want to congratulate one of our own: Daisy, congratulations on being the Woman of Influence!" I was so embarrassed. [*laughs*] They gave me a proclamation and everybody applauded.

In general, I don't think awards are important. If somebody tells me that they're going to give me an award for my work, I say no, because I am getting paid for it. But this award was for the work I do in the community, with no pay, because I am on so many boards and I raise money for them. That has nothing to do with work, because I have been doing it even before I started working here.

Right now, I am only on four boards, but I usually have six to eight board commitments. I started with the Mental Health Board and continued all the way to Future Milwaukee. I try to do the best I can. The reason is somebody has to do it, but in addition the more we do for our community, the better we'll be off. I am on the UCC Latino Arts Board because art is my baby; I love art, of all kinds.

Working to Expand Arts Programs

When arts funding is on the line, then I am there to fight for it. I've argued to the Common Council that, "A city without art is a city without soul!" They may think "Oh, that's just Daisy again," but we mobilize arts supporters and they can't ignore them. We asked many people to attend the last budget meeting, because the City only provides fifty to sixty thousand dollars for arts funding and it was on the chopping block. We use that money to provide grants to art groups in the communities for programs such as *Día de los Muertos* or Ballet for Kids. Well, somebody decided that we don't want to do that anymore, that we were going to take it out of the budget. We went to the mayor and said, "Mayor, we have to keep it." He said, "Yes, but the boys across the hall are the ones who do it, it's their job." We had an Art Board meeting coming up, and we called everybody and asked them to be at the meeting to testify for the arts. So many people showed up that we made the front page of the paper!

We had more people there to testify for the arts than the Police and Fire Department had. We had hundreds of people in line, and they all came and treated the aldermen with due respect. We showed how the arts create many jobs, including parking and restaurants. We gave it to the aldermen and we won. Everybody said, "Daisy, we did it again!" It was good, but you have to believe it and you have to do it, no matter what anybody tells you. I think, if you have a dream, you work for it. There's nothing wrong with art. There's everything right with it.

Milwaukee lags behind a place like Minneapolis in supporting the arts. They have a percentage for art. Milwaukee doesn't. We have to fight every year for a budget. The Wisconsin Arts Board doesn't have that much money, either. With 600,000 residents, if we just asked people to donate $1 of their tax money to the arts in the City of Milwaukee, we'd have at least $200,000. They say it would be a headache to organize it, but I say, no, other cities have done it. If even 50 percent of the people in the state did it, all those kids who are missing art because they can't afford an art teacher would have some art in their lives.

Politicians like to hear from constituents; if something is bad and they don't hear from anybody, they don't do anything. But you get two, three, four, twenty letters, then people pay attention. That's what I tell the people in there. Most people, especially us Latin Americans, we're not used to doing that. We don't get involved in politics, but politics are what run the world and we don't do that.

Dealing with Discrimination

A lot of people walk around with their heads down when it comes to discrimination, but for me it doesn't exist. Even if someone discriminates against me, it's their problem, not mine. Like when people say you are too fat. I say, "I'm too short for my weight." Many people tell me, "Oh, you speak too fast." I say, "No, you listen too slow." And everybody laughs! You should see the letters that the kids at a local school wrote me. They said, "We learned a lot from you, because you don't let anyone put you down." It's true. Because if you believe what you're doing is okay, it doesn't matter what they believe.

I've been by myself for such a long time, and in that time I've run into discrimination. When I change cars, I always buy a [brand] new one. When the [car] salesmen takes me to the used car area, I don't get upset; I just tell them that I want to talk to the manager, and I tell him that they are doing a bad job

Figure 14. Daisy Cubías featured on cover page for "Women of Influence" section in the *Milwaukee Business Journal*. June 18, 2010. Photo used with permission of *Milwaukee Business Journal*.

and I don't buy the car from them. I went to look for an apartment—with my two sons, because I took my sister's younger son to live with me, and my other sister took the other kids—and I went to this beautiful apartment. My son was going to high school. I always had a good paying job, with a good paying salary. The woman who was showing me the apartment was white. This was back in the 1980s. The apartment was over six hundred and fifty dollars. That was a lot of money. Then she said to me, "I didn't know the welfare check was so big." To my face! I said, "Excuse me?!" She said, "Well, I didn't know they give you so much money." The apartment had three bedrooms, and I wanted my boys each to have a bedroom of their own, so it was a big apartment. I said, "May I please talk to your manager?" She said, "I'm the manager." Then I asked, "Who is the owner?" I got in touch with the owner and explained to him what she said. I told her she was wrong, too. I said to her, "Don't think because I'm brown, I am on welfare. That's an insult. You should be trained." I told her that I didn't want her to lose her job, instead I wanted to educate her. "You are wrong," I added, "because I make more money that you do, okay?" I really told her, not shouting. My son said, "Mom, how could you do that?" I told him that if they don't have education, if they have a one-track mind then that's what they believe. The owner was a big company in Milwaukee with apartment buildings all over, very nice ones, and they were so apologetic. I just told them that they needed to educate their managers.

I've been insulted by other people, too. Once a plumber came over because of a drain break and he said, "Oh, your husband couldn't fix it, huh?" I mean, they feel you have to have a man to live? I'm sorry. Another time I went to the bank, when I was buying my house, which was pretty expensive. I met with a man who said, "Okay, we're going to lend you this money, but your husband has to sign." I said, "Are you going to give me a husband now?" [*laughs*] He asked, "You don't have one?" "No," I answered, "and I don't need one." "Oh, I'm sorry," he said, "I, I, I . . ." "I want to talk to your boss," I said. I always call and talk to the boss. This time they gave me a lady to talk to, and she was very nice. She said, "Some of those guys there are old. They are not used to women." I told her, "Yeah, well, they should get the idea that women can do it." We can do it. But that guy was fifty, sixty years old. You know, at that age they're not used to dealing with women, and I am strong, I don't let anyone put me down.

Look, if I chased the FBI out of my house, I'm not afraid of people wanting to discriminate against me. In the 1980s when I was going back and forth to Nicaragua, and involved in solidarity work, that's when the FBI came to visit me. Yeah. They told me that I was running around with Communists and I should stop. I chased them out of my house. I told them they don't belong in my house, they better get out. If I can throw the FBI out of my house, I can throw anybody out, right? They had guns! [*laughs*] It's true, you cannot let anybody put you down.

Education Never Ends

I'm always taking courses. Every year. At one point, I was working with recent Cuban refugees when I was at UMOS, and I had to take courses to help me in my work. When I was working at the Children's Hospital, I studied medical topics. When I worked in education, I took tons of courses. I'm *una estudiante eterna* [a perpetual student]. [*laughs*] There's so much to learn. You can never finish learning. Ever. I will never finish, because I don't just like doing this or doing that, I like taking on new projects. Then the next thing comes up, and the next thing comes up. I am always learning. It's exciting. Books can tell you one thing, that's a fair way, but the practice is completely different. I like to do all kinds of things. Always.

Once I took an art-making course, in Madison, for a whole week. I had a fellowship for that! I was, for the whole week, immersed in art in Madison, including jewelry, poetry, writing, dance. It was the best week in my life. If you want to be a whole person, you must learn many things. You can't learn just this or just that. There's so much to learn and you don't have five lifetimes to learn, so you learn what you can in the areas you like and in the areas you can be most effective with other people.

I'm very independent. I'm very strong. If I want to see something or learn something, I do it. If I don't like things, I change it. I don't like to be discouraged by another person, I can't be around someone who isn't encouraging. One way I learn is through travel, so I've gone to Italy, France, Spain, Cuba. I've been traveling with my friends Ardene Bunde and Liana Dolby recently, but I have several traveling companions. We just say, okay, let's go to France, let's go to Portugal, or whatever. I just came back from Puerto Rico. In September, we might go to Mexico. Why not? I was in Bolivia and Perú last year. We went to Machu Picchu. We also went to Colombia. I've been to Costa Rica ten times; I love Costa Rica. Oh, it's beautiful. Guatemala, too.

I plan on retiring soon, and in retirement I'm going to write, I'm going to travel, and I'm going to enjoy my garden. I have a beautiful garden. I took all the grass out and put flowers in everywhere. I have flowers. Everywhere. I'll have more parties at my house with my friends from different parts of the world who come and play the guitar until the wee hours of the night. We're always going out every place. Sometimes we go to Madison and here and there and everywhere. I'm going to do a lot of volunteer work, too, so I have a lot of things to do yet because age is a matter of the mind, and if you don't mind, it does not matter.

9. It Was Okay to Be Mexican, but I Wanted More

CARMEN ALICIA MURGUIA

Interviewed on July 5, 2010

Salesperson, Public Relations, Marketing, Grants Writer, Creative Writer/Poet, Performer, Activist, Teacher

Second- and Third-Generation Milwaukeeans

My name is Carmen Alicia Murguia, and I was born in the Chinese Year of the Horse in 1966 in Milwaukee, Wisconsin. My maternal grandparents came to Milwaukee during World War I and my mother Carmen Valdes was born in Milwaukee. Then my father, who was a boarder of my grandparents, came during the Korean War and that's how my mom and dad met. But it wasn't until years later that they got together as a couple, and were married and made a home in Milwaukee at 1638 South Seventh Street, which is where I grew up from birth until 1980. I went to one of the first bilingual bicultural Head Starts in the nation, called the Guadalupe Center, on Third and Washington. In the 1960s and 1970s, I participated in their summer school programs, where I got to meet other Latinos of Puerto Rican and Mexican American background. Then I went for kindergarten to Allen Field Elementary, and I remember that was the second time that I spent time with white kids, because we were raised in a Polish and Mexican neighborhood. We were well liked by a family of Polish American neighbors; I remember that vividly because we were a good family, that is, my father worked, and my mother was fluent in English, and we were all well-behaved kids, so we were "accepted."

I grew up with a mix of Mexican and American culture; both were always simultaneous in the house. On Saturdays and Sundays we'd hear *rancheras*[1] and Mexican music, whereas during the week my mom would play WOKYAM 920 AM, and it was music by Burt Bacharach and Carole Bayer Sager. That mixture happening in our house really played a role in my later life, and coming to understand that I'm a part of both cultures and embracing both cultures rather than putting one down over the other. I went through that negotiation for a long time.

Recognizing Gender and Sexuality in Elementary School

Then I went to St. Anthony's School for first through eighth grade, and that's where I realized a number of things. I was seven, which was about first grade, when I came out to myself. I realized that—well, I came out in different ways. I realized that I was a girl, and what that meant was that you're second-class, you're not as good as the boys. It also meant that there are other rules and regulations about being a girl. I also realized that I was Mexican, because that was really evident going to a private Catholic school where all the teachers were white, and most students were Polish or German, with some Mexicans and Puerto Ricans. It really stood out to me that I was from a working-class, Mexican family.

The third thing that I realized as a young girl was that I liked girls! [*laughs*] I remember one day we were on a break—we must've been out on the playground, and I was seven, and I remember going to the church, which was open. It must have been around noon or something. I walked into the church and I went to the front pew because I wanted to be as close to God and as close to Our Lady of Guadalupe as possible. I remember saying to them, "Okay, so you made me a girl and you know that's going to be tough, and you made me Mexican, and you know that's going to be tough, but you also made me like girls. So you better protect me. Amen!" I recognized as a child that I had a tough road ahead of me. [*laughs*] Then I just crossed myself, blessed myself, and I said, "So just please protect me." That was it. I knew. I had such insight as a little girl, perhaps in part because I was raised in a civil rights family.

I was raised in a very socially active family. My parents were very active. My grandparents, well, my maternal grandparents had passed away, and I didn't meet my paternal grandmother until we went to Mexico one year to bring her here. My dad brought her up to Milwaukee. My grandparents had passed away but I knew about rights from my parents. We'd go out into the community and we'd go to rallies for equal rights, and civil rights, and housing rights, and we'd go to celebrate Mexican Independence Day, and any Catholic events—we were always there. Then there were the *bailes*, the dances. With my parents as soon as we learned to walk, we had to learn to dance! There were five of us kids. I have older sisters who are twins, a younger brother, and then my brother David, who passed away in 2003. I remember other things, like learning in threes, learning about funerals because my parents didn't believe in babysitters and would take us to funerals. I remember funerals very vividly, and weddings and dances. It was a social way of life—to connect—it was a network.

Changes in the Ethnic and Racial Composition of Milwaukee Neighborhoods

In 1979 our lives shifted because my parents became foster parents and we started having brothers and sisters. We became a foster family. We were only a temporary foster home so kids would only stay with us for a maximum of three months, but we would get really close. Then in 1980 our lives changed again when my father announced that he would start taking us on drives. I remember a big thing in our life was going on a Sunday drive on Lake Drive, or to Bay View, or to Mequon—we'd go anywhere, or Holy Hill. He'd take us everywhere and on one of those drives I remember him pointing to a house on Sherman Boulevard. He said, "See that house? One day we're going to live in that house." And we did.

In 1980 he packed us up and we moved. The near South Side neighborhood where we lived was changing. There was ethnic change—more Puerto Ricans were moving into it while many white people were moving out, but there was also socioeconomic change: the neighborhood was becoming a neighborhood of renters rather than homeowners. I noticed that the Mitchell Street Festival became more Latino. You'd still see some white families there, but in 1979 and 1980 it became more Latino. Then they stopped having it.

When I told my friends that we were moving to Sherman Park, they said, "To the North Side? Where blacks are?" I said, "There's black and there's other kinds of people over there, too, and we're going to be there." I remember my father saying that it was time for us to let go of this neighborhood, and that was probably the hardest thing I had to do, because it was so much a part of who I was. For example, I remember around that time that I got my period for the first time. I was out playing tag, wearing white pants, and then all my girlfriends like stood around me and I said, "What? What?" and they said, "It's your time," and I was like, "What's my time?" Then they took me to their mother and their mother explained to me that I was bleeding because I had become a woman. I said, "But I don't want to become a woman. I want to play." They told me, though, "You gotta go in the house; you gotta go tell your mom." I told my mom and she said "Now you just have to stay in the house; you have to rest; you just have to lie down, and that's it."

Then we moved to Sherman Park, which was a mixed neighborhood but predominantly black and Jewish. There was a white family down the block; and the girl in the family befriended me. She was the first visual artist that I ever met and she was also a university student so it was a big thing for me to be her friend, even though she was a few years older than me. Around then, I also spent a lot of time at Finney Library, reading, drawing, and hanging out until it closed every night. When I started high school, I took the Number 30 Bus to St. Joan Antida High School. I was a freshman when my twin sisters were seniors so every time I got in trouble they would page the twins. I got into trouble because I was a loud person and I liked to yell in the hallway, and they considered that "acting up." I was not the quiet one with my legs crossed and all that. In grade school I had been very much into sports: volleyball, softball, basketball. Through sports I could let out a lot of my aggression about the inequality that I saw around me. When I got to high school, I turned to the arts, developing interests in painting and drawing. I did an abstract piece of art that a friend asked me to explain in writing. "Carmen? Like what are those about?" she asked. So I wrote something to accompany those pieces. After my friends read it, they'd say, "I want that." They liked what I wrote and I kept working on it. I really liked my creative writing, literature, and visual arts classes.

Normative Gender and Sexuality in a Catholic Girls' High School

In my senior year we lost our art teacher, because the school said that she was getting too close to the girls and the relationships that she was building were "too feminist." I just thought, "Oh, whatever that word means." I didn't know what the word meant until 1991, and this was the early 1980s. However, I knew that I had to follow the norm of being a girl, even though I had come out to my friend Guillermina in my sophomore year.

I remember telling Guillermina that I liked girls, and her response was, "Carmen you better keep that to yourself 'cause we've got four years of this," of an all-girl school. I think the girls knew it, and they just like liked me and my other girlfriends—Missy, Trina, and Wendy. It was cool, I was fine. It didn't become an issue but I didn't have it in their face either. I kept it to myself and I dated boys, which always surprised them. I was very picky about the guys who I went out with, and I dated some star athletes. If I was going to kiss any boys, the kisses had better be good and they better have something to them; I didn't want to waste my time. They often wondered how I wound up with those boys. It was very interesting.

They were cool with me, in part because one of the things that I could do besides make them laugh was write dedications for the radio. The radio station 102 FM had a program of love songs at ten o'clock at night during the week. If you submitted a whole letter they would read it on the radio. My girlfriends would always say to me, "Oh, write me a dedication." I would write and write and write and sign different girls' names to the letters and they would always get read on the radio. Everybody would talk about it at school the next day: the letter from Missy to "too tough Tony," from Trina to her boyfriend, and so on. The girls would just scream 'cause they heard their name on the radio and that made me cool. I wasn't real cool; I was pretty quirky.

Then in my senior year I was out. I had written a friendship card, to my friend Missy, just telling her how much she meant to me—we had become close—and how important she was to my life. Well, you can't say that when you're sixteen or seventeen and in high school. Missy got the card and she dropped it walking between classes. Christina picked it up and told everyone: Carmen Murguia is in love with Missy. Well, Missy freaked. She couldn't talk to me the whole rest of the day and that was at like 10:30 in the morning. To get to three o'clock was a very long day. It was awful. I went to go have lunch and nobody would sit with me. Then it was time for math class and when I went to go sit down, it was like the parting of the Red Sea. These girls literally picked up their chairs, on both sides, and moved away from me. I told the teacher that this girl had said that I was in love with Missy, because the terms "outed" and "lesbian" were not terms I knew or would have used in high school. I think "gay" was a term in use then, or just "a girl who likes girls." I guess that was how it was discussed.

I told the teacher that I had to leave, and I went from class to class looking for my best friend Connie, because I wanted to jump off the roof. I thought, "What am I going to do?" I was so scared. It's one thing when you know it; it's another having somebody out you. But there was also the issue of someone naming something in a way that wasn't accurate, because I wasn't in love with Missy. I went knocking on the biology door and asking the teacher to have Connie come out, but the teacher said, "I can't release her; she doesn't know anything." I said, "Please, I'm a senior, this is my life we are talking about," and I'm sobbing. Then I told Connie what happened. She's like "Carmen you've got to calm down and you can't jump off the roof, and you can't do anything drastic. Just wait for me until after school." Then I went down to the lockers, pacing back and forth, and some of our black friends were down there and they were just sort of staring at me and not saying anything. One girl was someone who used to kick it with me on the bus—we'd listen to Shalimar and Cameo and talk about the music, but suddenly she didn't know what to say to me. Then the bell rang; it was three o'clock and Christina was coming down to her locker and was snickering. I just grabbed her and I picked her up against the lockers and I just started pounding on her. It took four girls to get me off of her because I was just so mad and so emotional. Then Cindy, Missy's sister, said to me, "Carmen, let her go," and then she added, "Missy needs the weekend to think about it," so she didn't want me to try and talk to Missy then either, but she said, "It's going to be all right." On Monday I went to sit in the cafeteria for breakfast, and I was sitting all alone, knowing that if Missy and Trina came to sit with me it would be okay, and if they didn't it wouldn't be. Well, Missy and Trina sat down with me, and then the whole crew followed. I said, "Oh, my God!" Missy didn't know what to say except, "Hey, you know, it's okay," and then they were talking to me as if nothing had happened. Then they were laughing and joking about something and then without saying "let it go," we just sort of let it go. I was suddenly cool again. I had my crew of friends again, and that was pretty life changing. That weekend in my senior year was the longest weekend of my life. It was awful, just awful.

I came out to my parents, to my family on Thanksgiving, in my senior year. Oh, that was very traumatic. It was very traumatic. They sent me to my room. They were yelling. My brothers and sisters were like, "Are you kidding me?! Why did you say that?" My brother, who I had secretly told when I was thirteen, was so mad. He said, "Why would you call that kind of attention to yourself?! You know it's not going to go over. That was our secret!" But he also said, "You know Carm that I want to go to New York, and that means you have to leave the house first because you're my big sister."

The fact that I made it through high school was a big deal. It wasn't the academics that were the issue. I just liked to fool around a lot. My friends discovered that I was smart when I dropped my report card and somebody picking it up announced that it was a 3.7 GPA. "Carmen Murguia is smart!" they said, like that was a bad thing! [*laughs*] I was surprised that the fact that I was loud or creative, or different, meant to them and others that I wasn't really applying myself, but I told them that my parents made us do homework every night. We'd have dinner as a family every night. Then my parents would say, "Okay, it's time to do your homework," and we always had to do it around the dining room table. We couldn't go up to our room; we couldn't turn on the TV until everything was done. They were very strict, very strict. They were good strict.

When I was thirteen, I discovered alcohol. I remember how it made me feel and the fact that I could escape to it, and I could be myself and not be ashamed of who I was: girl, Mexican, lesbian. With alcohol I was fine. Later, at the age of twenty-five, when I was a student at Mount Mary College for the second time, I got into recovery. I found a priest and told him, "Okay, I'm ready. I'm ready to turn it over." For so many years before that I had not been ready. It had been my way of dealing with all the feelings that I had about who I was, but I knew that had to change, and I did change it.

Finding the Right College

In senior year, in religion class, we went around the room and each girl had to say what she was going to do after high school. Most girls were going to be secretaries or get married, but they knew that I would go to college even though I had kept my college applications secret. I was applying to all these really impossible schools like Harvard, Vassar, Chaminade University in Hawaii—all schools that I had seen on TV or in school and I was thinking, "Wow! I'd like to go there. Why not?" Then I got all these rejection letters, and I was like man this is crazy. I applied, too, to some art schools, like Minneapolis College of Art and Design, but my portfolio wasn't thick enough. There I was thinking, "Man! What am I going to do with my life then if I got all these rejection letters?"

Then my parents called the Dean of Mount Mary College, Sister Patricia Preston, who had been our family friend since we were little. They said to her, "Carmen is floundering and you have to take her, you have to do something with her because she's about to graduate high school and we're not having her at the house doing nothing." Sister Patricia said, "Okay, I'll take her and I'll keep my eye on her," and this and that. I went to Mount Mary for a year, but I was on probation the whole year, it was crazy.

I was on academic probation because St. Joan's did not prepare me for the papers, for sitting in two-hour classes, et cetera. Plus it was another all-girls school, and now I'm eighteen and my hormones are raging, and it's just like, "more girls!" Then, too, I wasn't prepared for the class differences there: it was a place where wealthy people from many different cultures sent their daughters. Mount Mary had an arrangement with schools in Guam, and so I made a lot of Chamorro friends there and met black girls from mostly upper-middle-class families. It was a crazy experience, a real culture shock. I think I was more absorbed in figuring out my surroundings than I was in my studies. I was in the art program. I didn't really make it that first year, but I made some good friends. When I was there I lived at home one semester and then one semester my parents let me live on campus. I don't really know what they thought, but since I had come out to them the year before I think they just wanted to keep a close eye on me.

After that year at Mount Mary, I went to MATC and I was in the marketing program. I really excelled at MATC, and that was good. It was a good year. I took creative writing classes, psychology classes, and marketing classes. I found it very enjoyable. I really liked the campus of Mount Mary and the atmosphere of college life there but the academics at MATC were more my level. At MATC I met other people who were working their way through college, like I was. I worked at Boston Store then, and met other students who were working and took the bus. Yet, I still felt unsure about whether I belonged there. I didn't know where I belonged.

Living an LGBT and Ethnic Life

I was feminine in that I wore lipstick. The reason I wore lipstick, and I wear lipstick to this day is because my mother insisted I wear lipstick and I just adapted. If I don't have lipstick on when I go out then my friends ask, "Carmen, what's wrong? Are you sick?" In the gay and lesbian bars I didn't know what my role was because I had been raised as a typical Latina girl, very feminine, but I had some masculine qualities. When I'd go to the bar I was so nervous. I didn't know if I was supposed to wait for someone to ask me to dance or if I was supposed to do the asking, because it became very clear to me the first time I walked into Fannie's or into the M&M, two bars that are no longer here, that the roles of the masculine girls and the feminine girls were very defined and there was very little in-between. I can recall sitting there with my legs crossed and then uncrossing them, and then crossing them again, and then uncrossing them . . . because I didn't know what to do. I thought to myself, "What the hell!?" Now, today, I know exactly who I am. I know that I love, and that I am more attracted to, feminine women.

I had my first real girlfriend at the age of twenty-one. I met her at the bar Fannie's. She was in town because her best friend was graduating from dental school. I just went up to her at the jukebox where she was, a very pretty girl, Puerto Rican, very feminine. She was wearing a linen dress. I said to her, "Oh, let me play that song for you, whatever song you want to hear." I played it for her and she thought that was so charming. Then we exchanged phone numbers. I thought she seemed really cool. She had just graduated from college. We had a long-distance romance for about a month. I was living with my parents then, but wasn't really contributing to the household, and I remember my parents getting the phone bill. Then one day she said, "I'm going to come up and see you." My brother went with me to the airport to pick her up. He said, "I want to meet this girl. I want to know who she is." He also volunteered to cover for me by telling our parents that we were going away for the weekend, because she had booked a hotel and we were going to be alone. She arrived and sat in the front with my brother and they got to talking and it was more of an argument than it was a discussion. When we got back to Milwaukee, we went to the hotel and we spent the weekend together. After that weekend, she sent me a ticket and asked me to come and live with her in Houston. "Okay!" I said.

I told my friend Stacie, who I was friends with since Mount Mary, that I was moving to Houston to be with my new girlfriend. Stacie said, "Carmen, you're still into that?" She thought that it was a phase, she thought that my being a lesbian was a phase. Then I told my parents that I was going to Houston for a job opportunity. They said, "*Pos, ojalá empieces una carrera y empieces con tu vida ya* [Well, hopefully you'll begin a career and get started with your life now]." But I was a baby. I was twenty-one and I was very amateur: to me it was party life or no life. I went down there with $100 thinking that my whole life was going to change. She had a career. Her university studies were behind her, and she had this great condo and this great car, and this great life. I was there maybe two weeks before she sent me back. She said, "You're just not ready for me, Carmen, and I can't take care of you. You're just sort of going from here to there and you don't have your degree yet. What do you want?" All I could answer was, "I don't know, but I want to be with you." She said, "You have to have more than that. I need somebody who wants more than that, Carmen." She sent me back to Milwaukee.

Deciding to Move to Minnesota

I came back and told my parents, "Oh, it didn't work, guys. It didn't work out."

Soon my friend Stacie came to tell me that she was going to be moving to Minnesota to study fashion and she wanted me to go with her. "You've got to leave Milwaukee," she said. "There's nothing here for you." Back then, basically, whenever a girl told me "you should do this" or "you should go do that," I would follow it, because I didn't have any direction really. I didn't have any models for how to be, and so I went from this woman to that woman, dating and partying, thinking that was life. Deep down I knew there had to be more. I said, "Okay."

I told my mother and she said she would tell my father. Well. I found out how she told him. One day I got home and my father was in the garage outside having a smoke. I said, "Hi, Pa." He said, "Licho"—they called me "Licho," from my middle name Alicia—"*métate*." I said, "Sure." He said, "It's late." I said, "Okay." I had sensed something was about to happen and then we were fighting. Then my mom and my older brother came down, and they separated us while we continued to yell in each other's faces. I was yelling, "Don't worry, I'm leaving!" But he said, "No, you have to leave tonight." I called Stacie and I told her that we had to leave that night, and I told her to call her sister and brother-in-law and ask them if we could go there that night. They came and got us. I left the house with a bag of clothes, $100, my box of thoughts, and my drawings. That was in 1989.

My box of thoughts was a collection of things I'd written down. They weren't poems, they weren't short stories, they were just a collection of different things I had written, some of them would eventually become my first poems. I took those with me: the box and the bag. We drove to Minnesota and I knew I had new responsibilities. I would be away from the community I knew and who knew me, though by then it was time.

Earlier in my life when we had moved to Sherman Park, I felt distant from the Latino/a community, even though we kept going to St. Anthony's Church. The South Side was very much related to my Mexican identity, but I felt like I didn't belong there entirely. High school and college then exposed me to other things. I was learning that I wanted different things out of life. Suddenly, it was okay to be Mexican but I wanted more. I was visiting the East Side, seeing how different people lived, visiting museums, galleries, and wanting to travel.

Finding Social and Religious Acceptance in Minnesota

Stacie's family really helped us out in Minnesota; we were able to stay with them for the first four months. Then we both got jobs at Saks Fifth Avenue and telemarketing jobs. We'd go to work during the day at Saks, then take the bus out to Edina for telemarketing, then come back and start all over again the next day. Our weeks were like that until we saved up for our own apartment. That was the first time I was on my own. I had my own apartment, paid the rent, and contributed to utilities and food. Stacie and I got along until she got a boyfriend and my Catholicism kicked in. I hadn't been to church since moving to Minnesota and I felt I had to go.

In Milwaukee, I went because I was forced to go, but I was getting pretty upset with God. I wanted to know, "What's my purpose?" and He wasn't giving me any answers. I had a pattern of excelling at something for a while and then falling ten steps back and having to start over. There was something in me that wanted something more, but I didn't know what it was exactly. In Minnesota, I found a Catholic church right outside the back door of our first apartment, St. Steven's Catholic Church, which was an eye opener, because it was all-encompassing of different cultures. I met Native American and cool white people and black people there and gay and lesbian people there; they were very embracing of everyone. I thought, "Wow. This is a Catholic church and it's very cool and very different." Before that, I was accustomed to mass in Spanish, in a very heterosexual environment, where social classes were very defined. I hadn't seen an embrace of all these different people in the Church. Women helped out at the church and during the service, which I thought was highly unusual.

I also joined a coming out support group that I saw advertised on a poster. It was at a place called Chrysalis Center for Women, which still exists. I went there and said, "I want to join the coming out support group." We'd sit in a circle and tell our coming out stories and then talk about supporting each other. It was very empowering. I think I was the only Latina in the group, but I still felt really welcome to Minneapolis. It was a completely different community than anything I had known before, and it seemed to me that they didn't have the social and racial segregation that I saw in Milwaukee. The arts community in Minnesota was huge. The feminist community was big—and that's the first time I heard the term "feminist." The gay and lesbian community was big there. The Walker Art Center is there. It was just a great life. It was the best.

Then Stacie and I had a falling out. She seemed to expect that my "phase" would pass, and it didn't. Then I moved to Lake Calhoun and West Thirty-Third, which was just two blocks from the water. I was bike riding in the neighborhood—because I really liked the neighborhood near the lakes—and I saw a sign on a door that said "Room for Rent." My new landlord, Cathy, was a very nice straight girl, blonde, blue-eyed, just the sweetest person. She worked in computing. I think that was the first time I met someone like her who accepted me. It was different. We were from two different worlds but at the same time she was just very cool with me.

I made several friends there, many of them gay men. I met my friend Romero, who later died of AIDS, while working in Minneapolis. We'd go out after work so many days a week it was ridiculous. My circle of friends there became gay men, mostly gay white men, which was very unique—at least to me. We went to parties, or played croquet on Labor Day weekend, or just hung out, or went dancing. That was a big thing to do then: go dancing. I kept thinking that when they discovered how Mexican I am they'd drop me but they liked me; they thought I was cool. With my friend George Rebolloso, who is also Mexican, I went to live jazz, theater, and independent movies.

In 1990 and 1991, AIDS was becoming more prevalent. As I dated I thought, "I have to be careful because of this AIDS thing." I didn't know anything about it except that it was a gay disease and mainly men had it, but I thought, "How could I be immune to it?" I started becoming more cautious. There was also lots of activism around AIDS. The Walker had a Day Without Art, where they covered all the art, to raise awareness around AIDS. It was a life-changing time, because I went to rallies and became a part of movements. I went to the Gay Pride Parade, the Gay Pride Picnic, and feminist rallies.

Discovering Chicana Literature

At the Amazon bookstore I discovered that they had a Chicana section. I had heard that word before from my brother David, who went to St. Lawrence Seminary High School, where there were students from Chicago and other parts of the country who used the term "Chicano." We never used that term in the house, though. Then here I see it in Minnesota, at the Amazon bookstore: a Chicana section! I was sort of looking over my shoulder as I pulled down Gloria Anzaldúa's book, *Borderlands/La Frontera*. Wow. I was so blown away. I read it while standing there in that section. Then Cherrie Moraga was in that section, too, and *Compañeras: Latina Lesbians*, an anthology of Latina lesbians that had an aqua cover with two women intertwined. It was edited by Juanita Ramos. That book I bought because it included essays, short stories, poems, and drawings—it was a really cool collection. Ana Castillo's books were there, too.[2]

Around that time, one of my friends, Greg, bought me Sandra Cisneros's book, *House on Mango Street*—and it was the first time that a Mexican American was published by a mainstream press.[3] I remember that. She was on NPR. I had started listening to NPR then. When Greg gave me the book he told me that he wanted me to write my stories, too, because he knew that I had just been accepted to The Loft's Letters of Color Program.[4] Greg had never read anything—none of my friends did—that I wrote; they just assumed that I wrote. I didn't do any readings until our work at The Loft culminated in a public reading. My brother flew in from New York to pick up my mother in Wisconsin to bring her to the reading. He told her, "We have to be at that reading; Carmen is going to do her first poetry reading."

Reconciliation with Parents

My landlord and roommate at Mirror Lake, Cathy, taught me how to drive a stick shift on her Camaro, and eventually I bought a Volkswagen, my first Volkswagen, and I drove it to meet my parents at their cabin. My parents vacationed in Northern Wisconsin in August, and I told them that I would visit them there, at the cabin. When I arrived, my dad got in the car and he said, "This is manual!" I said, "Yeah." "But I never taught you how to drive manual," he said. Then I told him, "I know. I learned myself." That was the first time since I had left—remember we had had that awful fight—that I saw him. The first time since then, and then he put his arms around me. He said he was very impressed that his daughter knew how to drive a stick.

I was driving him in my car—because the cabin was very secluded and hard to find so they had met me at a gas station so that I could follow them there. The fact that I had driven all that way by myself—it was six hours—and that I drove stick was very impressive to him, and he said, "Wow, my little girl is growing up." Then when we got out of the car, he put his arm around me and walked me into the cabin. He said to my mom, "Licho came in a stick shift car!" My mom was puzzled, "A stick shift car?" I showed her, and I showed her how you drive it, and she was just floored. "Oh, my God!" she said. They were just so happy

Figure 15. Carmen Murguia with parents Filiberto and Carmen Murguia in 2011. Photo used with permission of Carmen Murguia.

that I made it. It was the best four days that I had with my family in years, in years. Everybody was there, all five of us were there, and it was just the greatest time. We all left there happy.

Learning about the Work of Creating Art

Those of us accepted into The Loft's Letters of Color Program received a stipend to support ourselves while we worked on honing our writing skills. After several weeks, I went in search of my box of thoughts, the box I had brought with me from Milwaukee, where I kept the first poems I had written. I took some of these to The Loft workshop, including the very first poem I ever wrote, titled "Fear," and which I later published in a little chapbook titled *The Voices Inside: Mi Alma, Mi Cuerpo y Mi Espiritu* (1995). The thing is that after I wrote that—and it came out in one fell swoop—I remember looking up at the sky and I was like, I knew, I thought, "God is with me." Like whoa! Because it just came out and there was no editing. When I took it to the workshop, I remember that's the one poem that she didn't edit. Everything else, she commented on: "put this here," "what are you trying to say here?" et cetera, but that one poem she left alone. After that, I knew I had something and I wanted to go with it.[5]

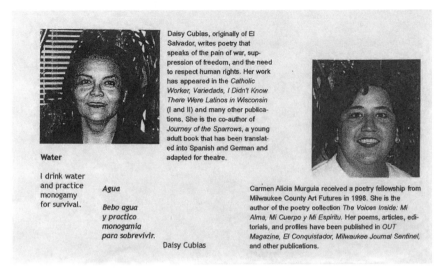

Daisy Cubias, originally of El Salvador, writes poetry that speaks of the pain of war, suppression of freedom, and the need to respect human rights. Her work has appeared in the *Catholic Worker, Variedads, I Didn't Know There Were Latinos in Wisconsin* (I and II) and many other publications. She is the co-author of *Journey of the Sparrows,* a young adult book that has been translated into Spanish and German and adapted for theatre.

Water

I drink water
and practice
monogamy
for survival.

Agua

*Bebo agua
y practico
monogamia
para sobrevivir.*

Daisy Cubias

Carmen Alicia Murguia received a poetry fellowship from Milwaukee County Art Futures in 1998. She is the author of the poetry collection *The Voices Inside: Mi Alma, Mi Cuerpo y Mi Espíritu.* Her poems, articles, editorials, and profiles have been published in *OUT Magazine, El Conquistador, Milwaukee Journal Sentinel,* and other publications.

Figure 16. Flier announcing poetry reading in Milwaukee. Photo used with permission of Daisy Cubías.

There were so many impressive people in the program, but we all thought that we didn't belong—that was the unique, connecting factor. We were all wondering what we were doing there, whether we were "really" writers. We thought our work wasn't worthy, or not Latina/o enough. I didn't think I belonged there either, because I didn't have a degree or a career, just a job. Yet the other Latina/o writers were well read and excited about life, and they brought that out in me, too. I became more excited about literature and writing and I found my purpose. When I lived in Minneapolis, I learned, too, that I have people skills.

Several Latina/o authors visited our group during that six-month period, including Sandra Cisneros, who I later had the honor of introducing both in Minneapolis and in Milwaukee; Luis Rodriguez from Chicago; and Martin Espada from Boston. The visiting writers would talk with us about preparing manuscripts. Their readings were just amazing, too, and their work inspired me to write.

Arrival: Pride in Being an Out Mexican American Woman and New Careers

Four months later, I moved back to Milwaukee, and I took advantage of every opportunity to meet Latina/o writers or to share my own work, because now I was totally Mexican American, and very proud to be female, very proud to be out, very proud to be an out female Mexican American. It was as if that had been my purpose in going to Minnesota and I had come full circle. When I returned I also worked to stop sweeping my alcoholism under the rug. When I turned my life over and came into recovery, it felt the same as when I came out. It was very much the same, another coming out process.

When I came back, I started writing for different newspapers in Milwaukee: *The Outpost, The Change* (our queer newspaper), and others. I went back to Mount Mary again for another year and then I was on the Dean's List the second time around—I was on the Dean's List! I was in the Art and Marketing Program. I did really well. Everything just changed.

Then I had to tell my parents that I was going to move out again, and that was really hard because my parents' viewpoint was that you don't come home to not live at home. Yet I realized that I didn't have a whole life because I was now out. I had met someone at work and we wanted to be together all the time. I moved out into a place of my own, then later into a place with my girlfriend. For a couple of years after that, my parents weren't real pleased with me, but then they sort of came around, because they saw I had settled down and I was with someone. My girlfriend was white, and her whole family embraced me, so that was great, though it took my family a little longer to come around. We were together for three years.

From 1996 through 1998, I put my writing skills to work as the Public Relations Coordinator for 9to5, the National Association of Working Women.[6] The Executive Director had heard me reading at a Women of Color Speak Out, where I read an essay on what it meant for me to be a woman of color in the work place, and she asked me to go to work for them, and I accepted. Suddenly I'm writing press releases and talking to the *Wall Street Journal*, and the *New York Times*, and the *Post* about women's issues in the work place—just like that!

Then I moved to the YWCA of Greater Milwaukee where I worked as the Marketing Director and focused, among other things, on the newsletter and website. Having my own office was really cool. These changes in my job situation were significant, and I was writing all the time in my positions at these two organizations, but I was also an activist in the LGBT and women's communities and I was often quoted in the media on those issues. At that time I was becoming more active politically, too. Then I became a spokesperson for LGBT issues, because there were few who were willing to do that. From the YWCA I went to work at the Medical College of Wisconsin, in their Marketing Department, and from there I shifted to doing freelance work, which was very successful. I was often hired by organizations around town to write their annual reports, press releases, or marketing materials, including the Hispanic Chamber of Commerce, United Migrant Opportunity Services, and Spanish Center.

From the Lesbian Variety Show to Poetry Readings

I also continued to write and read poetry, and to perform, which I felt was my calling—and I did a lot of readings and performed at the Broadway Theater Complex and in theater acts. It was a very busy time. When I released my chapbook *The Voices Inside* and had my first reading at the Lesbian Variety Show, I went in full charro outfit: the hat, the skirt, the tie, the vest, the little jacket, and cowboy boots that I'd gotten in Texas. The Lesbian Variety Show no longer exists, but LAMM, the Lesbian Alliance in Metro Milwaukee, still exists and they used to sponsor it at the Broadway Theater complex, where they have the Florentine Opera. It was my first time in a theater setting and it was packed! There were many different acts. I read poetry.

I also was smitten by a Mexican American woman I met at that event, and we became instant friends. That was the first time I met a Mexican American from Texas who was from a privileged background. Her parents had money but her dad, very Tejano, loved his *rancheras* in the pickup truck. She didn't know a lick of Spanish, but she'd pick up certain words because I did a lot of code switching—a term that Martin Espada taught me. She knew some Spanish vocabulary but she didn't know how to speak, read, or write Spanish, and here she was from Texas. I was just bowled over to meet another Mexican American lesbian—the first time that happened for me in Milwaukee. We were just magnets for each other!

Latina lesbians in Minnesota were very out, very public, but in Milwaukee the Latina lesbian community was very underground or they were at the bars. So it was surprising to meet someone like her and she was so open. That was really different for me, but we really loved each other. I remember the first time we danced together, a *ranchera*, was at this bar restaurant called *Pedranos* where my cousins were having a birthday party. Before that we had only danced together in the style of Madonna—separately, but during that party at *Pedranos* I took her in my arms for the first time. It was natural. Since I was a little girl I've always wanted to dance a Mexican dance as a couple with another girl, and that was the first time I did. I think I was twenty-eight at the time. There was something about it that was so life changing: after all, I was dancing a *ranchera* in a Mexican bar with a Mexican girl and my family was there. It was amazing. Then she had to leave. That was hard. Oh my God, we were bawling, just bawling but we knew it had to end somehow because she wasn't going to be with me.

My writing community at the time included elders like Luisa Lovert Gallous, Susanne Silvermarie, Antler, Harvey Taylor, and that whole group. Then there was another group around Joanne Chang. These different groups invited me to read with them at public poetry readings. The first time I read with Luisa's group it was out at the Audubon Court Bookstore—before they closed—and I was very honored by the invitation and the response. I was in my early thirties and I had been reading at open mics at lots of places but had never been a featured reader. They gave me a standing O! They really liked it. I began to make more connections with poets and writers at the University, at Woodland Pattern Bookstore, at different cafes, and to develop a wider audience for my poetry. I did a reading then at the University of Wisconsin in Madison when a professor there invited me to speak for both Chicano Studies and Women's Studies. I took my best friend Juana Vega with me, who had to get permission from her girlfriend to leave the city.

Friendship with Juana Vega

I had known Juana since Guadalupe Summer School, but we never came out to each other until one day when I was walking into the bar and dance club La Cage holding hands with my girlfriend, and she was walking out of La Cage with her girlfriend. Then we both looked at each other and said, "Hey, lesbiana what's up?" Before that we had the silent thing going on where we'd see each other at school or in the neighborhood, but we never hung out and we couldn't be friends, until that day that we ran into each other at a gay bar—and we were both with *gueras*! We thought that was the funniest thing. Later we went to this bar called The YP and ended up playing pool together.

When Juana and I first acknowledged each other as lesbians—in 1994 or 1995—I had returned from Minnesota and was in a steady relationship. I remember telling her that I was a poet, and it was funny that every time I told somebody that I wrote poetry it was like coming out. I was exposing a part of myself that before I had kept to myself. When I told her, I wasn't sure if she would think it was cool, but it was such a part of me that I felt that I had to tell her. I had just finished a reading at a little street festival in the Third Ward and I was headed home when I saw her at the bus stop. We talked and she asked me what I was doing there, and I hesitantly explained that I had been reading my poetry. Then she asked to see my poetry and I showed her "Border Crossing" and she was just blown away—and that was important to me because she was a South Sider to the core but she also traveled in other circles as a lesbian so she was very open minded. Juana asked me if I had more poetry, and after that I shared my poetry with her and invited her to my readings.

Fast forward to a year later, and Juana and I run into each other again. I was so happy to see her. She was always my best friend no matter what. It was several years later that she joined me for the Madison reading, which was an interesting experience for me, and for us as friends. Juana kept reminding me that I had a life in poetry and that I needed to keep at it even as events in my life were about to blow up.

Losing Romero to AIDS and Juana to Murder

In July 1998 I returned to Milwaukee from reading my work at "The Hijas del Quinto Sol Conference" in San Antonio, Texas, and I heard devastating news. My friend William called to say that my friend Romero, from Minneapolis, had only a week to live and was in a hospital in Pittsburgh, Pennsylvania. At that time I was teaching creative writing, English, and reading in a rural educational center, and so I had to take off two days, a Friday and Monday, to be able to go see Romero. I gathered together my things, told my mom—that was the first time I told her that I had a gay male friend who was dying of AIDS—and asked her for a blessing and prayers for him. She was very cool, and she gave me a blessing, then I drove to Pittsburgh and saw Romero. Before I went, though, I also made another stop. I visited the AIDS Research Center in Wisconsin to get some guidance on what to expect and how to act, because I didn't want to appear shocked or make Romero feel uncomfortable. When I did see him, he lifted his mask and said, "Hey, girl" and smiled. "Oh, Romero," I said and then I started crying. "It's okay, it's okay," he said. I spent the night there with him and William; we slept in the hospital. Then I came back to Milwaukee and he was gone within 72 hours, just like that.

In 2001 my friend Juana Vega was murdered in a hate crime. It received a lot of media coverage, and you'll still find many articles about it online including from *The Chicago Tribune, Seattle Gay News*, and the newsletter of the Southern Poverty Law Center. Every station in Milwaukee covered it, and a German magazine even covered it with a story called "Hate in the Heartland." It got media attention, in part, because I went from mourning to activism very quickly in defense of my friend. Juana had broken up with her controlling girlfriend, but she was murdered in a hate crime by her ex-girlfriend's brother. I saw her the night before she got murdered. I was out with my friend Genève who was in town for the National Gay and Lesbian Task Force meeting, held for the first time in Milwaukee in 2001. Genève and I connected and we went out dancing to Fannie's and Juana was there. Juana's last words to me were, "I'm finally free. I broke up with Ria and I'm finally free." I asked her, "Where are you going to sleep tonight? Do you want to stay at my place?" She said, "I have to go back and get my stuff." Well, it was when she went back to get her stuff that Ria was waiting for her.

She went to her apartment to get her things and Ria was there, waiting for her, and a fight ensued. They were fighting then Ria ran out of the house, with Juana following, and around the corner to her mother's house on Thirty-Sixth and Scott, where Ria's brother was waiting for her, and he killed Juana there. He had a gun and he shot Juana six times in the body and in the face at point blank range. They left her there. Didn't even call an ambulance or anything. Even so she was still alive. A boy coming home from work came upon her, and she asked him for help, and he called the ambulance, but by then it was too late.

I didn't want her to be just another poor, brown—she was dark-skinned—Mexican girl casualty on the South Side. I didn't want her to be just a statistic, or a one-liner. I didn't want that to be the end of it, the end of her, because there was more to this story. So I called the media. First, I called LLEGÓ, a national Latino/a LGBT organization,[7] and then I called the National Gay and Lesbian Task Force, because I had been reporting for them in our local gay and lesbian paper *The Wisconsin Light*. I said, "Hey, it's Carmen from Milwaukee and my best friend was just murdered and I know it's a hate crime." How did I know that? Juana had already told her brothers that Ria's brother had said to her, "I'm going to kill you because you're gay and because you turned my sister gay."

The neighbors who had witnessed the shooting were afraid and didn't want to come forward, so it was hard. The district attorney met with us about pressing charges for a hate crime, which was a historic event, because he had never met with anyone before about pressing charges on a hate crime and there had never been a prosecution for a hate crime in Milwaukee—in Madison, yes, but not in Milwaukee. Juana's family had hired an attorney, and the district attorney told them that if they went ahead and pressed charges for a hate crime, that the killer would get a smaller sentence. As a result, they said to me, "Carmen, you have to lighten up because we're not going to press for the hate crime." I argued otherwise but they didn't press for the hate crime. In the end, the killer got a sentence of sixty-five years to life for the crime.

I was afraid, too, because it was a nasty situation, but at the same time I felt that I had to act. I knew that I had gotten justice for Juana when the judge in the case said that he was appalled that it wasn't tried as a hate crime, because it clearly was a hate crime. That's all I needed to hear. It's on the record. We held an event to raise funds for Juana's headstone and we also established a scholarship in her honor for four years, the Juana Gloria Vega Scholarship, which awarded $3,000 to four lesbian or female bisexual college students each year.[8]

Writing, Teaching, and Performing Poetry

I earned my living as an automobile salesperson for a time. The ad said "women and minorities encouraged to apply" so I did, and I sold cars for five years and did very well at it. In 2009, I started working at the Latino Community Center on developing their website, writing the newsletter, and writing for the Executive Director. The Latino Community Center is a nonprofit that's been around for ten years and it serves children between the ages of five and nineteen in after-school and summer programs. I wrote the newsletter and maintained the website, served as photographer, and wrote reports for funders on our programming and outreach. I had actually started to work with kids more often in the years leading up to that job—as a poetry teacher in schools and at the Woodland Pattern Bookstore. The kids produced a lot of work, and I found it very rewarding, because I got to be myself and teach poetry. That, to me, is like everything coming together beautifully. Getting to be myself as a Latina, as a lesbian, and a poet—it's just great. I walk into a classroom and this is who I am; I just bring my whole self to the classroom. I'm not hiding anything or being too shy about this. I think it's important to be able to be a confident female for other girls, little girls and teenagers to see. I think I have a responsibility in that way.

I don't feel that I'm just supposed to write quietly by myself and then do readings. No. I feel like I have to teach this stuff so that others know that it's cool, that you can make a living of it, that you have a story to tell. In doing that, I'm doing what Sandra Benitez taught me, which was that if I'm the spirit of the group and if I'm a writer then I have to pass that on; I can't just sit with it and just do readings and get paid. I sat down with my friends who are teachers—like Sherry Jones, who taught in the public school system for many years—and I'd say, "Help me do a curriculum. How do I time myself?" She taught me how to do a curriculum and how to work backwards with time and how to create a disciplined classroom—there's that, too. Then I learned further by doing it. Emilio Lopez, the Executive Director of the Alternative High School approached me at one point about teaching for them, and they provided books and guides and training, too, to prepare me for it. I taught for them for a while, too, and all the while I continued to write and read my poetry, and when I wasn't teaching I sold cars.

Little by little these gigs would come my way, which I enjoyed. My biggest readings were at the Bronx Academy of Arts and Dance in 2003, where they held the BAADass Women's Festival every March for Women's History Month, and then in 2005 at the "Out Like That" June Festival of Art and Theater during Pride Month in New York. My friend Carmen Valentine had moved to New York, and he knew the directors of the Bronx Academy of Arts and Dance:

they're a gay couple, two men; one is a dancer, Arthur Aviles, and the other is Charles Rice-Gonzalez, who does all the marketing and direction for BAAD. They befriended Carmen, who told them about me, and so they invited me out to read at the festivals. I read with four other artists and that was when I learned about Spoken Word, because while I was reading from the page, they were performing. The other artists were Puerto Rican and Cuban and they were bold and powerful and they had a local fan base. They taught me a lot about being more physical with my work.

A Different Family

In terms of coming out of the closet as a lesbian, my parents and I have had a real journey. Now, my mother looks at me with such love and devotion and happiness. She's always happy to see me, and I feel that I bring her so much joy, but I remember the times when I didn't bring her joy, when I was just "a bad seed." With my father, well, we've we had our fights, we've had our differences, but now he's there for me no matter what I need. He's very supportive. He actually bought me my first computer when I decided to do freelance work as a writer. "What do you need?" he asked, and then he got it. He's also helped me out when I had trouble with the landlord, so he's been there for me. He's very fragile now, but we enjoy spending time together—just the other day we took a walk to the corner together, arm in arm, together, or sometimes I just sit with him because he's not feeling well. We couldn't do that back in the 1980s or 1990s, but it's different now; maybe we had to go through that Mexican family stuff, but then I don't think they ever stopped loving me, they just had difficulty accepting so many different things.

Epilogue

Contemporary Challenges for Latinas
in the Midwest

The oral histories gathered here provide insight into the many advances that Milwaukee's Latina/o communities have made in creating vibrant social, political, cultural, and business organizations and movements, and the role that women have played in these efforts. Although this volume does not include many of the women's descriptions of their children's successes, and their pride in them—except where children are direct participants in a shared project with their mothers—that, too, is an important contribution made by the women who here share their stories. Yet it is also important to note that many of the conditions that these life stories address, such as changing economic conditions, challenging educational settings for Latina/o students, access to health care, and limited opportunities for women in institutional and organizational leadership, persist. They persist not only in Milwaukee, or in the Midwest, but throughout the United States, suggesting that analyzing both their impacts and the creative ways that everyday people negotiate these situations may shed light on approaches to dismantling barriers to equal opportunity for all. The necessity for this in Milwaukee and Wisconsin grows more pressing as the Latina/o population has expanded. In 2013, the U.S. Census estimated that the population of Milwaukee County was 956, 023, with the "Hispanic or Latino" population comprising 14 percent of that overall total. In Milwaukee County in 2013, it is estimated that 16 percent of households speak a language other than English at home, though only 8.8 percent of persons surveyed were foreign-born.[1] While nearly half of that 8.8 percent foreign-born population is from Latin America (48.9 percent), the other half hails from Asian (27 percent), Europe (17.7 percent) and Africa (5 percent).[2] This suggests that not only will a variety of Latinidades continue to flourish in Milwaukee, but that Latinas/os will also increasingly share life experiences with other significant ethnic and racial groups in the county. The City of Milwaukee's 2010 Hispanic/Latino origin population numbered 103, 007, representing 17.32 percent of the overall city population, and, in 2010, half of that population was under the age of 19.[3] These shifting demographics suggest the continued importance of building educational institutions and settings, from kindergarten to college, where Latina/o students can flourish—work that many of the women included in this study engaged in for many years. As Daisy Cubías's life story reveals, Milwaukee is not the only place in the State of Wisconsin where Latinas/os settle. Demographic overviews of the state population show that the 2000 Census registered 3.6 percent of the state population as "Hispanic or Latino Origin," but the 2010 Census records 5.91 percent of the population in that category, with Milwaukee's Latina/o population accounting for only a third of that total.[4] This highlights the degree to which Latina/o Studies must include small town and rural areas in future research for a fuller understanding and analysis of the Latina/o experience in the region.

Young Latinas in Milwaukee face high, though gradually diminishing, rates of teen pregnancy, which poses unique health and educational needs. Adequate access to health care, including reproductive health care and mental health care, as well as preventative and family care, and an analysis of the health impacts of low socioeconomic status remain critical issues for Latina/o families in Milwaukee, though slightly less impactful for Latinas/os than for African Americans and Whites in the City.[5]

Foremost among the political issues that Latinas face in Milwaukee are immigration reform and political representation. Milwaukee participated in the 2006 marches and rallies across the nation in support of immigration reform with a historic 65, 000 person march from the Walker's Point neighborhood on the near South Side—a place remembered fondly by many of the women in this project—to downtown Milwaukee.[6] I recall seeing Olivia Villarreal's husband Ernesto participating in that march, alongside thousands of others, a testament to the broad appeal of immigration reform in many sectors of the population. Yet eight years later, there is still no immigration reform. Meanwhile, as the Latina/o population grows, so does its need for political representation. The life stories of Carmen Murguia, María Monreal Cameron, and Daisy Cubías highlight for us the significance of Latina/o political representation and activism. The Wisconsin chapter of The League of United Latin American Citizens, or LULAC, an organization founded in 1929 in Corpus Christi, Texas, has made the reconfiguration of Aldermanic Districts in the City of Milwaukee a key issue in its advocacy work to accord the Latina/o population political representation.[7] If these life stories are any indication of the talents, intelligence, and drive of Latinas, we can only hope that all those involved in these efforts work to cultivate the equal participation of women and men in the work of advocacy and representation.

The questions of immigration reform and political representation are not unrelated to patterns of segregation and unequal access to city services, such as police. As a recent report by Ben Poston in the *Milwaukee Journal Sentinel* indicated, "Milwaukee police pulled over Hispanic city motorists nearly five times as often as white drivers," while "a black Milwaukee driver is seven times as likely to be stopped by city police as a white resident driver."[8] Since, as the U.S. Census observes, multiple racial categories apply to Latinas/os, both of these figures are relevant to the Latina/o experience. In addition, Milwaukee remains among the most segregated cities in the country, with blacks, Latinas/os, and whites more likely to live in segregated residential areas,[9] suggesting the continued importance of building interracial and inter-ethnic coalitions and communities for greater social justice.

So much of what these oral histories also address is the ongoing process of social change among Latinas/os that makes it possible for families and communities to recognize the injustice of domestic violence directed against women, and act to change it; accept that preexisting biases against women might be misinformed and cultivate both consciousness to combat them and new practices to address them; include lesbian, gay, bi, and trans Latinas/os in our definitions of community and act to protect them from homophobia; have compassion for the coping mechanisms that people adopt to deal with stress and marginalization while also working to heal individuals and groups. While some women in this volume, immersed in the Latina/o experience, speak about the need to address these problems within Latina/o communities, none of the women express the view that these issues don't exist outside of the Latina/o community. Indeed, repeatedly, they point us to the evidence that these are larger social issues that Latinas also have a role in addressing, that speaking from a Latina experience one can, indeed, speak to the world.

Acknowledgments

It is not an easy task to open your life to another for public view, to share your stories and experiences, to remember both the difficult and the joyous times. Such speaking risks judgment and censure of others, by those both near to us and those we've never met, especially when addressing sensitive topics. For their courage and generosity in sharing their life stories, I remain grateful to all the participants in this oral history project.

I give thanks as well for the important assistance of my sister, María Elena Olveda, who has lived continuously in Milwaukee since arriving there in 1957 at a young age. Her long experience in the community was an invaluable resource to me in this project. She suggested possible participants, served as a sounding board for many an idea, and provided wonderful meals during research visits. One of the women interviewed in this volume observes that the oldest daughter in large Mexican families is often the "second mom," one role among many that my sister, María Elena, has often shouldered. For her love, compassion, wit, advice, and friendship I am grateful.

My parents, of course, were my inspiration for this project, as they have been for, and in, every step of my life. Their experiences, witnessed over my lifetime, and their stories, shared with me in so many conversations, are invaluable gifts in my life.

This work is also indebted to the path-breaking scholarship on Latinas/os in the Midwest that researchers in this field have created, many of whom I cite in both the introduction and throughout the volume. Mil gracias.

It was a great pleasure to work with several students in preparing this volume, emerging scholars who will undoubtedly have much to teach us in their own future work and scholarship: Christina García, Anabel Galán, Marvin Brown, and Nyanda Redwood.

A special thanks to family, friends, and fellow scholars who, over the past seven years, lent an ear to my ramblings about this project, shared their expertise, and supported me in this work, particularly all those who participated in the symposium titled "The Latino Midwest" at the University of Iowa, as well as Rosemary U'Ren, Miroslava Chavez-Garcia, Priscilla Ybarra, Lynn Itagaki, Jim Lee, Julie Cho, Valerie Smith, Janet Weaver, Lucila Ek, Tammy Ho, and Hyo Kim. Thank you to my students in Introduction to Latina/o Studies in Autumn 2013 for your inspiring enthusiasm for research on Latinas/os in the Midwest.

Colleagues and staff in the Department of Comparative Studies at The Ohio State University supported this project in many ways over the past several years, and I am grateful to all for their insight and care. The opportunity to preview this work in several venues was important in developing the final manuscript and I am fortunate to have received the generosity and interest of those who invited me to dialogue about this project with both scholars and the public while it was in progress. For those opportunities, thank you to Dorry Noyes of the Center for Folklore at OSU; Omar Valerio-Jiménez, Claire Fox, and Santiago Vaquera-Vásquez at the University of Iowa; Guadalupe A. Velasquez of the Community Relations Commission of Columbus, Ohio; Melinda Moreno of the Latino Empowerment Outreach Network of Columbus, Ohio (and former student); and the Asian, Hispanic, and Native American Center (AHNA) of Wright State University. I was also honored to share this work at both the inaugural national conference on Latina/o literature at John Jay College of Criminal Justice organized by Richard Perez and Belinda Rincón in 2013 and the annual conference of the American Studies Association in 2012 with copanelists Tami Albin, Janet Weaver, Sonia Saldívar-Hull, Thuy Vo Dang, Joseph A. Rodriguez, Linda Garcia Merchant, and Maylei Blackwell. Thank you all!

Finally, my deepest gratitude to the editors who encouraged and guided this work, Larin McLaughlin and Dawn Durante; the wonderful professionals at the University of Illinois Press who prepared the book in multiple stages; the anonymous reviewers whose comments and suggestions made this a better book; and the series editor, Frances R. Aparicio, for her vision. Any errors or omissions remain my own responsibility.

Notes

1. Latinas in Milwaukee

1. Larry Widen and Judi Anderson, *Silver Screens: A Pictorial History of Milwaukee's Movie Theaters* (Madison: Wisconsin Historical Society Press, 2007), x.

2. Frances R. Aparicio and Susana Chávez-Silverman, ed., *Tropicalizations: Transcultural Representations of Latinidad* (Hanover, NH: University Press of New England for Dartmouth College, 1997).

3. According to the Wisconsin Department of Natural Resources, Aztalan State Park is located on the site of thousands of years of successive Native American settlements. Early settlers "mistakenly thought the town was related to the Aztecs of Mexico," though archaeological evidence suggests that Native American inhabitants were related to Mississippian culture in what is now Southern Illinois (Wisconsin Department of Natural Resources website, http://dnr.wi.gov/topic/parks/name/aztalan/history.html, accessed 15 May 2014). Following the U.S.-Mexico War and the surrender of what are now several southwestern states to the United States, newly incorporated Mexican Americans experienced dispossession, violence, and disenfranchisement in a region where they soon became a minority.

4. Joseph A. Rodriguez and Walter Sava, ed., *Latinos in Milwaukee*, Images of America Series (Charleston, SC: Arcadia, 2006), 10; Dennis Nodin Valdés, *Barrios Norteños: St. Paul and Midwestern Mexican Communities in the Twentieth Century* (Austin: University of Texas Press, 2000). Valdés dates Mexican migration to midwestern cities and towns back to approximately 1906 by tracking the emergence of Mexican colonias, or neighborhoods lacking the full resources available to other residential areas (25). His study offers a rich consideration of the industries that drew Mexican migrants and the communities they formed in the north. Zaragosa Vargas, however, dates Mexican migration to Milwaukee to 1917, bringing individuals to serve as contract workers for local railroads and the Illinois Steel Company (Zaragosa Vargas, *Proletarians of the*

North: A History of Mexican Industrial Workers in Detroit and the Midwest, 1917–1933 [Berkeley: University of California Press, 1993], 89).

5. Zaragosa Vargas, *Proletarians of the North*, 1.

6. Ibid., 3.

7. For example, the introduction to *Mexican Chicago* offers documentation of Latino/a agricultural workers in nineteenth-century Illinois, while *The Mexican Community in Lorain Ohio*, published by the Western Reserve Historical Society of Cleveland, Ohio (1999), dates the Mexican American community in that city to 1921.

8. Valdés, 41.

9. Joseph A. Rodriguez and Walter Sava, ed., *Latinos in Milwaukee*, Images of America Series. (Charleston, SC: Arcadia, 2006).

10. Vargas, *Proletarians of the North*, 90.

11. Valdés, 221.

12. Valdés, 221–22.

13. "Community Organizations, Puerto Rican, 1954–1968." Latino/Hispanic American Collection. Milwaukee County Historical Society. MSS-3035. Box 1. Folder 6.

14. The experience of Latina/o groups with other Latina/o groups, such as Puerto Ricans and Mexican Americans, or Cuban Americans and Salvadoran Americans, might be more accurately described as inter- rather than panethnic, though the term *inter-ethnic* is often employed to describe relations between Latina/o and Asian American or African American groups; therefore, this work adopts the plural *Latinidades* as a way of capturing both the commonalities and the differences within this heterogenous group. See "Latinidades" by Mérida M. Rúa and "Latino Identities and Ethnicities" by Suzanne Oboler et al., both in *The Oxford Encyclopedia of Latinos and Latinas in the United States*, ed. Suzanne Oboler and Deena J. González (New York: Oxford University Press, 2005).

15. Vicki L. Ruiz, introduction to *Memories and Migrations: Mapping Boricua and Chicana Histories*, ed. Vicki L. Ruiz and John R. Chávez (Urbana: University of Illinois Press, 2008), 1.

16. Valdés, 15–19.

17. Marcelo M. Suárez-Orozco and Mariela M. Páez, "Introduction: The Research Agenda," in *Latinos Remaking America*, ed. Marcelo M. Suárez-Orozco and Mariela M. Páez (Berkeley: University of California Press, 2002), 9.

18. I use *intra-ethnic* following Frances R. Aparicio's usage of this term in her new work-in-progress on the question of relations among Latina/o groups in Chicago.

19. David G. Gutiérrez also discusses the racialization and immigration experience in shifting self-identifications of Mexicans and Mexican Americans. See David G. Gutiérrez, "Migration, Emergent Ethnicity, and the 'Third Space': The Shifting Politics of Nationalism in Greater Mexico," *Journal of American History*, 86.2 (September 1999): 481–517.

20. Susan Bibler Coutin, *Nations of Emigrants: Shifting Boundaries of Citizenship in El Salvador and the United States* (Ithaca: Cornell University Press, 2007); Sherri Grasmuck and Patricia R. Pessar, *Between Two Islands: Dominican International Migration* (Berkeley: University of California Press, 1991); David G. Gutiérrez, *Walls and Mirrors: Mexican Americans, Mexican Immigrants, and the Politics of Ethnicity* (Berkeley: University of California Press, 1995); Maria de los Angeles Torres, *In the Land of Mirrors: Cuban*

Exile Politics in the United States (Ann Arbor: University of Michigan Press, 1999); and Mary Waters and Reed Ueda, *The New Americans: A Handbook to Immigration Since 1965* (Cambridge, MA: Harvard University Press, 2007).

21. Robert W. Wells, *This Is Milwaukee: A Colorful Portrait of the City that Made Beer Famous* [Original Edition: Garden City, NY: Doubleday, 1970] (Milwaukee: Renaissance Books, 1981).

22. The 1989 chapbook was published by "Friends of the Hispanic Community" in Milwaukee, Wisconsin, copyright Focus Communication, second volume of *I Didn't Know There Were Latinos in Wisconsin*, also edited by Mireles, was published in 1999 by Focus Communications, and recently a third volume was published by Cowfeather Press in 2014, also edited by Mireles.

23. For discussion of the significance of these new documentary books in self-consciously crafting a Latina/o narrative for inclusion in U.S.-national narratives, see Theresa Delgadillo, "The Ideal Immigrant," *Aztlán: A Journal of Chicano Studies* 36:1 (2011): 37–67.

24. In addition to the theoretical and methodological works and models of oral history discussed in this introduction, see the Oral History Association's series of useful Practices in Oral History handbooks, including Linda P. Wood, *Oral History Projects in Your Classroom* (Carlisle, PA: Oral History Association, 2001); John A. Neuenschwander, *Oral History and the Law* (2002); Linda Barnickel, *Oral History for the Family Historian* (2006); and Laurie Mercier and Madeline Buckendorf, *Using Oral History in Community History Projects* (2007).

25. Vicki L. Ruiz, foreword to *Songs My Mother Sang to Me: An Oral History of Mexican American Women*, by Patricia Preciado Martin (Tucson: University of Arizona Press, 1992), xii.

26. Ibid.

27. Leonard Ramírez, *Chicanas of 18th Street: Narratives of a Movement from Latino Chicago* (Urbana: University of Illinois Press, 2011), xi.

28. On how historians make use of oral histories, see Vicki L. Ruiz, *From Out of the Shadows: Mexican Women in Twentieth-Century America* (New York: Oxford University Press, 1998), xvi.

29. Genaro M. Padilla, "Recovering Mexican-American Autobiography," in *Recovering the U.S. Hispanic Literary Heritage*, ed. Ramón Gutiérrez and Genaro Padilla (Houston: Arte Público Press, 1993), 153–78, 153.

30. Ibid., 156–58, 170–71.

31. Ibid., 172.

32. Rosaura Sánchez, *Telling Identities: The Californio Testimonies* (Minneapolis: University of Minnesota Press, 1995), 8.

33. Ibid., 18, 31.

34. Genaro M. Padilla, "The Mexican Immigrant as *: The (de)Formation of Mexican Immigrant Life Story," in *The Culture of Autobiography: Constructions of Self-Representation*, ed. Robert Folkenflik (Stanford: Stanford University Press, 1993), 125–48, 128.

35. Ibid., 131–33.

36. Ibid., 130–31.

37. Ibid., 133.

38. Ibid.

39. Ibid., 144.

40. Ibid., 147.

41. Sidonie Smith and Julia Watson, *Reading Autobiography: A Guide for Interpreting Life Narratives* (Minneapolis: University of Minnesota, 2001), 27.

42. Ibid., 7.

43. Robert Folkenflik, ed., introduction to *The Culture of Autobiography: Constructions of Self-Representation* (Stanford: Stanford University Press, 1993), 1–20, 11–12.

44. Ronald J. Grele, "Movement without Aim: Methodological and Theoretical Problems in Oral History," in *The Oral History Reader*, ed. Robert Perks and Alistair Thomas (London: Routledge, 1998), 38–52.

45. Michel Foucault, *The Archaeology of Knowledge* (New York: Pantheon, 1972), 26.

46. Kimberlé Williams Crenshaw, "Mapping the Margins: Intersectionality, Identity Politics, and Violence Against Women of Color," in *Critical Race Theory: The Key Writings That Formed the Movement*, ed. Kimberlé Crenshaw, Neil Gotanda, Gary Peller and Kendall Thomas (New York: New Press, 1995), 357–83, 376.

47. Ibid., 360.

48. Ibid., 357.

49. Ibid., 358.

50. S. Berger Gluck and D. Patai, introduction to *Women's Words: The Feminist Practice of Oral History* (New York: Routledge, 1991), 9.

51. Theresa Delgadillo, "Latina Oral Histories of Milwaukee Project," July 2008.

52. Alessandro Portelli, "What Makes Oral History Different," in *The Oral History Reader*, ed. Robert Perks and Alistair Thomas (London: Routledge, 1998), 63–74, 64, 66.

53. Joan Sangster, "Telling Our Stories: Feminist Debates and the Use of Oral History," in *The Oral History Reader*, ed. Robert Perks and Alistair Thomas (London: Routledge, 1998), 87–100. Sangster notes that among the methodological questions that surface in oral history work are the need for careful contextualization of interviewees' words, how to interpret silences and omissions or intonation and tone, how ideology constructs memory, and when the researcher's focus, status, or point of view might impinge on interview.

54. Doris Sommer, "'Not Just a Personal Story': Women's Testimonios and the Plural Self," in *Life/Lines: Theorizing Women's Autobiography*, ed. Bella Brodzki and Celeste Schenck (Ithaca: Cornell University Press, 1988), 107–30. John Beverley, *Subalternity and Representation: Arguments in Cultural Theory* (Durham: Duke University Press, 1999); John Beverley, *Testimonio: On the Politics of Truth* (Minneapolis: University of Minnesota Press, 2004).

55. Sonia Saldívar-Hull, *Feminism on the Border: Chicana Gender Politics and Literature* (Berkeley: University of California Press, 2000).

56. Elizabeth Lapovsky Kennedy, "Telling Tales: Oral History and the Construction of Pre-Stonewall Lesbian History," in *The Oral History Reader*, ed. Robert Perks and

Alistair Thomas (London: Routledge, 1998), 344–55. Elizabeth Lapovsky Kennedy and Madeline D. Davis, *Boots of Leather, Slippers of Gold: The History of a Lesbian Community* (New York: Routledge, 1993).

57. Katherine Borland, "'That's Not What I Said': Interpretive Conflict in Oral Narrative Research," *The Oral History Reader* (London: Routledge, 1998), 320–32, 320.

58. Marianne Hirsch and Valerie Smith, "Feminism and Cultural Memory: An Introduction," *SIGNS: Journal of Women in Culture and Society* 28:1 (Autumn 2002): 1–19, 5.

59. Doris Sommer, "Resisting the Heat: Menchú, Morrison, and Incompetent Readers," in *Cultures of United States Imperialism*, ed. Amy Kaplan and Donald E. Pease (Durham: Duke University Press, 1993), 407–32, 408.

60. Gloria E. Andzaldúa, *Interviews/Entrevistas*, ed. AnaLouise Keating (New York: Routledge, 2000), 242.

61. This work does not partake in all aspects of the collective model of gathering oral histories that Benmayor describes but shares in the ethos of that work. See Rina Benmayor, "Testimony, Action Research, and Empowerment: Puerto Rican Women and Popular Education," in *Women's Words: The Feminist Practice of Oral History*, ed. Sherna Berger Cluck and Daphne Patai (New York: Routledge, 1991), 159–74, 160.

62. The Latina Feminist Group, *Telling to Live: Latina Feminist Testimonios* (Durham: Duke University Press, 2001), 2.

63. Vicki L. Ruiz, *From Out of the Shadows: Mexican Women in Twentieth-Century America* (New York: Oxford University Press, 1998), xiii, xvi.

64. Vicki L. Ruiz and Virginia Sánchez Korrol, *Latina Legacies: Identity, Biography, and Community* (New York: Oxford University Press, 2005), 4.

65. Theresa Delgadillo, *Spiritual Mestizaje: Religion, Gender, Race, and Nation in Contemporary Chicana Narrative* (Durham, NC: Duke University Press, 2011), 35.

66. Comments of Mr. Peter F. Murphy Jr. at "Puerto Rican Institute" on January 20, 1954. "Community Organizations, Puerto Rican, 1954–1968." Box 1. Folder 6. Latino/ Hispanic American Collection. Milwaukee County Historical Society. MSS-3035. These comments belie Milwaukee's strong identity for much of the twentieth century as a city of political openness and diversity as made evident in its election of a socialist mayor Frank Zeidler, who held office from 1948 to 1960.

2. Antonia Morales

1. Morales is describing the near South Side neighborhood around Sixth and National known as the Walker's Point area, where Mexicans, Mexican Americans, and Puerto Ricans have lived for a century. In recent decades, the Latina/o population has expanded well beyond this area.

2. Mercy High School, an all-girl Catholic school, operated in Milwaukee from 1926 to 1973.

3. A national department store chain in operation from 1887 to 1987.

4. Schuster's opened a store on Sixth and Mitchell in 1914, joining Goldmann's. Gimbel's first store in Milwaukee opened downtown on Grand Avenue in 1887.

5. United Migrant Opportunity Services (UMOS) was founded in 1965 and remains an active social service provider to migrants, immigrants, and Latinas/os in Milwaukee, Wisconsin.

6. Archival photo of site: http://resources.msoe.edu/library/archive/digital/mss01/Photos/image7.htm.

3. Elvira, Gloria, Margarita, and Rosemary Sandoval

The chapter title comes from a Mexican song whose lyrics are:

Hilitos, hilitos de oro que se me viene quebrando.
Que manda decir el rey que cuántas hijas tendréis.
Que tenga las que tuviera, que nada le importa al rey.
Ya me voy muy enojado a darle la queja al rey.
Vuelva, vuelva, caballero, no sea descortés
de que las hijas que yo tengo escoja la más mujer.
No la escojo por bonita, ni tampoco por mujer.
Lo que quiero es una Rosita acabada de nacer.

1. Listed in 1930 U.S. Milwaukee Census.

2. Dante Navarro arrived in Milwaukee in the mid-1940s from Mexico via Chicago, and was well known in the community for his Mexican music weekend radio program as well as community and civic activities. He died in 2013 at the age of 93. Georgia Pabst, "Dante Navarro Gave Milwaukee Latino Community a Voice." April 23, 2013. Obituaries. *Milwaukee Journal Sentinel*.

3. St. Rita school and parish is located on Sixty-First Street and Lincoln Avenue in West Allis, Wisconsin, a city contiguous to Milwaukee on the near southwest side where many Latinas/os began settling in the 1970s.

4. James G. Muellenbach was a well-known dress designer in town and owner of Milwaukee's Muellenbach's Fashions. He passed away in 2008 at the age of 79. http://www.churchandchapel.com/obituary/James-George-Muellenbach/Sussex-WI/550338.

5. Aurora Weir was an advocate for and leader in Milwaukee's Latina/o communities, an important voice in debates on desegregation and other matters. Weir was Panamanian American. She was killed in 1985 outside the Community Enrichment Center, which she founded, at the age of 45. See Barbara J. Miner, *Lessons from the Heartland: A Turbulent Half-century of Public Education in an Iconic American City* (New York: New Press, 2013), 84–85; "Honors Set for 9 Graduates." September 12, 1983. Community News Section. *The Milwaukee Sentinel*; "Santiago released on bond." January 3, 1986. Part Two. *The Milwaukee Journal*.

6. On August 27, 1970, Latina/o students and community activists staged a sit-in and occupation of Chancellor J. Martin Klotche's office in Chapman Hall, demanding greater access to UWM for Latina/o students and more curricular offerings in Latina/o Studies. In response, UWM established the Spanish Speaking Outreach Institute (SSOI) to address these issues. In 1996 this became the Roberto Hernandez Center. Source: Joseph A. Rodriguez, "Latinos at UWM: A History of the Spanish Speaking Outreach

Institute and the Roberto Hernandez Center," Revised December 2005. Online digital publication. https://pantherfile.uwm.edu/joerod/www/ssoi.html

4. *María Monreal Cameron*

1. Personal files of María Monreal Cameron.

2. María Monreal Cameron is now retired.

3. By 2008, the Hispanic Chamber of Commerce of Wisconsin had been selected for thirteen consecutive years as the Region IV (IA, IL, IN, KY, MI, MN, OH, WI) Large Hispanic Chamber of the Year "Best in the Midwest" by the United States Hispanic Chamber of Commerce (USHCC) in Washington, DC. Personal files of María Monreal Cameron.

4. As of 2013, the HCCW had invested $571,240 in area young adults entering or completing undergraduate studies. Sean Ryan, "María Monreal-Cameron, Hispanic Chamber of Commerce of Wisconsin," March 15, 2013, *The Business Journal: Serving Greater Milwaukee*.

5. This luncheon and conference regularly features city leaders and Latina entrepreneurs, professionals, and artists. Topics addressed have included: women in education, women in administrative roles, women in elected positions, women in the arts, women in unconventional careers, continuing education, Latina health and well-being, domestic violence, empowerment, financial independence, and others. Personal files of María Monreal Cameron.

6. These establishments were all in the vicinity of Sixth and National, on the near South Side of Milwaukee.

5. *Olga Valcourt Schwartz*

1. "The Madonna Medal represents the highest honor bestowed upon an alumna by the Mount Mary University Alumnae Association. Awards are given to alumnae who clearly demonstrate a long standing commitment to their profession or volunteerism as evidenced by outstanding and unique accomplishments, previous awards, organizational memberships, and substantive relationships. Awards are given to highlight alumnae accomplishments in one of three areas: Professional Excellence, Community Service, Service to the University and/or Alumnae Association." Source: "Madonna Medal and Tower Award," Mount Mary University website, www.mtmary.edu/alumnae/association/madonna-tower.html.

2. The Spanish Center was the common name for the Council for Spanish Speaking, Inc., a nonprofit community-based agency serving Latino/a Milwaukee since 1964. It is known today as Centro Hispano. UCC stands for United Community Center, a comprehensive social service agency in the Latino/a community that dates back to the early 1970s. SER (Service, Employment, Redevelopment) Jobs for Progress began in 1965 as a nonprofit organization with federal funds from the U.S. Department of Labor to provide employment opportunities for the poor.

3. In 2010, the Arizona legislature passed two controversial laws. One, SB-1070, directed against immigrants, allowed police to force anyone suspected of being undocumented to provide papers. The second, HB-3281, targeted Mexican American studies classes in Tucson's K–12 educational system, making them illegal.

6. Ramona Arsiniega

Translated from Spanish by Theresa Delgadillo.
1. Literally co-mother, this term connotes a very close and intimate friendship.
2. An organization dedicated to celebration and preservation of world ethnic life.

7. Olivia Villarreal

1. The South Side of Milwaukee has long been where most Latinas/os reside.
2. Lanette Johnson-Elie "Latinas Finding Place in Market: Entrepreneurship Growing among Hispanic Women," September 14, 2005, *Milwaukee Journal Sentinel*.
3. Mark Hobbman, "Adiós, Original El Rey," March 8, 2011, *Milwaukee Journal Sentinel*.
4. Villareal did not discuss this, but employees and customers were treated very harshly in a police raid. See Jesse Garza and Leah Thorsen, "Police Raid El Rey for Antibiotics," *Milwaukee Journal Sentinel*, September 19, 2002.

8. Daisy Cubías

1. *La Matanza* refers to the 1932 massacre of over thirty thousand Salvadoran indigenous and peasants. For further reading see *Remembering a Massacre in El Salvador* by Héctor Lindo-Fuentes, Erik Ching, and Rafael A. Lara-Martínez (Albuquerque: University of New Mexico Press, 2007); *El Salvador: The Face of Revolution* by Robert Armstrong and Janet Shenk (Boston: South End Press, 1982).
2. "Nicaragua to Get Donated Items," *The Milwaukee Sentinel*, November 20, 1986.
3. Marie Rohde, "Nicaragua's Problems Worsen as Help Drops," *The Milwaukee Journal*, October 10, 1992.
4. Daisy Cubías is now retired.
5. Doyle McManus, "EMBARGO: U.S. to Bar Trade: Reagan Embargo to Halt U.S. Trade with Nicaragua," 1 May 1985, *Los Angeles Times*; Bill Neikirk and Raymond Coffey, "Reagan Puts Embargo On Nicaragua To 'Mend Their Ways,'" 2 May 1985, *Chicago Tribune*.
6. Gretchen Schuldt, "Parental Involvement Project Gets to Pupils Where They Live," *The Milwaukee Sentinel*, April 17, 1991; Michael Derus, "School Life: Parents Making a Difference," *The Milwaukee Sentinel*, January 29, 1992; Curtis Lawrence, "Team Strives to Make Parents Feel at Home in Kids' Schools," *The Milwaukee Journal*, January 25, 1995.
7. Virginia Hart (1914–2007), Wisconsin's first woman cabinet member, served as secretary of the Department of Regulation and Licensing; chairperson of the Department of Industry, Labor, and Human Relations; and chairperson of the Labor and Industry Review Commission. The Virginia Hart Award was established by friends and colleagues upon her retirement. The award seeks to recognize women who share the following qualities: esteem from peers; acceptance of responsibility beyond the limits of their job descriptions; sustained, extraordinary achievement of assigned tasks; performance recognition from clients; community service; self-improvement; and the ability to overcome obstacles to performance. Source: Virginia Hart Award Program Booklet. http://oser.state.wi.us/docview.asp?docid=7455.

9. Carmen Alicia Murguia

1. Traditional Mexican music genre.

2. Gloria Anzaldúa, *Borderlands/La Frontera* (San Francisco: Spinsters/Aunt Lute, 1987). Juanita Ramos, ed., *Compañeras: Latina Lesbians* (New York: Latina Lesbian History Project, 2004 [1987]).

3. Sandra Cisneros, *The House on Mango Street* (New York: Vintage, 1991 [1984]).

4. The Loft Literary Center in Minneapolis, Minnesota, is the nation's largest independent literary center and has existed since 1975.

5. Murguia was enrolled in the INROADS Program for Hispanic/Chicana writers at The Loft from April 6, 1991, to May 24, 1991. Her mentor was Sandra Benitez. Lewis Mundt, education associate, The Loft Literary Center, e-mail correspondence, November 5, 2014.

6. 9to5, the National Association of Working Women formed in Boston in 1973. The Milwaukee chapter has existed since 1983.

7. LLEGÓ, the National Latino/a Lesbian and Gay Organization dedicated to organizing Latino LGBT communities through mobilization and networking existed from 1987–2004 and was headquartered in Washington, DC.

8. The Juana Gloria Vega Scholarship Fund was administered by the Milwaukee Lesbian Gay Bisexual Transgender Community Center.

Epilogue

1. U.S. Census Bureau: State and County QuickFacts. Last Revised Tuesday, 08-Jul-2014.

2. U.S. Department of Commerce, United States Census Bureau, American Fact Finder, "DP02: Selected Social Characteristics in the United States: 2008–2012 American Community Survey 5-Year Estimate. Wisconsin and Milwaukee." http://factfinder2. census.gov/faces/tableservices/jsf/pages/productview.xhtml?src=CF.

3. Census Viewer, "2010 Census Population of Milwaukee, WI." http://censusviewer. com/city/WI/Milwaukee/2010.

4. Census Viewer, "Population of Wisconsin: Census 2010 and 2000 Interactive Map, Demographics, Statistics, Quick Facts." http://censusviewer.com/state/WI.

5. See reports and graphs of Center for Urban Population Health, Milwaukee, Wisconsin (www.cuph.org).

6. Georgia Pabst, "A Mass Appeal for Immigration Reform: Milwaukee's 'Day Without Immigrants' Is Part of National Effort," May 2, 2006, *Milwaukee Journal Sentinel.*

7. LULAC, "Milwaukee Latino Redistricting Committee," www.lulac-wisconsin.org/ redistrictingmilwaukee.html

8. Ben Poston, "Racial gap found in traffic stops in Milwaukee: City's disparities are greater than other large metro police departments," December 3, 2011, *The Milwaukee Journal Sentinel.*

9. Stephanie Lecci and Michelle Maternowski, "New Ranking: Milwaukee Still Country's Most Segregated Metro Area," Regional News, WUWM: Milwaukee Public Radio, 89.7, November 27, 2013 (http://wuwm.com/post/new-ranking-milwaukee -still-countrys-most-segregated-metro-area).

Index

THERESA DELGADILLO is an associate professor in the Department of Comparative Studies at The Ohio State University. She is the author of *Spiritual Mestizaje: Religion, Gender, Race, and Nation in Contemporary Chicana Narrative.*

Latinos in Chicago and the Midwest

The University of Illinois Press
is a founding member of the
Association of American University Presses.

Composed in 10.5/13 Adobe Minion Pro
by Kirsten Dennison
at the University of Illinois Press
Manufactured by Cushing-Malloy, Inc.

University of Illinois Press
1325 South Oak Street
Champaign, IL 61820-6903
www.press.uillinois.edu